THE APOSTOLICITY OF THE CHURCH

Study Document of the
Lutheran–Roman Catholic
Commission on Unity

The Lutheran World Federation

Pontifical Council for Promoting Christian Unity

Lutheran University Press
Minneapolis, Minnesota

The Apostolicity of the Church
Study Document of the Lutheran–Roman Catholic Commission on Unity

Copyright 2006 Lutheran University Press, an imprint of 1517 Media.
The Lutheran World Federation, and
The Pontifical Council for Promoting Christian Unity

All rights reserved. Except for brief quotations in articles or reviews, no part of this book may be reproduced in any manner without written permission of the publisher: 1517 Media Permissions, PO Box 1209, Minneapolis, MN 55440-1209, or copyright@1517.media.

Published under the auspices of:

> The Lutheran World Federation
> 150, rte de Ferney, PO Box 2100
> CH-1211 Geneva 2, Switzerland

> The Pontifical Council for Promoting Christian Unity
> 00120 Vatican City, Vatican

Library of Congress Cataloging-in-Publication data
Lutheran-Roman Catholic Commission on Unity
  The apostolicity of the church : study document of the Lutheran-Roman Catholic Commission on Unity [of] The Lutheran World Federation [and] Pontifical Council for Promoting Christian Unity.
    p. cm.
  Includes bibliographical references.
  ISBN-13: 978-1-932688-22-1
  ISBN-10: 1-932688-22-6 (perfect bound : alk. Paper)
  eISBN: 978-1-942304-83-8
  1. Church—Apostolicity—History of doctrines—20th century. 2. Interdenominational cooperation. 3. Lutheran Church—Relations—Catholic Church. 4. Catholic Church—Relations—Lutheran Church. 5. Lutheran-Roman Catholic Commission on Unity. I. Title.
    BV601.2.L88 2006
    262'.72—dc22

                                                        2006048678

CONTENTS

Introduction 7

Part 1
The Apostolicity of the Church – New Testament Foundations

1.1 Introduction. 14
1.2 The Following of Jesus and the Mission of the Twelve 15
1.3 The Commission of the Risen Christ and the Promise of.
 the Holy Spirit 18
1.4 The Apostles 19
 1.4.1 Terminological Observations 19
 1.4.2 The Pauline Corpus 20
 1.4.3 Luke-Acts 24
1.5 Ecclesial Structures and Patterns of Ministry 27
 1.5.1 Spiritual Gifts and Ministries 28
 1.5.2 The Ministry of Episkope 29
 1.5.3 The Emergence of a Threefold Order 31
 1.5.4 Rites of Laying-on of Hands 32
1.6 Living Tradition and Remaining in the Truth 34

Part 2
The Apostolic Gospel and the Apostolicity of the Church

2.1 Introduction 42
2.2 Biblical Orientation 43
2.3 The Apostles and the Church in Early Medieval
 Interpretations 48
 2.3.1 Early Affirmations of Apostolicity 46
 2.3.2 The Special Apostolicity of Rome and its Bishop 47
 2.3.3 Apostolicity in Lifestyle, Art, and Liturgy 49
 2.3.4 Calls for Reform 50
2.4 Developments in the Reformation and Afterwards 50
 2.4.1 The Lutheran Reformation 50
 Continuity and Critique in the Lutheran
 Reformation 52
 2.4.2 Apostolicity at Trent and in Post-Tridentine
 Catholic Theology 53
2.5 Developments toward Resolution and Consensus 55
 2.5.1 A Catholic Ecumenical Vision of Participated
 Apostolicity 55

		The Gospel and the Episcopal College	55
		A Renewed Understanding of Tradition	57
		The Catholic Church and the Other Churches and Ecclesial Communities	58
	2.5.2	An Ecumenical Lutheran Account of the Apostolicity of the Church	60
		The Full Dimensions of the Word of God	60
		The Elements of Apostolicity and their Configuration	61
		The Substance of the Gospel and its Contingent Forms	62
		Diversity and its Reconciliation	63
		Lutherans and the Roman Catholic Church	64
2.6	Conclusions on Ecclesial Apostolicity		65
	Introduction		65
	2.6.1	Shared Foundational Convictions of Faith	66
	2.6.2	Shared Understandings Discovered	67
	2.6.3	Differences Calling for Further Examination	70

Part 3
Apostolic Succession and Ordained Ministry

3.1	Introduction		74
3.2	Biblical Orientation		77
3.3	Ordained ministry in the Early Church and the Middle Ages		83
3.4	The Ordained Ministry in the Lutheran Reformation and the Council of Trent		88
	3.4.1	The Lutheran Reformation	88
		The Priesthood of All the Baptized	89
		The Relation between the Priesthood of All the Baptized and the Ordained Ministry	91
		The Authority of the Ministry	94
		The Problematic of the Episcopate at the Time of the Reformation, and the Reaction of the Reformers	96
		The Theological Definition of the Relationship between the Pastorate and the Episcopate	97
		Ordination and "Apostolic Succession"	100
	3.4.2	The Threefold Ordained Ministry of Bishop, Priest, and Deacon according to the Council of Trent (1545-1563)	103
3.5	The Ordained Ministry according to Vatican II and in Lutheran Teaching Today		108
	3.5.1	Vatican II on the Ordained Ministry	108
		The Common Priesthood of All the Baptized	108
		Apostolic Mission and Church Ministry	110

		The Episcopal Office	111
		Presbyters and Deacons	112
	3.5.2	The Ordained Ministry in Lutheran Teaching Today	116
		The Ordained Ministry and the Priesthood of all the Baptized	116
		Differentiation of the Ministry	119
3.6	Conclusions: Apostolic Succession and Ordained Ministry		123
	3.6.1	Agreements	123
	3.6.2	Differences	127
	3.6.3	An Ecumenical Perspective on These Differences	130

Part 4
Church Teaching that Remains in the Truth

4.1	Introduction	136
4.2	Biblical Orientation	137
4.3	Doctrine and Apostolic Truth in Early and Medieval Developments	142
	4.3.1 Early Testimonies to the Gospel, Doctrine, Teachers, and Scripture	142
	4.3.2 The Rule of Faith	143
	4.3.3 Creeds for Professing the Apostolic Faith	144
	4.3.4 The Canon of Scripture	145
	4.3.5 The Councils of the First Eight Centuries	148
	4.3.6 Interpreting the Truth of Scripture for the Church: Early and Medieval Approaches	149
4.4	The Church Maintained in the Truth According to the Lutheran Reformation	154
	4.4.1 Canon, Interpretation of Scripture, and Teaching in the Lutheran Reformation	154
	4.4.2 The Ministry of Teaching in Lutheran Churches	164
4.5	Catholic Doctrine on the Biblical Canon, Interpretation of Scripture, and the Teaching Office	171
	4.5.1 The Canon of Scripture and its Basis	171
	4.5.2 Biblical Interpretation: Trent to Vatican II	175
	4.5.3 The Teaching Office in Catholic Doctrine	180
4.6	The Church Maintained in the Truth: Conclusions	186
	Introduction	186
	4.6.1 Shared Foundational Convictions of Faith	186
	A. The Gospel of God's Grace in Christ	186
	B. The Gospel and the Church	187
	C. The Gospel, the Canonical Scriptures, and the Church's Teaching and Life	188

4.6.2 Topics of Reconciled Diversity 188
    A. The Canon of Scripture and the Church 188
    B. Scripture and Tradition 190
    C. The Teaching Office: Its Necessity and Context in
       the Church 192
    C.1 The Existence of a Ministry of Public Teaching
        at the Local and Supra-local Levels 192
    C.2 The Teaching Office Among Several Instances
        of Witness to God's Word 194
    C.3 The Teaching Office in its Constructive
        and Critical Functions 195
Abbreviations 196
Participants 197

Introduction

With the present study document on the apostolicity of the church, the Lutheran–Roman Catholic Commission on Unity completes, after working from 1995 into 2006, the fourth phase of the Lutheran-Catholic world-level dialogue. The Commission was mandated and its members were appointed by their churches, as these acted through the Lutheran World Federation and the Pontifical Council for Promoting Christian Unity. The study document is presented to these two mandating bodies, and so to the respective churches, but as well to the wider public of persons and groups engaged in the ecumenical movement. The Commission hopes that the study will open fresh perspectives in the area of ecumenical ecclesiology and will throw light on pathways along which significant steps may be taken toward the goal of full communion between the Catholic Church and the Lutheran churches of the world.

The document offers, first, a careful examination of New Testament texts pertaining to the apostles and the main aspects of apostolicity (Part 1), and then sets forth the outcome of investigations from three specific perspectives on apostolicity, namely as a creedal attribute of the church (Part 2), as a characteristic of church ministry (Part 3), and as a decisive quality of the teachers and doctrine which our churches require in order to remain in the truth of the gospel (Part 4).

The History of this Phase of Lutheran-Catholic Dialogue

In the early years of this phase, the Commission discussed two topics in addition to the topic of apostolicity, namely, first, ethics and moral teaching in our churches and their significance for ecumenical relations, and, second, the degree of Catholic-Lutheran doctrinal agreement on the Eucharist. But the Commission soon recognized that both these topics are so extensive and complex in themselves that it could not do justice to them while carrying out its investigation of apostolicity. It was decided, therefore, to concentrate all the effort on the topic of apostolicity. Thus we present only one text, which however has grown to notable length.

The make-up of the Commission provided the ample geographical background of the members themselves, who represent Catholic and Lutheran perspectives formed by life and work in their local churches. They come from Argentina, Canada, Finland, Germany, Hungary, Italy, Japan, Nigeria, Norway, Poland, Tanzania, and the United States.

During its years of dialogue, the Commission entered into exchanges with local churches in the places where its annual week-long meetings were held, namely in Germany (Rottenburg-Stuttgart, Würzburg and Tutzing-Munich), Scandinavia (Finland and Denmark), Hungary (Dobogokö near Budapest), Poland (Opole), Italy (Bose, Milan, and Cassano delle Murge near Bari), and the United States (Baltimore). Reports were heard on ecumenical efforts in these locales and the Commission sought to communicate to others in these places something of its commitment to Christian unity and of its dialogue method. The Commission hopes that these meetings have enriched local churches and fostered the ecumenical dedication of their members in the places where the Commission met.

While meeting in Baltimore in July 2004, the Commission heard a report on the then just-concluded Round X of the Catholic-Lutheran dialogue in the USA, which has since been published as *The Church as Koinonia of Salvation. Its Structures and Ministries*.[1] Here the Commission found points of contact and a complementarity between that text and Part 3 of its document which treats church ministry and apostolic succession. Also, support was found in the project of the German Ecumenical Working Circle of Evangelical and Catholic Theologians (*Jaeger-Staehlin Kreis*), in which two Commission members are active participants. Several sections of Part 4 of the present study, on how the church remains in the truth of the apostolic gospel, were aided by the Working Circle's ample study, *Verbindliches Zeugnis*.[2]

The decade of this dialogue was marked by the major event of the Lutheran-Roman Catholic *Joint Declaration on the Doctrine of Justifi-*

---

[1] Eds. R. Lee and J. Gros, FSC (Washington, D.C. 2005).
[2] Eds. G. Wenz & T. Schneider, 3 vols. (Freiburg & Göttingen 1992-98). In 2002 the German Working Circle took up the topic that the present study document treats in Part 3, namely, the church's ministry in apostolic succession. The Working Circle has published two volumes of papers, but as yet no agreed conclusions, in *Das kirchliche Amt in apostolischer Nachfolge*. I. *Grundlagen und Grundfragen*, eds. T. Schneider & G. Wenz (Freiburg & Göttingen 2004), and II. *Ursprünge und Wandlungen*, eds. D. Sattler & G. Wenz (Freiburg & Göttingen 2006).

cation, signed amid considerable solemnity on October 31, 1999, in Augsburg, Germany. During the first years of its work on apostolicity the Commission accompanied and discussed the processes by which our churches received the *Joint Declaration* and reached agreement to proceed to the signing in Augsburg. Some members of the Commission contributed to the drafting of the *Joint Declaration* itself and they along with others helped present it to the churches.

The Context of this Study

The world-level official dialogue between Lutherans and Catholics began immediately after Vatican Council II and completed its third phase in 1993. The Commission that has now completed its work thus represents the fourth phase of this dialogue. The present work should be understood as a further step along the path of the three previous phases and as extending what they proposed in the documents they produced. It relates especially to the Lutheran-Catholic world-level dialogue reports, *The Gospel and the Church* of 1972, *The Ministry in the Church* of 1981, and *Church and Justification* of 1994.[3]

An important characteristic of the present work is its connection with the *Joint Declaration on the Doctrine of Justification*. The *Joint Declaration* has a notable weight and authority, because with its signing in 1999, the two churches in dialogue formally received the results of several Lutheran-Catholic dialogues which had treated the doctrine of justification both on the world-level and in national dialogues in the United States and Germany.

The Methods of the Joint Study

The investigation of the New Testament witness to the apostles and to their mission on behalf of the gospel of Jesus Christ contributes extensive and important results to our document. Scholarly exegetical study has been central in the effort to avoid an older style of using Scripture as the source of proof-texts. Part 1 presents the New Testament texts in their complexity and allows them to speak for themselves.

---

[3] Given in Growth in Agreement, eds. H. Meyer and L. Vischer (New York/Ramsey & Geneva 1984), pp. 168-89 (*The Gospel and the Church*) and pp. 248-275 (*The Ministry in the Church*), and in *Growth in Agreement II*, eds. J. Gros, FSC, H. Meyer, and W. G. Rusch (Geneva & Grand Rapids 2000), pp. 485-565 (*Church and Justification*).

Then Parts 2, 3, and 4 each contain sections of "biblical orientation" in which the relevant New Testament texts are placed within the horizon of the topics and questions of each of these Parts. The Commission was attentive to the dynamic of development within the New Testament itself. In a real sense, the entire process went ahead in the Commission as an intense dialogue grounded in Scripture as the primary testimony of our faith.

Parts 2, 3, and 4 also survey developments in the church of the patristic and medieval periods. Many detailed studies exist concerning the issues taken up in these sections. These studies have been drawn upon in a selective manner in the different sections, without any presumption of giving complete and fully nuanced accounts of the relevant topics.

The surveys of the centuries between the apostolic age and the outbreak of the Reformation aim to be more than just a historical narrative. These centuries are for both Lutherans and Catholics a common history of the development of doctrine and church order. The Lutheran churches see their tradition as rooted in the mission and founding work of the apostles, but also as carrying forward through the Reformation essential elements of the doctrinal and structural developments that occurred, after the apostles, in the early-church and medieval periods.

While not exhaustive, the historical surveys have nonetheless produced unsuspected benefits, as appears in Part 3, regarding the transformation of the episcopal ministry in the fourth century, from which an important contribution has been provided to the interpretation of both the Reformation and more recent Catholic developments.

The sections on Luther and the Lutheran Reformation rest on detailed studies, but not simply as historical accounts, but also for systematic theological explanations and arguments. Similarly, detailed studies have been carried out on the modern Catholic doctrinal tradition as shaped by the Councils of Trent, Vatican I, and especially Vatican II. Important points are taken over from Trent on the Sacrament of Order in Part 3, while Vatican II contributes to Part 2, on the ecclesial "elements" originating from the apostles, and to Part 4, on the place and role of the Bible in Catholic life.

Introduction

Limits of This Study of Apostolicity

The Commission agreed from the beginning not to take up a point of serious difference between Lutherans and Catholics, namely, the ordination of women to the pastoral ministry and their appointment to the episcopal office. The Lutheran members of the Commission emphasize, however, that when the text speaks of "ministry" they have in mind men as well as women as office bearers.

Concerning another controversial issue, namely the special apostolic ministry of the Bishop of Rome, this does in fact enter into our study at several points. But the Commission does not presume to provide an ecumenical treatment of the papacy at a fundamental level or in a comprehensive manner. Other Lutheran-Catholic dialogues, conducted in the United States, have focused directly on the Roman primacy and on infallibility in teaching.[4] Moreover, the recent dialogue-study brought out in Germany, *Communio Sanctorum* (2000), contains a substantial Catholic-Lutheran exchange on the papacy.[5] The Commission recognizes that it could not aspire to add new insights to this discussion. Furthermore, we are aware that Pope John Paul II's encyclical on ecumenical commitment, *Ut unum sint* (1995), has led to a broad discussion and many publications on the papal ministry, which we could not hope to work through and integrate into our study.

A Note on Language

This dialogue document has been prepared, at all stages of the Commission's work, in both English and German. The two versions aim to respect the stylistic requirements of each language and thus do not stand in literal, word-for-word correspondence with each other. But an editorial sub-group of Commission members carefully examined the two versions in order to be sure that the two texts agree fundamentally with each other.

---

[4] See the publications of Rounds V and VI of the Lutheran-Catholic dialogue in the USA, *Papal Primacy and the Unity of the Church* (Minneapolis 1974) and *Teaching Authority and Infallibility in the Church* (Minneapolis 1980).

[5] Bilateral Working Group of the German National Bishops' Conference and the Church Leadership of the United Evangelical Lutheran Church of Germany, *Communio Sanctorum. The Church as the Communion of Saints*, trans. M. W. Jeske, M. Root, and D. R. Smith (Collegeville 2004), treating the Petrine Ministry on pp. 51-68.

Thus, both the English and the German versions of this study may be considered original texts of the Commission and may be cited in reports on and analyses of its contribution toward hastening the recognition of greater communion between the Catholic Church and the Lutheran churches of the world.

Bishop Béla Harmatí
Budapest, Hungary
Lutheran Co-Chair

Archbishop Alfons Nossol
Opole, Poland
Roman Catholic Co-Chair

Study-Document of the Lutheran-Roman Catholic Commission on Unity

PART 1
THE APOSTOLICITY OF THE CHURCH

NEW TESTAMENT FOUNDATIONS

1.1 Introduction

1. The witness of Scripture is of decisive importance as we strive together to explore the apostolicity of the church as expressed in its apostolic foundation and by its apostolic message. The church adopted the Holy Scriptures of the Jewish people and established the canon of the New Testament as a normative witness to the apostolic gospel, that is, to the primary and authentic proclamation of God's revelation in Jesus Christ by the first who were sent to "bring good news" (Rom 10:14-15). Under the guidance of the Holy Spirit, both individual Christians and the church at large have read the Scriptures time and again to gain insight and guidance as they continue to carry out the divine commission to proclaim the gospel anew in every place and at every time. Throughout the centuries, the church has thus aspired to honor its apostolic foundation and to remain faithful to it. The conviction has always been essential that the Holy Spirit would guide and maintain the church in the truth, and that the content of the faith, kindled by the Spirit within the confessing community of believers, was primary and essential to any outer form. The ways in which being a Christian was practiced and in which the ministry of reconciliation was carried out have always had to correspond to the gospel.

2. The interpretation of Scripture has identified and paid tribute to the rich variety of voices and forms found within the New Testament in speaking of discipleship as a following of Jesus, and of the apostles and the gospel they were commissioned to proclaim, both while they were with Jesus in Galilee and by the risen Lord after Easter. The New Testament texts also speak in various ways of the charisms and ministries in the early Christian communities in which these texts were written and to which they also were addressed. The examination of this diversity within the New Testament witness makes the question of how it all combines to constitute a unified canon all the more compelling.

3. Our churches have different traditions of interpreting certain passages. There are also differences as to which writings are given greater emphasis, while different readings may even challenge one another within each church. The hermeneutical task, however diverse it may be, is rooted in the shared conviction that the witness of Scripture is normative. The awareness of how Scripture, Tradition and traditions must be clearly differentiated, while at the same time understood in their state of continual interaction, is a crucial issue for the ecumenical dialogue and an area in which considerable consensus has already been reached.

4. The New Testament witness as it is presented in this study document has a long history of reception in our churches - part of which, but far from all, has been one of division. This applies especially to the question of whether any concept or practice of apostolic succession can be found in the New Testament and, if so, what this would mean for the apostolicity of the church. The question may be further sharpened by asking whether the later apostolic succession in ministry has a basis in the New Testament. The selection and theological emphasis of the New Testament witness will inevitably take account of the dogmatic questions and framework of the study document as a whole. It is not, however, a matter of proof-texting certain dogmatic positions. The New Testament is itself fundamental in its witness to the Word of God and is hence an invitation to examine dogmatic traditions critically and to discuss seemingly contradictory expressions, which could even give rise to conflict.

1.2 The Following of Jesus and the Mission of the Twelve

5. Jesus preached the Gospel of God, saying "The time is fulfilled, and the kingdom of God is at hand; repent, and believe the gospel" (Mk 1:15), and he called disciples, both men and women, to follow him and become "fishers of people" (Mk 1:16-20 par.; Mt 4:18-22 and Lk 5:1-11; 8:1-3). In the gospel narratives, discipleship is described as the following of Jesus as he, in obedience to his Messianic calling, goes up to Jerusalem to be rejected, to suffer and be crucified, and to rise again after three days (Mk 8:31-38). The following of Jesus is thus a following under the cross; it demands self-sacrifice and readiness to suffer, and to aspire to no other greatness than that of serving (Mk 10:38-45). However, the gospel narrative of disciple-

ship is also a story of fear and failure, as many of the disciples do not persevere to the end but desert and even deny their relationship with Jesus. In the end, therefore, it is the risen Christ himself who appears to them and redeems them, re-calls them into his following, and re-establishes his community, as described in no. 30, below.

6. As they are together on the road, Jesus teaches the disciples about the kingdom of God in parables, exemplifies God's mercy and power in wondrous acts, and authoritatively expounds the will of God as it is expressed in the Law and the Prophets. One key characteristic of Jesus' following is that the initiative comes from him and that the disciples respond to his call: "You did not choose me but I chose you" (Jn 15:16). He is their teacher (Mt 23:8; Jn 13:13), and imparts to them a share in his authority as well by commissioning them, as his followers, to proclaim the kingdom of God and to heal the sick and possessed like he does himself. (Lk 9:1-2, cf. also Mk 6:7-13; Mt 10:1). However, his discipleship is essentially service, as they follow and are marked by him who "came not to be served but to serve and give his life as ransom for many" (Mk 10:44-45, and also Lk 22:24-27).

7. All four Gospels recount that Jesus already selected a group of twelve disciples during his Galilean ministry. Mark reports that they were appointed "to be with him, and to be sent out to proclaim the message, and to have authority to cast out demons," (3:14-15) and he presents their names as "Simon (to whom he gave the name Peter); James son of Zebedee and John the brother of James (to whom he gave the name Boanerges, that is, Sons of Thunder); and Andrew, and Philip, and Bartholomew, and Matthew, and Thomas, and James son of Alphaeus, and Thaddaeus, and Simon the Cananaean, and Judas Iscariot, who betrayed him." (3:16-19). The number twelve derives its significance from the twelve tribes of Israel, and following the Q-source, both Matthew and Luke interpret the Twelve to have a part to play in the eschatological restoration of the people of God, "in the new age, when the Son of Man is seated on his throne of glory, will yourselves sit on twelve thrones judging the twelve tribes of Israel" (Mt 19:28; Lk 22:29-30).

8. At times, Jesus selects from among the Twelve a smaller group of three to witness particular events, most often Peter, James, and John (Mk 9:2; Mk 14:32; par. Mt). On occasion, Peter speaks on

behalf of the larger group, and he is mentioned first in all the lists of the Twelve, corresponding to the fact that, in the Synoptic tradition, he and his brother Andrew were the first to be called (Mk 1:16-20 par.). In the Gospel of Matthew, Jesus responds to Simon Peter's confession of him being the Messiah, the Son of the living God, by giving him, *Simon Bar-Jonah*, the name *Petros* (in Aramaic *Kephas*, cf. Jn 1:42) and stating that Peter is "the rock *(petra)* on which I will build my church *(ekklesia)*". Peter will also receive the power of the keys to bind and loose (Mt 16:16-20). At the last supper in Lk 22:24-34, Jesus teaches the apostles a different ethos of leadership from that which is common in the world: "the greatest among you must become like the youngest, and the leader like one who serves." He then confers on the Twelve their eschatological role as described further in no. 7, above, and no. 30, below. While alerting them to the trials ahead, he reassures Simon Peter that "I have prayed for you that your own faith may not fail; and you, when once you have turned back, strengthen your brothers." When Simon Peter responds by pledging that he will not fail Jesus, come prison and death, Jesus pronounces that his failure is imminent - before the cock crows that very day. All the Gospels unanimously report that Peter denies Jesus three times at the crucial time of Jesus' trial (Mk 14:66-72). When some of the resurrection stories focus particularly on Peter, this may be read to convey that the risen Christ forgives him his betrayal, restores him to the communion of love and care, and calls him to follow Christ to his death (Mk 16:7; Jn 21:15-22).

9. The Synoptic tradition is in agreement that the Twelve were sent out on a mission during the Galilean ministry of Jesus. Their mission represents an extension of Jesus' own ministry of proclamation and healing (Mk 6:7-13; Matt 10:1-11:2; Lk 9:1-6). Luke has also included, at even greater length, the commissioning of seventy others (Lk 10:1-20). They, too, represent Jesus himself so that "whoever listens to you, listens to me and whoever rejects you, rejects me . . ." (10:16). In its present form, the commission in Mt 10:5-42, by applying the language of an eschatological crisis, merges the sending of the Twelve "to the lost sheep of the house of Israel" with the experience of the church at a later time. The temporal transparency at work in the Gospel of Matthew results, all through-

out, in the time of Jesus illuminating the later experience of the church and vice versa.

1.3 The Commission of the Risen Christ and the Promise of the Holy Spirit

10. The early Christian community was convinced of the abiding presence of the Lord even after Jesus no longer appeared to them. The church is the locus where the Christian faith is maintained and renewed time and again, from one generation to another. The Gospel of Matthew concludes with the promise that the risen Christ will always be with his disciples wherever they go to the end of the age/world (Mt 28:20). In the Gospels of Luke and John, as well as in Paul's writings, this continuous divine presence is perceived in pneumatological categories. The Holy Spirit unites the church, lastingly and ever anew, with Jesus Christ and with its apostolic foundation. By the power and guidance of the Holy Spirit, the church is equipped for its mission in manifold but ever present ways. It is thus enabled to meet the needs of each time and place, and the Spirit creates bonds of shared love and community among all Christians.

11. In the Gospel of John, Jesus speaks, in his farewell address to the disciples, of the Paraclete or the Spirit of Truth, who will come when Jesus himself is gone and who will "guide them into all the truth" (Jn 14:16-17,26; 15:26; 16:7-15). The Paraclete will teach the disciples everything and remind them of all that Jesus has told them. The Spirit does not add to the revelation of Christ but expounds, uncovers, conveys and applies the meaning and implications of this revelation as they are led into the whole truth. The emphasis lies on the maintenance and preservation of that which was once said and taught by Jesus as well as on the pneumatic witness to its meaning. Indeed, the Gospel of John is itself an expression of the sustaining presence of the Paraclete and the conviction that "blessed are those who have not seen and yet have come to believe" (Jn 20:29).

12. In Luke-Acts, Christ, ascended into heaven, pours the Spirit promised by the Father upon his disciples as they are all gathered in Jerusalem (Lk 24:49; Acts 2:1-4,33). They can be his witnesses "to the ends of the earth" only in the power they receive when the Holy Spirit comes upon them (Acts 1:7-8). In the narrative about

the two disciples on the road to Emmaus (Lk 24:13-35), the two are kept from recognizing their fellow traveler. Not until he breaks the bread are their eyes opened. Faith is re-established, as the presence of the Lord is revealed in this eucharistic act. The questioner thus proves to be the teacher while the guest acts as host. The disciples do not themselves seek out and find the living Christ. As in all the appearance stories he is the one who comes to them and reveals himself, and the disciples remain receivers even as they recognize him. The risen Christ does not remain with the two disciples at Emmaus beyond the moment of recognition. They are left with the broken bread, the Scriptures that have been opened to them, and the story of their encounter to tell. As the Lord vanishes, they change their plans and return to Jerusalem that very evening in order to join the other disciples who are already gathered there; community is being restored. It is to this full assembly of disciples that the Lord again appears, and on the day of Pentecost when they are all gathered (and not only the Twelve), the Holy Spirit is given to all of them.

13. Matthew and Luke, and also John (who does not mention a previous commission in Galilee), attest to a final, universal commissioning of the apostles by the risen Christ. They were not Jesus' disciples only when he still was with them. Despite their fear and even denial, their calling is reaffirmed and they are given a still greater commission for the post-Easter period. This is their apostolic brief, which corresponds to Paul's emphatic statement that he received his apostolic calling from the risen Lord himself (1 Cor 15:8-11). The mandate may vary in wording and in content but the authority it extends is fundamentally similar. According to the Great Commission in Mt 28:19-20 their task is to make disciples by baptizing and teaching; in Lk 24:48 and Acts 1:8.21-22 they are to be witnesses to the resurrection, which also implies the proclamation of the repentance and forgiveness of sins; and according to Jn 20:21-23, they are to forgive or retain sins.

1.4 The Apostles

1.4.1 Terminological Observations

14. In the New Testament apostolicity is not yet an attribute of the church as such. However, the terms *apostolos* and *apostole* occur,

always applied to individuals and to their mission. Most New Testament references to *apostolos* are found in the Pauline letters and in Luke-Acts. Scattered references elsewhere also indicate that the term was well established and widely used in the Early Church.

15. The terms *apostole* and *apostolos* as used in the New Testament undoubtedly carry titular connotations although this was apparently unknown to pre-Christian Greek, including the language of the Septuagint-traditions. The Greek term *apostolos* means a messenger or an ambassador, "one who is sent", and is a derivative form from the verb *apostello*. The verb is the primary term - without someone to do the sending, no one is an *apostolos*.

16. The specifically Christian usage of the term has been explained by reference to a Jewish convention of commissioning (*shaliah*), namely the authorized representation of an individual or a group in legal or religious matters: the envoy is equated with the sender himself. In carrying out the mission, the representative or agent has full authority and commands the same respect as the principal. The dignity of a representative thus depends entirely upon the authority and status of the sender. However, as a legal institute, *shaliah* is corroborated only by rabbinical sources from the late second century A.D., but some have argued that Mt 10:40 and especially Jn 13:16-19, which seem to refer to a commonly used turn of phrase, provide evidence that the convention of *shaliah* was already known in New Testament times.

1.4.2 The Pauline Corpus

17. The meaning as well as the implications of the term *apostolos* were a matter for debate and interpretation in the Early Church. In Paul's letters, the earliest Christian texts known to us, he assumes a previously established wider usage in the congregations. Among the ministerial functions in the church at Corinth, Paul refers to apostleship as the first charism (1 Cor 12:28f.), and in the long list of personal greetings concluding his letter to the Romans, a couple, Andronicus and Junia, are said to be "prominent among the apostles" (Rom 16:7). Recent research considers it likely that *Iounian* is the accusative case of *Iounia*, which is a woman's name - thereby retrieving an insight held by many of the Church Fathers, among them John Chrysostom, Origen, and Jerome. Rom 16:7 hence seems

to support the possibility of women having numbered among the broader group of apostles, and that Paul simply accepted this.

18. Traces of a similar broad use of *apostolos* for Paul and Barnabas can be found in Acts 14:4 and 14:14. In 2 Cor 2-6 and 10-13, Paul defends his right to the title of apostle with intensity and even some bitter irony. The way in which he defends himself indicates that his opponents, whom he ironically calls "super-apostles" (2 Cor 12:11), operated according to the wider and generic understanding of the title as well as a different set of criteria for apostleship: besides enjoying certain exceptional charismatic gifts, they required material support from the congregations they established or visited. Most likely they had also a local base from which they were sent out and to which they referred and returned. This may reflect an Eastern (Syrian) practice, which is also to be assumed in 2 Cor 8:23 and Phil 2:25. It is likely that Barnabas and Paul were also initially sent out by the congregation in Antioch (Acts 13:1-3). This remained their base of support to which they returned during their early missionary activity. At some stage it seems that in Paul's case this connection broke off so that he no longer had any particular base. The way in which Paul understands the nature of his apostleship, especially in Galatians and in 1 and 2 Corinthians, confirms and emphasizes his independence and supports a more narrow and privileged interpretation of the title *apostolos*.

19. Some have identified in Paul's writings a distinction between those "apostles" who were envoys sent out by local congregations/churches and a more exclusive set of "apostles of Jesus Christ" who had been commissioned by the risen Christ and among whom Paul counts himself. This distinction is, however, not consistent as Silvanus and Timothy are both referred to as "apostles of Christ" together with Paul in 1 Thess 2:7. A further possibility is therefore that Paul also used the term in a wider sense before his apostolate was challenged. Once he was compelled to give grounds for and defend his credentials as an apostle, he insisted on a more exclusive set of qualifications. Whatever the explanation may be, there is clearly some ambiguity in the Pauline usage of the title *apostolos*, which Paul adopts, both using the wider sense as well as a more narrow definition, which he further develops to apply to and qualify his own ministry.

20. It is essential to Paul's specific and developed understanding of apostleship that the apostle proclaims the gospel as one so commissioned by Christ. An apostle is defined as a messenger authorized and appointed by Christ. In this sense an apostle is a missionary, but there is no indication that every missionary is an apostle. The prevailing view seems to be that the apostolic charge should be issued by Christ directly, and that an appearance of the (risen) Lord was a necessary locus for the commissioning or *apostole* (Rom 1:4-5; Gal 1:11-17; 2:7-9). In the later reception of the church, this is the all-predominant understanding.

21. When Paul's opponents question his right and status as an apostle, his Damascus road experience is crucial in his defense; he received his commission to be an apostle to the gentiles from the risen Christ directly and without any human mediation (Gal 1:1; 1:15f). He is, however, also concerned with demonstrating how important it was that his divine commission was recognized and supported by the "pillars" in Jerusalem, even if he did not depend on their recognition. Indeed, Paul takes care not to present himself as submitting to some supposedly superior authority in Jerusalem. The fact that he was accepted by them, is rather described in collegial terms: "James and Kephas and John, who were reputed to be pillars, gave me and Barnabas the right hand of fellowship"(Gal 2:9). The collection which Paul took in his congregations as a ministry to the poor among the saints in Jerusalem (Gal 2:10; 2 Cor 8-9), shows their solidarity with Jerusalem and is an acknowledgment of Jerusalem's significance in having shared its "spiritual blessings". Paul's anxiety as he is on his way to deliver the gift (Rom 15:25-33) however indicates that there is mutuality involved. By accepting the gift - assuming they do so - the community (German: *Urgemeinde*) in Jerusalem recognizes Paul's mission and his congregations. The gift, once received, becomes a token of mutual recognition and of the unity of the whole church.

22. For Paul, the apostolic mission is fundamental as an *ekklesia* is established; the apostle is a *Gründer*. Through an apostle's proclamation, the word of God becomes effective in faith and Jesus Christ is laid as the foundation of the church in ever new places. In this, the apostle, like those who follow him and who build on this foundation, is a servant of God (1 Cor 3:5-11). But the apostle does not

belong to one particular place or to one specific congregation. The apostle's mobility is a sign of the solidarity and unity of the whole church. He may even address congregations he had never visited, as Paul does when he writes his letter to the Romans.

23. An interdependent communion is established between the apostle and the congregations he helped found. The faithful life of the congregations where he proclaimed the word of faith is therefore a clear measure of his apostolic achievements. The congregations are the "the seal" of his apostleship (1 Cor 9:2) or his "letter of recommendation" (2 Cor 3:1). In this there is also an aspect of mimesis, of imitation of the apostle and a reflection of the apostolic life (*vita apostolica*) to which Paul often encourages his congregations (1 Thess 1:6; 1 Cor 11:1; Phil 3:17 and 2 Thess 3:7,9). As some of these references show, this apostolic mimesis is in fact an imitation of the Lord. It is to lead a life according to the teaching and example of Jesus Christ and even to make the life and suffering, and indeed the death of Jesus visible "in our mortal flesh" (2 Cor 4:11). In this sense there is a succession, a following in the apostolic faith just as in life.

24. Paul had numerous co-workers whom he mentions in his letters. These also included women as the examples of the deaconess Phoebe (Rom 16:1-3) and Prisca (Rom 16:3-5a; 1 Cor 16:19) demonstrate. Some of his co-workers were also co-authors of the letters, which Paul wrote to his churches: Silvanus (1 Thess 1:1; 2 Thess 1:1), Sosthenes (1 Cor 1:1), and Timothy (2 Cor 1:1; Phil 1:1; 1 Thess 1:1, Phm 1:1). Timothy (2 Cor 4:17; 16:10; 2 Cor 1:19; Phil 2:19; 1 Thess 3:1-10) and Titus (2 Cor 7:5-16; 8:6,16-17,23; 12:18) are given important assignments in the apostle's communication with the churches and they are sent to provide guidance to the congregations on Paul's behalf. In the Pastoral Letters, which assume Timothy and Titus as the addressees, their role is developed into followers of the apostle in the leadership they provided to the church (2 Tim 3:10-15).

25. The foundational role of an apostle is a matter of priority in time and in sequence, but it also has a formative function. It implies a responsibility of setting a norm that may subsequently be further explored, developed, and applied, but not abandoned and distorted. This is why the apostle Paul writes his letters to congregations he

26. The Pastoral Letters go further in spelling out the apostle Paul's role as a founder both in view of his exemplary way of life (2 Tim 4:7) and his teaching "in faith and truth" (1 Tim 2:7). Thus Timothy is said to have observed Paul in his teaching, conduct, life goals, faith, patience, love, steadfastness, persecutions and suffering, and he is encouraged to continue that which he has learned and firmly believed, knowing from whom it was that he had learned it all (2 Tim 3:10-14). The Pastorals assume that Paul had in this manner established measures by which the churches could continue to safeguard the truth of the gospel and sound doctrine as well as the purity of faith once Paul himself was no longer there. The instructions concerning bishops, presbyters, and deacons indicate various responsibilities in this regard, notwithstanding the lack of a consistent pattern.

27. In the Pauline tradition represented by the Letter to the Ephesians, the church itself becomes a thematic focus of reflection. Apostles are mentioned in Eph 4:11 in a context similar to 1 Cor 12. The various gifts of Christ to be apostles, prophets, evangelists, pastors, and teachers in his church, all serve to build up the body of Christ. Significantly, in Eph 2:20 the language of the foundational role of the apostles is further developed in that they, together with the prophets, are regarded as part of the foundation of the church whereas Jesus Christ is the "cornerstone", which holds the whole together. A similar image is found in Rev 21:14 where the names of the twelve apostles of the Lamb are written on the foundations of the city wall of the New Jerusalem. This language indicates that the apostles belong to the past. However, not only the church of the present but also the future eschatological city of God's glory is built on that past.

1.4.3 Luke-Acts

28. As Paul already makes clear, the apostleship is a part of the post-resurrection period. However, the Synoptic tradition sometimes uses the term "apostle" for those who belonged to the group of the Twelve. In Mk 3:13 and Mt 10:1-2 the terms "apostle" and "disciple" seem to be equivalents. This terminological usage is most likely explained, according to many, as a retrojection back into the time

of the public ministry of Jesus. The title *apostolos* has retrospectively been applied to the Twelve since their selection is so closely related to their mission in Galilee, to their first sending by Jesus. However, in the view of others, already Jesus himself called his disciples "apostles", and they regard it as at least functionally representing what is later expressed in the Jewish institution of *shaliah* as well as in the Early Christian understanding of the apostolate.

29. In the two-volume work of Luke, the Gospel and the Acts of the Apostles, "the Twelve" and "the Apostles" are programmatically identified. The title *apostolos* is (but for Acts 14:4,14) restricted to the Twelve, who exclusively constitute the *collegium* of apostles. The Lukan composition of this *collegium* has influenced the Christian tradition in a decisive manner and has become the predominant configuration in iconography as well. In the semantic context of Luke the position of Paul as an apostle becomes problematic. In the last part of Acts in particular, Luke portrays Paul as the main protagonist, and Paul preaches and heals much in the same manner that the twelve apostles had done. But because of the specifically Lukan notion of apostleship as a privilege limited to the Twelve, Paul cannot be included. Even though the wider usage that occurs in other New Testament writings is also found in Acts 14:4 and 14, Paul's special claim to apostleship has little support in the prevailing terminology of Acts, even if Paul, like the Twelve, has decisive importance as a witness of Jesus Christ.

30. The selection of the Twelve during Jesus' ministry in Galilee and the mandate they receive at the last supper (Lk 22:22-38) prepare them for their role in the restoration of Israel, as is described in eschatological terms: in the kingdom of God they will sit on thrones judging the twelve tribes (v.30). After the betrayal and death of Judas, the group of Twelve is no longer complete and therefore, immediately after the ascension of Jesus, a new apostle is elected to replace Judas and take his "place in this ministry" (Acts 1:15-26). At the election, at least two candidates appear to meet the criteria, Joseph and Matthias, and the lot falls on Matthias, an otherwise unknown disciple.

31. In preparation for the election, the eligibility criteria for service as an apostle are listed (Acts 1:21-22): the person must have been among the followers of Jesus from the day he was baptized by John

until the ascension. Significantly, the criteria are such that they cannot be fulfilled beyond the first generation. According to Luke, the *collegium* of the twelve apostles has a unique and singular function in the history of the people of God, that is in the period in which those who believe in Jesus build the community in Jerusalem, which is the point of departure and the center of the worldwide mission to which the apostles are called (Acts 1:8). Not only are the criteria by which candidates are identified clearly stated, but the special commission and service of the apostles is explained as well. The criteria and the commission are related but they are not identical. The assignment is to become (note the use of *genesthai* in 1:22) a witness to Jesus' resurrection (Lk 24:48 and Acts 1:8,22). Having been an eyewitness (*autoptes*) is a requirement, but just having been an eyewitness does not make an apostle. It requires a special commission and represents a unique function; it is the result of selection and limited to the Twelve. Their task is to attest to the continuity between the crucified Jesus they knew and the resurrected Lord, and to bear witness to the resurrection of Lord Jesus.

32. After the election of Matthias, the *collegium* of the Twelve is again complete and ready for its mission. When the Spirit is poured out and the Jerusalem community established, they harvest mass conversions of Jews both from the Diaspora and from Palestine, as described in the first part of Acts 2:1-8:25. The apostolic ministry of the Twelve is focused on Israel, and their eschatological role becomes effective as the fallen dwelling of David is rebuilt (Acts 15:16). Once this mission is accomplished, an apostle can die (James in Acts 12:2) without a new apostle being elected in his place. After the Jerusalem council in Acts 15, at which the conflict in Antioch over the circumcision of gentiles was resolved, the twelve apostles disappear from the narrative as Paul's continued mission gains focus and attention. It is noteworthy that each step forward takes place because the Holy Spirit sets events into motion or precedes human action, as when the God-fearing Cornelius is baptized by Peter as the first non-Jew (Acts 10-11).

33. In the Jerusalem community, the apostles serve as leaders, as does James, the brother of Jesus. They teach, they defend the faith, and they work miracles. They also take part in the laying-on of hands

so that those who have been baptized may receive the Holy Spirit (Acts 8:16-17). They install "the Seven" through prayer and the laying-on of hands, as reported in Acts 6:6. The Seven are sought out and selected by the whole community at the apostles' request so that these "seven men of good standing, full of the Spirit and of wisdom" can serve at tables. This leaves the apostles themselves free to devote themselves to prayer and to the service of the word. This delegation of duties on the part of the apostles allows for a division of labor. The intention is thus not to replace any of the apostles by the Seven, even if the meaning of the Greek word *diakonos,* referring to an intermediary function or a go-between, comes strikingly close to that of the term *apostolos*. The subsequent accounts in Acts of Stephen and Philip, two of the Seven, indicate that they do indeed serve in a way similar to that of the Twelve. They may not be the successors of the apostles, but there is an apostolic message to which they too bear witness.

34. It is important that, despite the Lukan focus on the apostolic *collegium* of the Twelve, the apostles function within the whole community, all of whose members (cf. the emphatic *pantes,* Acts 2:3f) receive the gift of the Spirit at Pentecost. Their common life is formed by devotion to the apostles' teaching, to fellowship and the sharing of resources, to the breaking of bread, and to prayers. This condensed description of the Jerusalem community in Acts 2:42 has been understood as a list of marks of the apostolic community.

1.5 Ecclesial Structures and Patterns of Ministry

35. The canonical writings of the New Testament reflect a phase during which different ecclesial patterns developed, coexisted, and interacted. Some writings (e.g. the Johannine Literature and the Letter to the Hebrews) reveal little interest in ecclesial structures and leadership, and even the picture painted by those which do show interest may seem unclear and even inconsistent to us. A lack of interest does, however, not preclude that structures were already in place, and a lack of consistent or common patterns does not necessarily indicate a critical or indifferent attitude to ecclesial structures as such. The church has never been without persons holding specific responsibilities and authority, and functions and tasks make sense only when persons carry them out.

1.5.1 Spiritual Gifts and Ministries

36. In the Pauline churches, a charismatic profile should not be understood to exclude order and governance. Nevertheless, there is a strong affirmation in the New Testament of the calling of the whole people of God. The Holy Spirit bestows on the whole people of God - be they young or old, slave or free, man or woman - a diversity of gifts and ministries. In 1 Cor 12:4-11, Paul speaks, following a Trinitarian structure, of the diversity of charisms (*charismata*) given by the one Spirit, the diversity of services (*diakoniai*) inspired by the one Lord, and the diversity of activities (*energemata*) - all worked by the one God. The divine unity is the source and holds together this diversity of expression, which is to serve the same purpose of building up the community. Paul applies the well-known image of the body to the church as the body of Christ (1 Cor 12:12-27), and unfolds it to show that the gifts are not there for people to boast over against each other, but to teach them to appreciate and serve one another as they recognize their interdependence. The most excellent gifts are therefore faith, hope, and love, and the greatest of these is love (1 Cor 13). This is pursued further in Rom 12:3-8 when Paul emphasizes that the exercise of the different gifts should be determined by the purpose for which they were given.

37. By means of these gifts of the Spirit, God creates and maintains the church and gives birth each day to faith, love, and new life. Those who are baptized are therefore called upon to offer themselves as a living sacrifice and to intercede for the church and the salvation of the world. This constitutes the priesthood of all believers and the calling of the whole people of God to ministry and service (1 Pet 2:5,9).

38. In several writings there are indications that ecclesial offices and titles were being formed, but they were not yet precisely defined or generally accepted. The list in 1 Cor 12:28-30 contains a series of titular positions, which may have been carefully ordered, "first apostles, second prophets, third teachers" (*apostoloi, prophetai,* and *didaskaloi*); they are followed by a mixture of responsibilities borne by people with particular charismatic gifts. Whereas these first three may have had a more official and established status, the others probably refer to more occasional functions. Sometimes there is a more general men-

tion of "leaders" such as *proistamenoi* in 1 Thess 5:12 (cf. also *prostatis* in Rom 16:2) and *hegemonoi* in Heb 13:17.

1.5.2 The Ministry of Episkope

39. In biblical Greek, *episkope* is used to refer to God's visitation (cf. Luke 19:44; 1 Pet 2:12). In the rare cases where the subject is not divine but human, it may also refer to an ecclesial task. In Acts 1:16-20, the election of a new apostle to replace Judas is explained as a fulfillment of Ps.108:8 and the term *episkope* occurs in the scriptural quotation. In 1 Tim 3:1, however, where *episkope* is most likely coined on the basis of the title *episkopos*, it refers to a distinct office, which one may seek.

40. Whereas *apostolos* was a rare term in pre-Christian Greek, *episkopos*, meaning overseer, watcher, and protector, was a common one and was frequently used to describe those who held various official posts. It was, however, not the title of a specific office. The Christian usage may have been influenced by a corresponding Essene term in Hebrew, but that remains an open question.

41. The term *episkopos* is used five times in the New Testament. In 1 Pet 2:25, Christ is called "the shepherd and *episkopos* of your souls". In the other cases the term refers to leaders in a local church. From Phil 1:1 we learn that Philippi has both *episkopoi kai diakonoi*, without specifying further. Paul's farewell speech to the elders of the church in Ephesos (Acts 20:17-38) implies that *presbyteroi* and *episkopoi* (again both in plural) refer to the same group of persons. But, although *hoi presbyteroi tes ekklesias* are the explicit addressees of the speech and seem to constitute a distinct group, it is not equally clear whether the use of *episkopoi* in the speech (20:28) refers to a specific title or rather, in alliance with *poimen*, is a convenient Greek term used to describe a certain task or function of the presbyters (cf. the same combination in 1 Pet 2:25). The image of a shepherd serves to illustrate their role as the protectors and guardians of the flock - and of themselves as well. This is important because of both external and internal threats to the communities. The source of their authority is the Holy Spirit who has made them *episkopoi*. The proximity between this speech in Acts 20 and the Pastoral Letters indicates that the speech reflects the Lukan rather than the Pauline period and situation. However, local traditions may have been influential in both cases as well.

42. The Pastoral Letters are concerned about the protection of the apostolic (Pauline) heritage in a situation in which it is perceived as being under threat and attack by distorted speculations and subversive behavior. They teach "God's household management (*oikonomia*) that is in faith" and call for instruction that aims at "love that comes from a good pure heart, a good conscience, and sincere faith" (1 Tim 1:3-5). They further defend the tradition by establishing firmly a church order. This occurs in close interaction with an insistence on what was considered to be proper discipline for a respectable household, which also entailed the submission of women. The church is ordered as "a household of God" with moral expectations and clearly set standards of behavior according to one's place and with a defined allocation of authority (1 Tim 3:14-15). God is the master/owner (*despotes*) of this household (2 Tim 2:21) and has entrusted its management (Tit 1:7) to a steward (*oikonomos*) in the person of the bishop (*episkopos*).

43. The interaction between the proper ordering of a household and ecclesial order is made clear in 1 Tim 3:1ff in the form of a list of rather mundane qualifications which a candidate for the office of bishop (*episkope*) should have. They represent expectations, which were commonly found in society concerning the conduct of a man of good standing, and apart from the fact that the person should not be a recent convert, no specific Christian requirements are mentioned. At the same time, little is told about the election procedure or about the special duties of the bishop. Titus 1:5f provides a similar list of the requirements for a presbyter. This list reveals more about a presbyter's obligations: he should be a man with "a firm grasp of the word that is trustworthy in accordance with the teaching, so that he may be able both to preach with sound doctrine and refute those who contradict it." In v.7 the term *episkopos* occurs, which shows that the terms *presbyteros* and *episkopos* can still be interchangeable. 1 Pet 5:1-2 may also attest to a similar lack of differentiation. According to a well-supported textual variant, the *presbyteroi* are exhorted to tend the flock of God that is in their charge, exercising oversight (*episkopountes*) - thus reflecting the language of 1 Pet 2:25 referring to Christ as shepherd and *episkopos*.

44. It is noteworthy that the term *presbyteros* occurs in plural (*hoi presbyteroi*) in the Pastoral Letters, while the term *episkopos* is

always found in singular. On the whole, it remains unclear in these letters whether all presbyters could also be called bishops, which could be argued from Titus 1:6f, or whether the bishop was always one of the presbyters as 1 Tim 4:14 may seem to suggest. At this early stage both may be true, and there may have been local and regional differences as well.

45. In the Pastoral Letters, the *episkope* is thus a distinct pastoral office. Its responsibilities may have included the installation of deacons and widows by the laying-on of hands, even if this is not clearly stated. But its crucial responsibility was the official teaching of community, holding fast to the sound doctrine (Tit 1:9). This sound doctrine is the depositum (*paratheke*) that they have received from Paul through his disciples and messengers, Timothy and Titus, whose task it has been to guard it faithfully (1 Tim 1:11f.; 6:20). The apostolic legacy also includes the formative example of the apostle himself (1 Tim 1:16).

1.5.3 The Emergence of a Threefold Order

46. In the Synoptic tradition one may trace the interface between itinerant preachers whose authority was primarily based on charism and emerging local structures in settled communities. In *Didache (The Teaching of the Twelve Apostles)* this interface and the potential tension involved are approached in a pragmatic manner with concrete advice given (Did 12-13). The itinerant charismatics were referred to as *prophetai* and *didaskaloi,* or *parodioi,* but they were never called *episkopoi, presbyteroi* or *diakonoi*. These terms and titles all developed as part of the local established structure.

47. An often held view has been that while a twofold order employing the established Greek terms of bishops (*episkopoi*) and deacons (*diakonoi*) emerged in primarily Gentile (Pauline) congregations in a Hellenistic setting, a structure in which "the elders" (*hoi presbyteroi*) were honored as leaders reflects an original Jewish background and terminology. In the end, the challenge was to unite these two different structures and terminologies, resulting in a threefold order of bishop, priest, and deacon, first developed in the East (Antioch and Asia Minor).

48. Contrary to the previously assumed distinction between Hellenistic and Jewish influences and patterns, recent research has sug-

gested that respect for "the elders" was not a particular Jewish custom but a prevalent feature in Greco-Roman society as well. In both contexts "elder" is more a way of speaking of leaders than of a specific office as such. Some have, however, argued that the Christian usage of *episkopos* is due to a translation into Greek of a Jewish-Aramaic term (*mebaqqer*) used by the Essenes and found in the Damascus Document and the Community Rule of Qumran. This view has not gained any broad support although it is often mentioned.

49. One recent attempt at explaining the diversity within the New Testament witness posits a three-step development. First, as the Christians gathered in private houses, the *kyrios* of the house or the *paterfamilias* served as the patron of the group and may have been referred to as the *episkopos*. This could explain why presbyters are never mentioned in the Pauline writings. As the number of house-churches multiplied, the patrons/*episkopoi* would sometimes have had to act together. As a *collegium*, in the second stage of development, they were called *presbyteroi*. The third stage evolved in the face of the threat of dissent and division. A single bishop then emerged as the overall leader of all the house-churches within a city, which did not, however, render the other patrons/bishops/presbyter colleagues superfluous. The bishop continued to preside with them together. This, however, first developed with the turn of the first century. This historical outline might help explain the flexible and interchangeable use of the titles *episkopoi* and *presbyteroi* in several New Testament writings as well as the variance between the singular and plural forms. There is, however, no convincing evidence to support the first stage of the explanation, which in the end leaves this attempt at (re)constructing these developments questionable as well. The textual evidence is complex and it remains an open question as to how the ministerial structures developed.

1.5.4 Rites of Laying-on of Hands

50. The Pastoral Letters attest to a rite of ordination through the laying-on of hands. In 2 Tim 1:6, Timothy is reminded to "rekindle the gift (*charisma*) of God" that he has within him through Paul's laying-on of hands. A similar rite, seemingly referring to the same occasion, is mentioned in 1 Tim 4:14, but in this case it is a council

of elders (*presbyterion*) laying on hands. How these differing versions can be reconciled remains unresolved. 2 Tim 1:6 describes neither the charism to be rekindled nor its effects and manifestations in any detail. In 1 Tim 4:14, three elements seem to be involved in the rite: a gift (charism), a prophecy, and the laying-on of hands. It is not however easy to ascertain the relation between these elements or whether they all belonged within the framework of one liturgical event, even if this is likely to be the case.

51. What does seem to be clear is the fact that the notion of charism occurs in the Pastorals only in connection with an act of ordination. The enabling gift of the Spirit is conferred through the laying-on of hands and it is perceived as the charism of ministry (German: *Amtscharisma*). Accordingly, the rite of ordination is to be interpreted in epicletic terms, and the laying-on of hands functions as a rite of initiation into a position of spiritual leadership. The rite is mentioned retrospectively within an exhortative context, and it is thus effectively connected to the truth of the doctrine that Timothy is called upon to proclaim and defend. The Pastoral Letters do not isolate this rite from the life of the church as a whole or from the authentic preaching of the gospel and the teaching of sound doctrine. The rite demonstrates that the church is permanently subject to the guidance of the Spirit by means of an ordered transition through the personal transmission from one generation to another.

52. The Acts of the Apostles also affirms a connection between the laying-on of hands and the gift of the Spirit. This connection however varies. In Acts 8:14-17 and 19:5-6, the laying-on of hands is an act which is somehow associated with or which follows baptism. When the Seven who will "serve at tables" are selected in Acts 6, one of the requirements for eligibility is that they are "full of Spirit". The laying-on of hands by the Twelve, which follows the election of the Seven by the community, is an act which confirms their election and authorizes them to carry out a specific assignment. According to Acts 13:2-3, Barnabas and Paul are, by the directions of the Holy Spirit, "set apart" by fasting, prayers, and laying-on of hands as they are sent off from Antioch on their first mission. There are obvious differences between Acts and the Pastoral Letters, but instances of installation to special missions or offices through the laying-on of hands are also attested to in Acts.

53. The Pastoral Letters leave many questions open concerning the particular features of the ecclesial structure, which the letters strongly advocate and to some extent reflect. They do, however, attest to the disciplining and gradual transformation of the church's charismatic activity into an orderly ministry wearing also the prophetic mantle. Within the canon, the Pastoral letters come closest to expressing the position which became predominant in the mainstream of the Early Church: the formation of ecclesial structures in which specific offices, some with supervisory authority, became responsible for the church's steadfastness in faith, at first, however, without any firmly fixed terminology.

1.6 Living Tradition and Remaining in the Truth

54. The assurance of an abiding divine presence empowered and guided the apostolic community. This assurance helped the Christian communities to retain and retell the deeds and words of Jesus time and again; it moved them to ponder the meaning of his life and death; it moved them to remain his followers, while it shaped their lives; it helped them find their way forward and encouraged them in their teaching and witness. Jesus' proclamation was embedded into their proclamation of Jesus the Christ, the Word of God, Lord and Savior. The teaching of the apostolic community was thus not merely a repetition of the teaching of the historical Jesus himself. While remaining faithful to his message, they recognized him as being the message himself. At the heart of the apostolic proclamation and teaching were the life, death, and resurrection of Jesus Christ.

55. In doing this, they were convinced that God's continuing guidance was not only a promise for the future but also the present fulfillment of the promises given to God's people in the past. A major theological concern in the New Testament is the exploration and identification of God's actions in the present as they relate to the prophecies and promises in the Scriptures. The divine plan of salvation is traced time and again to give witness to the faithfulness of a God in whom there is no contradiction. This develops as they make Scripture and history meet, recognizing the unswerving will and plan of God in the Holy Scriptures shared with the Jews, and trusting the intervening guidance of the Spirit. Their proclamation is a witness to the living Word of God.

56. While emphasizing the unity of its source, the early proclamation took on diverse forms, shaped by the diversity of the local communities and the cultures of the time. It served a variety of functions and purposes such as missionary preaching and apologetics, the introduction to and further instruction in the faith, ethical guidance and, not least, the liturgical life of the church.

57. The Christians told the parables of Jesus; they remembered his words of wisdom and his guidance for life; they rejoiced in his acts of healing, liberation, and forgiveness as they proclaimed the gospel of his life, death, and resurrection. When they gathered for worship, they expressed their faith in hymns, in prophecies, in creedal and doxological formulas, and in the celebration of baptism and the eucharist; they read and expounded selected passages from the Scriptures and soon came to read from specifically Christian texts as well. The writing of letters providing advice, encouragement, and theological reflection was not only a way for the "founding father" of the community to exercise his authority but also an important bond of unity, as it brought local churches into correspondence with each other. Complex compositions were used as a means to compile, reappraise, and retell traditions about Jesus within a comprehensive narrative framework, not just in order to preserve them, but to proclaim the message of Jesus and ponder its meaning time and again (Luke 1:1-4; John 20:30-31). This type of narrative was later referred to as an *euaggelion,* "glad tidings". There were several such narratives, which differed from each other to various extents but this lack of uniformity was not in itself a problem.

58. The church has ever since endeavored to remain faithful to the apostolic witness and the canon of the Bible eventually became a normative exposition of this concern. The formation of the canon grew out of the practice of reading particular Christian texts in the liturgy alongside the treasure of the Holy Scriptures shared with the Jews. But it was also motivated by the wish to safeguard the content of the apostolic tradition from attempts to reduce or distort it. The canon, however, still incorporated a variety of expressions; normativity did not necessarily entail uniformity. Some gospels were not included into the canon, but neither was only one gospel chosen. Even though gospel harmonies were widely spread

and read, the canon endorsed the diverse versions of the gospel according to Matthew, Mark, Luke and John.

59. Faithfulness to the apostolic witness was not at any time taken for granted, and controversies occurred as early as the time of the apostles about the right interpretation and application of the Christian message. Paul was worried that the Corinthians were surrendering to a spirit different from the one they had received or to a gospel other than the one they had accepted (2 Cor 11:4). The incident in Antioch in which Paul confronts Peter (Gal 2:11-21) shows that not even a prominent apostle was exempt from criticism. For Paul, the authority of the gospel resides in the gospel itself; the proclaimer, be it Paul himself or an angel from heaven, is no guarantee of the faithfulness of the proclamation (Gal 1:8f). There is indeed no other gospel than the true gospel; "another gospel" is nothing but a perversion of the gospel of Christ (Gal 1:7).

60. Paul's polemical insistence in Galatians on the inherent self-authorization of the gospel does not prevent him from exercising his authority elsewhere and commending his own example as "the father" of the congregations (1 Cor 4:14ff). He is also able to reinforce his line of argument at decisive points by referring to the tradition and using conventional Jewish language of transmission (1 Cor 11:23; 15:1-11). He has passed on to the Corinthians what he himself has received, and they should not abandon what they have received and came to believe when he first proclaimed it. In 1 Cor 15:11, the statement that this is a tradition shared by Paul and all the other apostles transforms the entire passage (v.1-11) into a statement about unity in the community of faith, which holds fast to this tradition. Since the tradition is shared, it does not depend on any particular one of them.

61. The almost technical terminology of transmission in some New Testament passages is a clear pointer to early creedal statements in the Christian communities. Such statements (also called homologies or *pistis/credo* formulas) or allusions to such statements occur not infrequently in the New Testament. Most of them are Christological in content, and they most often serve as reference to a conviction already shared between sender and receiver. But they are not untouchable treasures, and Paul made both additions and other changes to underscore his theological concerns. They also serve

as a source for further reflection. In 1 Cor 15:3ff. the transition between the underlying formula and Paul's expansion and further use of it is blurred. In Rom 1, Paul slightly amends a pre-Pauline Christological confession (1:3-4) and develops it soteriologically to lead on to the theme of the letter which is stated in 1:16-17.

62. The Pastoral Letters, written in Paul's name, represent a new application of that which the author understands Paul's teaching to be for the next generation. In these letters, there is a growing concern for the forms of transmission since a continuity with the teaching of the apostles (and especially that of Paul) is a measure of faithfulness and a ground of credibility. The paramount task for those in leadership positions is therefore to teach and to safeguard the transmission of sound doctrine, which is constantly under threat. They are entrusted with the apostolic legacy, in Greek *paratheke*, (1 Tim 6:20; 2 Tim 12-14), and in Latin *depositum*. This is a *depositum fidei* but it also comprises a *depositum vitae*, inviting the community to imitate the apostolic life in its spiritual discipline and practices. More than other writings in the New Testament, the Pastoral Letters intertwine the question of the faithful transmission of doctrine with the orderly conferral of ecclesial office.

63. The New Testament speaks in a variety of ways of "those called apostles", but this variety converges in a common emphasis of their foundational role. They play a unique part in the post-resurrection period by mediating the transition from Jesus' own proclamation and the saving acts of his life to the formulation and communication of the message about Jesus the Christ. The church was founded on their initial proclamation of the gospel, and the living memory of this origin should never cease to sustain and nurture us. At the same time, the witness of the apostolic era is maintained and continued by new witnesses being called and sent out at every time and place: "How are they to hear without someone to proclaim him? And how are they to proclaim him unless they are sent?" (Rom 10:14-15).

64. No human authority is able to guarantee the truth of the gospel since its authenticity and its power to evoke faith is inherent to the gospel itself (its *extra nos*). On the other hand, however, the faithfulness of the church requires certain forms of traditioning and a

particular ecclesial ministry of proclamation, reconciliation, and teaching in order to ensure the orderly transmission of the apostolic teachings. This leads to dynamic tension that has constituted a challenge to the church from the very beginning.

Study-Document of the Lutheran-Roman Catholic Commission on Unity

PART 2
THE APOSTOLIC GOSPEL AND THE APOSTOLICITY OF THE CHURCH

2.1 Introduction

65. This second Part treats the apostolic character of the church, as our churches confess this in the Creed and understand it in their theological traditions. The task is to work together as Lutherans and Catholics toward answering the question, what makes a church apostolic? In fact, long-standing differences over the respective claims of our churches to stand in continuity with Christian apostolic beginnings constitute an obstacle preventing the establishing of communion between our churches. Therefore, with the aim of grasping better the dimensions of this obstacle, and of moving toward overcoming it, this Part will examine in detail the relation between the apostolic gospel of our salvation in Christ and the ecclesial attribute of apostolicity.

66. What follows articulates first our churches' conceptions of ecclesial apostolicity as these are grounded in Scripture and have developed in history, with special attention to changes in emphasis in recent times. The elements that constitute today's churches as continuous with the once-for-all apostolic beginnings need to be considered in their multiplicity. But this Part will also examine the degree of agreement over the configuration among themselves of the components of apostolicity.

67. The difficulty of this task is the overcoming of an all-too-simple alternative in interrelating and evaluating different components of apostolicity. One often hears that Lutherans see the church legitimated as being in apostolic succession *only by* its preaching and teaching of the gospel, with ministry playing no essential role. Catholics, on their side, are thought to hold that the unbroken line of rightful episcopal succession is *of itself* a guarantee of the apostolicity of the church. But both assertions are misleading.

68. An important step on the way toward overcoming this all-too-simple alternative will be to show the importance in the two traditions of

Apostolic Gospel and Apostolicity of the Church

a larger complex of components, in doctrine, worship, and forms of life and service, which together constitute apostolicity as an attribute of the church.

69. A second question to be answered in this Part concerns the present resources of our churches for acknowledging in dialogue the apostolic character of the partner church which is not now united in full communion. This study will show that Catholics and Lutherans are in greater agreement on ecclesial apostolicity than is ordinarily supposed. What follows in this Part will show this from our common biblical foundation and from the historical ways the apostolic gospel has been understood in relation to the church. Then, from this basis, this Part will deal with the issue of mutual recognition, which is clearly a critical step toward the visible union of our churches, toward which our dialogue aims.

2.2 Biblical Orientation

70. The Gospels keep alive the memory of Jesus' proclamation, as Part 1 presented in detail. Jesus' message of God's reign and kingdom, along with his accounts of God the Father, of sin and forgiveness, of faith and human hopes, and of Israel and the nations, remained foundational and was essential in the apostles' preaching The apostolic church then continued to transmit this message and doctrine. The Gospels keep fresh as well the recollection that Jesus called individuals to discipleship (Mk 1:16-20 par.) and sent them on mission (Mk 6:6b-13 par.; Lk 10:1-16). Even with the transforming impact of Easter, these events continued to characterize the apostolic mission of the church. Acts 1:3 tells of Jesus speaking to the disciples of the kingdom of God during the forty days of his appearances. In Lk 24:47 the risen Messiah interprets Scripture as promising "that repentance and forgiveness of sins is to be proclaimed in his name to all nations, beginning from Jerusalem." According to Mt 28:19-20, he sent them to all nations, to baptize them "in the name of the Father and of the Son and of the Holy Spirit and teaching them to obey everything that I have commanded you."

71. The Easter Gospel not only renews Jesus' message of God's reign. Interwoven with worship, catechesis, service, and the whole life of the church, it also includes the message of Jesus' saving death and

resurrection, his pre-existence and incarnation (Jn 1:1-18), his exaltation (Phil 2: 6-11), and his awaited return (1 Thess 1:9-10). Only through Jesus' death and resurrection, did the disciples come to regard his announcement of the gospel as an eschatological saving event, now to be further proclaimed. By renewing after Easter Jesus' preaching of the reign of God, the apostolic message underscores the identity of the Risen One with the earthly and crucified Jesus of Nazareth.

72. Early formulations of faith give witness to the Easter Gospel. According to Acts 4:12, Peter confesses before the Jewish authorities, "There is salvation in no one else, for there is no other name under heaven given among mortals by which we must be saved." In First Corinthians, Paul cites one of the earliest Christian confessions of faith, extending it to include his own vocation: "that Christ died for our sins, in accordance with the Scriptures, and that he was buried, and that he was raised on the third day, in accordance with the Scriptures, and that he appeared to Cephas, and to the Twelve. Then he appeared to more than five hundred brothers and sisters at one time, most of whom are still alive, though some have died. Then he appeared to James, then to all the apostles. Last of all, as to one untimely born, he appeared also to me" (1 Cor 15:3-8). Thus Jesus' resurrection not only renews the disciples' earlier mission within Israel, but also expands it to become a worldwide mission to all peoples (Mt 28:16-20; Acts 1:8; cf. Mk 16:15).

73. The first community of believers, gathered together by the work of the Holy Spirit, was according to Acts 2:42 distinctive in that "they devoted themselves to the apostles' teaching and fellowship, to the breaking of the bread and the prayers." According to Luke, these four aspects represent the constitutive elements of the community as church.

a. The *apostles' teaching* comes first, because the apostles, according to Luke, have by the gospel message also renewed and actualized fundamental aspects of the preaching of Jesus, while Jesus' death and resurrection was at the very center of their proclamation. On Pentecost Peter is said to be the first to begin public proclamation in Jerusalem. Paul, although for Luke not an apostle in the strict sense because not one of the Twelve, is still one who in Acts announces the same gospel as do the Twelve. This teaching of the apostles has to be defended in disputes about correct belief and be interpreted in fresh ways in new situations. But the apostles' teaching is essentially connected with other fundamental actions of the church.

b. The *fellowship* indicates the bond of faith uniting those who have all received the Holy Spirit, along with their community of goods, which served to help the poor and gave essential expression to their bond of union (Acts 2:44-45; 4:32-35).

c. The *breaking of the bread* is best understood in connection with the Lord's Supper, which in Luke's account includes the mandate, "Do this in remembrance of me" (Lk 22:19; cf. 1 Cor 11:24.25).

d. The *prayers* recited in common would include the Our Father, which Jesus had taught his disciples (Lk 11:1-4; cf. Mt 6:9-13), as well as the Psalms, which were treasured as prayers in the early community from the beginning (cf. 1 Cor 14:26; Col 3:16; Eph 5:19), as this community continued using Jewish forms of prayer.

These four characteristics of the church in Luke-Acts are not a complete account. But they are fundamental. They link teaching with the practice of the faith, both in service and in worship. The proclamation of the gospel, leading to conversion and baptism, preceded the first community's life of faith. And the same Spirit who led the members to hear God's word in faith then strengthens them as the community of believers to give in word and deed their own witness to the gospel.

74. The gospel of Jesus Christ must be proclaimed, as Paul writes about those who come to faith, "How are they to call on one in whom they have not believed? And how are they to believe in one of whom they have never heard? And how are they to hear without someone to proclaim him? And how are they to proclaim him unless they are sent? As it is written, 'How beautiful are the feet of those who bring good news!'" (Rom 10:14-15, citing Isa 52:7). There is no preaching of the gospel without persons who preach, but no preacher may act as master over the gospel, since all must place themselves in its service.

75. The apostles are the first Christian preachers, sent out by the Risen Lord himself (1 Cor 15:1-11; Gal 1:15-16). The Creed's later designation of the church as "apostolic" serves to indicate that the church

is, according to Eph 2: 20, "built on the foundation of the apostles and prophets" whose essential task was the proclamation of the gospel (1 Cor 1:17; Acts 9:15). The church is apostolic because the gospel that she hears in faith and to which she gives witness is apostolic.

76. The New Testament does not offer a unified concept of apostle, as already shown in Part 1. Common elements are the moment of commissioning and the proclamation of the gospel in word and deed. Luke's image of the twelve apostles brings out their eschatological significance, for they point to the hoped-for restoration of all Israel, while at the same time the Twelve can offer assurance that the Risen Lord is indeed the same one who lived on earth and was crucified. The Twelve link the proclamation of the church to Jesus' preaching. But also according to Luke, it is by the mandate of the Risen Lord that they announce the gospel "in Jerusalem, in all Judea and Samaria, and to the ends of the earth" (Acts 1:8).

77. Paul's understanding of the apostolate is narrower, as has been carefully described in Part 1 of this study. To him the apostolic mission is based in an appearance of the risen Lord (Gal 1:15-16; 1 Cor 15:1-11) while also for him the identity of the risen Christ with the crucified one is decisive. Because Christ died "once-and-for-all" (Rom 6:10) and "for all" (2 Cor 5:14), the mission is not only to Israel but also to all peoples. The apostles are sent to proclaim the gospel so that in every place Christ may become the foundation of the church (1 Cor 3:5-17; cf. Eph 2:20-21, 4:7-16). In this, the Pauline apostolate is of lasting importance.

78. In his conflict with his Galatian opponents, Paul asserts that there is no other gospel than the gospel of Jesus Christ (Gal 1:7). The apostolic gospel, no matter who preaches it, is one and the same as a definite message (1 Cor 15:11) centered on Jesus' death and resurrection (Gal 1:1.4; 1 Cor 15:3-5). This gospel founds community (Eph 4:4-5) and builds up the church (1 Cor 15:1). It must be firmly maintained by the word that is proclaimed (1 Cor 15:2).

79. The evangelist Mark placed his work under the heading, "The beginning of the gospel of Jesus Christ, the Son of God" (Mk 1:1). All the evangelists give witness in their gospels, different as they may be, to the one gospel of God, which Jesus announced and in which Jesus is proclaimed. In the New Testament the one gospel of Jesus

comes to us in the four canonical Gospels, into which numerous particular traditions about Jesus have been incorporated. In the preface to his gospel narrative, Luke states that this happened after critical examination (Lk 1:1-4). In Acts, Luke tells how the witness to Jesus came to Jerusalem and Judea, to Samaria, and to the gentiles as far as Rome (cf. Acts 1: 8). The apostolic letters relate how, in faith in Christ, a way of life took shape in the first communities, or how this should occur, amid difficulties of disputes in the communities and threats to them from outside. The book of Revelation makes its readers look ahead to the realization of God's Reign in a world of sin and chaos, until the descent to earth of the heavenly Jerusalem (Rev 21-22). All of these writings belong to the chorus of many New Testament voices witnessing to the gospel.

80. Luke tells Theophilus that his new account of Jesus is written "so that you may know the truth concerning the things about which you have been instructed" (Lk 1:4). The Fourth Evangelist declares the intent of his gospel: "These are written so that you may come to believe that Jesus is the Messiah, the Son of God, and that through believing you may have life in his name" (Jn 20:31). In his letters, Paul repeatedly speaks of wanting to reach his readers by proclamation, consolation, requests, admonitions, and instruction. The New Testament books express the living faith of all those who have been drawn by Jesus' message, by his death, and by his resurrection to hope to share in the "universal restoration" (Acts 3:21). The New Testament keeps alive Jesus' call to discipleship and his mission mandate, along with the truth of his teaching and his loving service. The books of the New Testament understand the Scriptures of Israel, the Old Testament, in the way pointedly expressed in Second Timothy: "All Scripture is inspired by God and is useful for teaching, for reproof, for correction, and for training in righteousness, so that everyone who belongs to God may be proficient, equipped for every good work" (2:16-17).

81. The apostolic gospel encounters us basically in the witness of Holy Scripture, which both presupposes and is further ordered to the *viva vox evangelii*. The New Testament, produced amid the life of the Early Church, and meant to be read in the context given by the Scriptures of Israel, communicates the gospel of Jesus Christ. The canonical conclusion of Paul's letter to the Romans asserts the fun-

damental significance of the apostolic gospel for the church of all ages: "To God who is able to strengthen you according to my gospel and the proclamation of Jesus Christ, according to the revelation of the mystery that was kept secret for long ages, but is now disclosed, and through the prophetic writings is made known to all the gentiles, according to the command of the eternal God, to bring about the obedience of faith – to the only wise God, through Jesus Christ, to whom be the glory forever" (Rom 16:25-27).

2.3 The Apostles and the Church in Early and Medieval Interpretations

2.3.1 Early Affirmations of Apostolicity

82. Early post-apostolic expressions of the churches' relationship to the apostles present only fragments, but these are important. *First Clement*, written from Rome around 96 A.D., called on the faithful of Corinth to submit to those whose ministry comes in an orderly sequence from those whom an apostle appointed. But Polycarp, bishop of Smyrna, urged the church of Philippi, which had been instructed in the "word of truth" by Paul, "to turn back to the word delivered to us from the beginning", that is, to the apostolic message of Christ's coming in the flesh and his cross, with the transmitted sayings of the Lord.[6]

83. More explicit attention to continuity with the apostles' doctrine emerged in second and third century arguments against Gnostic masters, like Valentinian and Basilides, who claimed to be transmitting to their disciples revealed doctrines originating with Jesus. Hegesippus, writing about 180 A.D., asserted that the bishops of his day, who succeed the apostles in Jerusalem, Corinth, and Rome, agreed in proposing the same public teaching from which the Gnostics were diverging. Irenaeus, shortly after, claimed that Christian public instruction is basically the same in different locales, where bishops adhere to the canon of truth, or rule of faith, passed on from the apostles. Sure access to God's word is had in the churches being led by bishops whose ministry stands in continuity with those whom the apostles appointed to transmit Christ's truth.

---

[6] "Letter to the Philippians", nos. 3 and 7, dated in the second decade of the second century, not long after Ignatius of Antioch passed through Smyrna as a prisoner.

84. The canon of truth, neglected by the Gnostics, provided the apostolic scheme of teaching and principles of Scriptural interpretation, for example, in holding the identity of the God of Israel with the Father of Jesus Christ. But one early teacher, Marcion, questioned the use by Christians of the Scriptures of Israel, leading to his excommunication at Rome in 144 A.D., after which a number of writers reinforced the role in Christian faith of Israel's Scriptures, with their Creator-God of righteousness and promises. In time, the ongoing presence of the apostles was sensed in the churches through the apostolic instruction heard by the faithful from readings of the apostolic texts of the eventual New Testament canon. In the fourth and fifth centuries, great preaching bishops brought the Scriptures to bear on both doctrinal questions and Christian life, so as to make the churches apostolic in an intense manner, without however linking this with the notion of apostolicity.

85. Among early creeds, much like the Apostles' Creed professed today in our churches, some baptismal formulae confess, among the works of the Holy Spirit "the holy and catholic church". The Council of Nicaea (325) issued against those using Arian slogans the anathema of "the catholic and apostolic church". The widely received and still recited Creed of the Council of Constantinople (381) confesses the church to be "apostolic", which is an attribute effected by the Holy Spirit who unites, sanctifies, and maintains believers over time in continuity with the apostles' faith, teaching, and institutional order.

2.3.2 The Special Apostolicity of Rome and its Bishop

86. In the patristic era, the churches considered to have been founded by apostles (*sedes apostolicae*) had normative roles in clarifying the content of true faith in Christ. But from the second century onward, the Church of Rome, where Peter and Paul were venerated as apostles and martyrs, claimed to be "apostolic" in a singular manner. The bishops of Rome, claiming to fulfill responsibilities Christ gave to Peter, were active in the fifth century in convalidating doctrines and norms issued by local Western synods. In Late Antiquity, bishops, presbyters, or synods, from both the West and the East, repeatedly appealed to Rome requesting an intervention in situations of conflict. They sought support for their positions, asked advice, and hoped to obtain from Rome a decisive solution of disci-

The Apostolicity of the Church

plinary and doctrinal disputes. As time went on, being in communion with Rome gained ever greater importance.

87. Rome's special apostolicity found expression in principles which were for the most part uncontested in the West through Late Antiquity and the Middle Ages, as encapsulated in the maxim, *Prima sedes a nemine iudicatur* ("The First See is judged by no one"), to which, however, medieval canonists formulated an exception regarding the Pope: *nisi deprehendatur a fide devius*. ("... unless found deviating from the faith"). Pope Hormisdas formulated in 515 the basis for Rome's normative role in teaching, *quia in Sede Apostolica immaculata est semper catholica servata religio* ("because in the Apostolic See the catholic religion has always been preserved immaculate"). But Pope Gregory the Great (590-604) designated himself *servus servorum Dei* ("the servant of the servants of God") and recognized Antioch and Alexandria as Apostolic Sees also exercising "petrine" authority in the ecclesial *communio* of churches founded by Peter and the other apostles.

88. In the Early Middle Ages, the older structures of collegial church governance, such as provincial councils, largely disappeared in the West, which eased the passage of local churches under imperial and princely power. Contesting this, the popes of the Gregorian reform, beginning in the eleventh century, intervened in the name of the freedom of the church, spreading their effective influence over much of Western Europe. Medieval canonical codifications, expressing the ecclesiology of the era, formulated the changed structure with the popes at the apex of the hierarchy, leaving few remaining traces of the church seen as the communion of local churches led by bishops who were keeping alive the apostolic gospel. Individuals, such as Ockham (d. 1347), Wycliffe (d. 1384), and Huss (d. 1415), protested against the prevailing juridicism on behalf of a radically spiritual church. But it was the crisis of the Western Schism (1379-1417) that occasioned the revival of older ideas of a corporate locus of authority, whether in the universal church or concretized in a general council, which could end the Schism and, it was hoped, promote general church reform. But the papal restoration after the Council of Constance, given ecclesiological formulation in *Summa de ecclesia* (1452) of J. Torquemada, O.P., had the effect of subordi-

nating both councils and reform to the governing policies of the popes.

2.3.3 Apostolicity in Lifestyle, Art, and Liturgy

89. During the Western Middle Ages, the apostolicity of the church extended beyond the hierarchy. Movements beginning in the late eleventh century sought to revive the *vita apostolica* ("apostolic lifestyle") in communities without private property and dedicated to work and prayer on the model of the founding community of Jerusalem. The Waldensian movement expressed this yearning for apostolic simplicity and for preaching based on vernacular portions of Scripture. Their preaching without episcopal approval, however, led to censure in 1182 and their marginalization. But the thirteenth century approval of the programs of Dominic and Francis of Assisi assured the on-going presence in the church of the ideal of living and spreading God's word in conformity with the church's apostolic beginnings.

90. Iconography made the apostles and their foundational role present to Christians of Late Antiquity and the Middle Ages. Always twelve in number, their membership could vary, as when Paul replaced Matthias. Early frescoes showed Christ teaching the word of revelation to the Twelve and mosaics depicted Christ amid the apostles as giver through them of the new law of life. All major Gothic cathedrals include statues of the apostles, for example, at portals in groupings with the prophets who witnessed to Christ before he came. The liturgical calendar distributed the feasts of the apostles throughout the year, to create a regular rhythm of remembrance of Jesus' chosen emissaries to the whole world.

91. Medieval carvings, paintings, and illuminated bibles at times link each apostle with an article of the Creed and also show the apostles departing on mission from Jerusalem to preach the gospel and baptize after Christ's Ascension. The Roman Canon names the twelve apostles in the *Communicantes* prayer, just after the *Te igitur* had qualified the offering as being for the benefit of all who hold "the catholic and apostolic faith". On these prayers Gabriel Biel, in a work studied by Luther, commented that the apostles are foundational of the church as the principal witnesses of Christ's passion and resurrection, but their founding depends on Christ, the ulti-

mate foundation from whom the faith began and has its present solidity.[7]

2.3.4 Calls for Reform

92. Individual churchmen had issued memoranda and appeals for reform of the church all through the fifteenth and into the early years of the sixteenth century.[8] Perceptive observers could see that a wealthy and powerful hierarchy was no longer in harmony with its apostolic mission. Often these appeals called for a return to observance of the older codes of law, while a few, like Wycliffe and Hus, called for renewed biblical preaching. But the desire of reform of the head, and thereby of the members, remained an unsatisfied aspiration.

2.4 Developments in the Reformation and Afterwards

2.4.1 The Lutheran Reformation

93. Among early modern exponents of religious reform, Martin Luther was distinctive in the force of his appeal to the biblical basis of reform, especially as found in the apostolic writings of the New Testament. Luther called an apostle "one who brings God's word" and understood the apostolic legacy wholly from the gospel and the commission to make it known. The church lives by the specific word coming to it from the risen Christ, through the apostles and the witnesses who follow. "Where the word is, there is the church."[9] The church remains apostolic by proclaiming the good news concerning Christ who "has died for our sins and is risen for our righ-

---

[7] *Canonis misse expositio*, Lectio XXXII, Par. G, and XXIV, C-G; ed. H. A. Oberman & W.J. Courteney (Wiesbaden, 1963-67), 1, 334 and 227-232. The work was printed some fifteen times beginning in 1488 and Luther studied it before ordination to the priesthood in 1507.

[8] Some representative titles: *De squaliboribus Romanae curiae* (Matthias of Cracow, 1404), *Monita de reformatione ecclesiae in capite et membris* (Pierre d'Ailly, 1414), *Advisamenta super reformatione papae et romanae curiae* (D. Capranica, 1447), *Libellus de remedies afflictae ecclesiae* (R. Sánchez de Arévalo, 1469), *Libellus ad Leonem X* (T. Giustiniani & V. Quirini, 1513). To these may be added the reform preaching of Savanarola in Florence and the complaints over papal appointments and taxes formulated in the *Gravamina nationis Germanicae*, regularly revised at late fifteenth century diets of the Empire. A new and widely attractive program of reform emerged after 1500 in Erasmian biblical humanism, calling for a transforming impact of the apostolic writings of the New Testament, known in their original Greek, on theology, spirituality, and preaching.

[9] "Ubi est verbum, ibi est Ecclesia." WA 39/II, 176,8f.

teousness" (Rom 4:25).[10] Thus, "where two or three are assembled, if only they hold to God's word in the same faith and trust, there you certainly have the authentic, original, and true apostolic church."[11]

94. The gospel word displays the power of the risen Christ by gathering and shaping the church as *creatura evangelii* ("creature made by the gospel"),[12] in which pastors, preachers, and all the faithful are called to continue the succession of witness to Christ's saving Lordship. Christ, now at the right hand of God, rules visibly on earth through the preaching of the gospel and celebration of the sacraments in the church. Receiving the apostolic gospel in faith entails as well receiving the practices such as baptism, the Lord's Supper, the power of the keys, and mutual consolation, through which the message of Christ engages human life with divine power.[13] By the apostolic word and practices, as Luther set forth in the *Large Catechism* (on the Creed, Third Article), the Holy Spirit is distributing, through the ministry of those properly called, the treasure of forgiveness of sin and sanctification acquired by Christ's death and resurrection

95. Luther himself rarely spoke of the "apostolic church". But he understood the reality that we designate the church's apostolicity as continuity in proclaiming the same message as the apostles and as continuity in practicing baptism, the Lord's Supper, the office of the keys, the call to ministry, public gathering for worship in praise and confession of faith, and the bearing of the cross as Christ's disciples.[14] These are the marks of the church by which one can recognize it, since they are the means by which the Holy Spirit creates faith and the church. Among these marks, the gospel mes-

---

[10] *Commentary on Galatians* (1519), WA 2, 452; LW 27, 154. *Smalcald Articles*, II, 1.

[11] WA 47, 778,9-12.

[12] WA 2, 430, 6-7, from *Resolutiones Lutherianae super propositionibus suis Lipsiae disputatis* (1519). Also, WA 6, 560,33-35; LWF 36, 107, WA 77, 721,9-14; and 17/1, 100,2-3.

[13] *Exposition of Psalm 110* (1535), WA 41, 131; LW 13, 272. *Smalcald Articles*, III, 4, BC 19.

[14] See Luther's defenses of the continuity of the Lutheran churches with the ancient church of the apostles in *On the Councils and the Church* (1539), WA 50, 628-644; LW 41, 148-167, and *Against Hanswurst* (1541), WA 51, 479-487; LW 41, 194-199.

sage, however, is the decisive criterion of continuity in practice with the apostolic church.

96. The apostolic legacy is handed down based on and always related to Holy Scripture which is the touchstone of all preaching, teaching, and practice. Scripture, when read as centered on God's grace in Christ, makes present the right understanding of apostolic teaching,[15] which includes the trinitarian and christological doctrine of the Ancient Church. It is the doctrine of justification by faith that expresses and orients this understanding.

97. The gospel serves as the basis of all authority in the church. Since apostolic authority is concrete service of the message of Christ, the rank or role of a person does not suffice to legitimate teaching, for the latter must be tested for its coherence with the gospel originally delivered by the apostles. But for one to undertake in public to speak this message, which is God's means of life-giving promises, one must be authorized by a definite call.

Continuity and Critique in the Lutheran Reformation

98. The aim of the Reformation was to re-establish continuity with the true church of the apostles by a new reception of the apostolic gospel and the practices bound to it. This entailed rejecting the misconceptions of the gospel and deformations of practice by which the church of the day had broken continuity with the apostles. For the good news had been falsified by making God's favor dependent on good works, by centering the Lord's Supper on sacrifice offered to propitiate God, and by the papal hierarchy's claiming the right to add new articles of faith and impose practices binding in conscience.

99. The Reformation rejected what it found contradicting and obscuring the gospel in the church under the papacy, but its critique was not total, for Luther could say, ". . . in the Papacy there are the true Holy Scriptures, true baptism, the true sacrament, the true keys for the forgiveness of sins, the true office of proclamation, and the true catechism."[16] The Catholic Church possessed and was pass-

---

[15] WA 41, 562,14-16: "Hoc vero est apostolice tractare scripturas, et statuere illam universalem sententiam, quod omnes qui credunt verbo Dei sunt iusti."

[16] *Concerning Rebaptism* (1528), WA 26, 146f, LW40, 231f. Also, *Commentary on Galatians* (1535), WA 40/1, 69; LW 26, 24.

ing on the elements of the apostolic legacy which the Reformation was now using in correct ways.

100. Reformation critique thus served re-focusing church life on the gospel and reorganizing it to serve the communication of the gospel. Reform aimed at renewed continuity with the apostolic church by centering church life on Scripture and its exposition in preaching, by the administration and daily remembrance of baptism, by the common celebration of the Lord's Supper, by pastoral exercise of the keys to deal with sin, and by reaffirming ministry as an office of communicating the gospel. By preaching and these basic forms, the gospel of Christ makes itself present in the church.

101. The gospel purely taught and the sacraments rightly administered are necessary for the existence of the church (*Augsburg Confession*, Art. 7). This basic affirmation defines the church by reference to the apostolic mission, while also establishing what is needed for its unity. But an agreement on the teaching of the gospel also embraces the practices coming from the apostles by which the message impacts on life and gives form to the life of the community (cf. nos. 94-95, above). Beyond the apostolic nucleus, "traditions" may be accepted, but not as necessary for constituting the church and its unity.

102. Maintaining the church's continuity in the message and in the essentially connected practices received from the apostles comes to be centered in catechesis, which is instruction and initiation aiming to shape life and devotion by the basic texts of the Commandments, the Creed, prayer, the sacraments, and confession and absolution by the power of the keys. By these, the apostolic legacy remains present and alive in the church.

2.4.2 Apostolicity at Trent and in Post-Tridentine Catholic Theology

103. To prepare its doctrinal clarifications and reform decrees, in 1546 the Council of Trent first stated that the gospel of Christ, preached by the apostles, is the source of all saving truth and norms of Christian practice. This gospel gave rise to a body of doctrine and norms expressed in both Scripture and the unwritten traditions transmitted by the apostles to the church (DS 1501; Tanner, 663). But this same gospel is not only an external word, but is also interior, planted

by the Holy Spirit in the hearts of believers.[17] Regarding Scripture, Trent specified the canon and indicated that interpretations concerning faith and practice must not diverge from a perennial ecclesial understanding, exemplified by the Church Fathers, which remains present today and empowers the teaching office to judge the adequacy of biblical interpretations (DS 1507; Tanner, 664).

104. Trent did not present a dogmatic ecclesiology, but left this area open. Theologians responded to the immediate needs of controversy by developing an apologetical treatment of apostolicity, that is, a presentation of evidence to prove that the Roman Church is alone the *vera ecclesia* ("true church"), with rightful authority in teaching and a legitimate corps of bishops and presbyters.[18] Later Catholic manuals of ecclesiology were dominated by apologetics, arguing from numerous external "marks" or "notes" by which to ascertain the true church of Christ, especially through the papal and episcopal succession in office from Peter and the other apostles to the present day.

105. Post-Tridentine Catholic theology was narrowed by constraints of argument to give practically no place to the ecclesial endowments of Scripture, creeds, worship, spirituality, and discipline of life, which in fact shaped the lives of Catholics but which were also shared in different ways with Christians of the separated churches. Ecclesiology was dominated by concern with the formal issue of *legitimacy* in holding these and other gifts. Interior gifts appeared less important than the verifiable marks employed by an apologetics drawing on history. In the argument, the aim was to identify the institutional entity in which Christ's truth is normatively taught, his efficacious sacraments administered, and a pastoral governance exercised in a legitimate manner, especially by reason of apostolic succession of Pope and bishops in a church assuredly still sustained by Christ's promised assistance.

---

[17] Cardinal Legate M. Cervini, the future Pope Marcellus II, spoke of the gospel written on hearts, in the programmic address of 18 February, 1546, which initiated deliberations on Scripture and the traditions. CT 1 (Freiburg 1901), 484f.

[18] This narrowed theological perception, abstracting from preaching, the spiritual life, and missionary zeal, has been magisterially presented by G. Thils, *Les notes de l'Église dans l'apologétique catholique depuis la Réforme* (Gembloux 1937). An emblematic exposition of "apostolicity" in the form of historical proof is the entry by J.V. Bainvel in the monumental *Dictionnaire de Théologie Catholique*, 1 (1903), 1618-1629.

2.5 Developments toward Resolution and Consensus

2.5.1 A Catholic Ecumenical Vision of Participated Apostolicity

The Gospel and the Episcopal College

106. In the mid-twentieth century, important works of biblical theology, along with newly circulating patristic and liturgical sources, gave Catholics the resources for fresh developments in ecclesiology. But the gospel is basic to the church, as Vatican II indicates at the beginning of its dogmatic text on the church (LG 1) by referring to Christ as the "light of the nations" (*Lumen gentium*) to be brought to all humanity by proclaiming the gospel to every creature (cf. Mk 16:15).

107. When Vatican II restates Trent's declaration on the gospel as source of all saving truth (DV 7), "the gospel" is the concentrated expression of God's revelation which gives believers, out of the fullness of God's love, access to the Father through Christ in the Holy Spirit. The truth revealed about God and human salvation "shines forth in Christ, who is himself both the mediator and sum total of revelation" (DV 2). Christ completed and perfected revelation by his words and works, signs and miracles, but above all by his death on the cross and glorious resurrection, which express the gospel message "that God is with us, to deliver us from the darkness of sin and death and to raise us up to eternal life" (DV 4). The gospel of salvation is thus articulated in Vatican II's Constitution on Divine Revelation (*Dei Verbum*), which is prior to all else that the Council taught on the church and its life.[19] This recovery of the soteriological focus of revelation was one factor in opening the way for Catholics to join Lutherans in adhering to a common understanding of justification in *The Joint Declaration on the Doctrine of Justification* (esp. nos. 14-18).

108. Regarding the papal and episcopal ministry serving the public proclamation of this gospel, Catholic doctrine now features further recovered insights. In Vatican II, the apostolic primacy of Rome and its bishop must be seen *within* the entire body of bishops, who form

---

[19] In a 1964 response to a proposed amendment, Vatican II's Doctrinal Commission stated that *De revelatione*, the future *Dei Verbum,* is "in a way the first of all the Constitutions of this Council." *Acta Synodalia Sacrosancti Concilii Vaticani Secundi*, vol. IV/1 (Vatican City 1976), 341.

a structured *collegium*, which succeeds the college of the apostles in missionary and pastoral responsibility, and in governing and teaching authority (LG 22-24). The unity of the church has the form of *communio* among particular churches whose bishops are united in the episcopal college, which is a corporate locus of apostolic succession in union with the bishop of the primatial apostolic See of Rome, who is both a member of the college and its head. This college perpetuates itself in order to carry out its responsibilities to the gospel by including new members, firm in their profession of the church's faith, who corporately ensure the continuity over time of what the college has been commissioned by Christ to proclaim to and preserve in his church.

109. Being an ordained member of this college does not guarantee an individual bishop's faithful transmission of the apostolic gospel and tradition, for one can fall into disaccord with the transmitted faith and so lapse from episcopal *communio*, but the Catholic conviction is that the college as a whole, in union with the primatial bishop, is protected in transmitting the apostolic message and forms of worship and life. This heritage of teaching, liturgy and witness, that is, the living tradition, is thus bound to a corporate body of living teachers, whose apostolic succession makes them normative witnesses to what comes from Christ through the apostles.

110. Vatican II echoes a major Reformation concern by linking the episcopal office, before all else, with the preaching of the gospel of Christ (LG 25.1). Bishops are evangelists, called to exemplify preaching for the presbyters whose ministry of word, sacrament, and pastoral care (PO 2.4, 4-6) they promote and oversee. Since the petrine office is within the episcopate, its primary role is also to proclaim Christ, in the image of Peter's foundational witness to the resurrection of Christ, as the central event announced in the gospel. Thus, episcopal and papal apostolic succession in office serves a *successio verbi* ("succession in the word"), to build up the church from its foundation of faith in Christ.

111. Part 3 of this report will present how Catholic doctrine views a pastoral ministry of word and sacrament outside the corporate episcopal succession. But this must rest on a view of ecclesial tradition, about which contemporary Catholic teaching features insights recovered from long-neglected sources, which lead to a conception different from what

predominated in the post-Tridentine era, but which in fact fulfills essential intentions of the Councils of Trent and Vatican I.

A Renewed Understanding of Tradition

112. Beginning in the initial Catholic arguments against Reformation claims and continuing well into the twentieth century, an apologetically framed Catholic theology stressed the existence of certain non-written traditions conveyed to the churches by the apostles by means other than Scripture. A text like 2 Thess. 2,15 was cited to show that Paul also transmitted "traditions taught by word of mouth", while John 20,30 and 21,25, on the "many other things that Jesus did", opened a broad panorama of possible practices not attested in the gospels. These traditions, emphasized against the Reformation *sola Scriptura* ("Scripture alone"), entered the church as doctrines and instituted community practices, which the apostles communicated orally but did not set down in the New Testament, with these leading in time by the dynamic of development to required liturgical and disciplinary ordinances and even to dogmatic propositions of the doctrine of faith.

113. Historical studies motivated Vatican II to avoid ratifying the notion of unwritten traditions which supplement Scripture with further teachings and practices of apostolic origin. The Council carefully avoided a doctrinal decision on the contents of the "unwritten traditions", while stressing instead an intimate correlation, permeating the whole life of the church, between Scripture and the dynamic process of tradition (DV 8.3, 9). By the interaction of these two in the church, the apostolic tradition of the gospel and life is perpetuated, which Scripture expresses in a special manner (DV 8).

114. Here apostolic tradition itself is depicted in a fresh manner. In the churches they founded, the apostles communicated the gospel, thereby communicating *dona divina* ("divine gifts") to believers, by the ensemble of "the spoken word of their preaching, by the example they gave, by the institutions they established, [as] they themselves had received" (DV 7.1). This complex reality, the apostolic patrimony, passed into the post-apostolic churches and thus began its further life in history: "what was handed on by the apostles comprises everything that serves to make the People of God live their lives in holiness and increase their faith." This reality consti-

tuted of many elements is then perpetuated in and by the church "in her doctrine, life, and worship" as she continuously transmits "all that she herself is, all that she believes" (DV 8.1).

115. The patrimony of the apostolic tradition is multifaceted and vital, being closely linked with the corporate reality of the community. A many-sided *depositum vitae* ("deposit of life"), illustrated suggestively by the Pastoral Epistles, represents what Vatican II sees as the apostolic tradition, which has its center in the gospel and finds in the New Testament its pre-eminent testimony to Christ, in whom appeared "the goodness and loving kindness of God our Savior" (Titus 3,4-7, also 2,11-14).

116. The apostolic tradition comprises many interwoven strands of teachings which foster faith and life consonant with faith, and many practices inculcated in the community to promote its witness in its locale. These traditions make up the authentic Tradition manifested in the church's communal life.

The Catholic Church and the Other Churches and Ecclesial Communities

117. The renewed Catholic doctrine on Scripture and tradition leads, in our ecumenical context, to the recognition that these components pertain to the means of sanctification and formation in truth that are present both in the Catholic Church and in other communities now in real but imperfect communion with the Catholic Church.

118. These developments in Catholic ecclesiology, concerning the episcopate and tradition, open avenues of advance, not only toward doctrinal agreement with churches of the Reformation about the church, but also toward acknowledging the apostolicity of these churches whose ministerial pastoral leadership does not stand in historical apostolic succession.

119. Vatican II took important initial steps toward considering as apostolic churches now outside the Catholic communion, when it affirmed that "many elements of sanctification and truth are found outside its [own] visible confines", that is, in other churches and ecclesial communities, and when it called these "gifts belonging to the Church of Christ" (LG 8). The Council developed this in LG 15, with reference to the "elements" that are central components of

life in the separated churches and ecclesial communities: baptism, the Scriptures, faith in the Triune God, sacraments, the sanctifying activity of the Holy Spirit, and the witness of martyrdom.

120. Vatican II's Decree on Ecumenism (*Unitatis redintegratio*) laid a central foundation of our dialogue by acknowledging that the other churches and ecclesial communities "have been by no means deprived of significance and importance in the mystery of salvation. For the Spirit of Christ has not refrained from using them as means of salvation ..." (UR 3). The same passage mentions again "the elements of sanctification and truth", with amplification on liturgical worship among the endowments which come from Christ and constitute the separated communities as means by which the Spirit of Christ works out the salvation of their members.

121. From this conciliar affirmation of the Christian endowments of the separated churches, Catholic ecumenical theology is justified in concluding to an implicit recognition of these churches and ecclesial communities as apostolic, since the very elements listed are not meteorites fallen from heaven into the churches of our time, but have come from Christ through the ministry of his apostles and are components of the apostolic tradition. Beyond our common sharing in Christ's salvation by grace and personal faith, we are also in real, but still imperfect, ecclesial communion (UR 3) because we share the mediating elements of sanctification and truth given by God through Christ and the apostles. The Catholic Church and the churches and ecclesial communities of the Reformation both participate in the attribute of apostolicity because they are built up and live by many of the same "elements and endowments" pertaining to the one and multiple apostolic tradition.[20]

122. This affirmation involves for Catholics an analogous or differentiated application of the qualification "apostolic" to other churches and ecclesial communities, because of Catholic convictions about

---

[20] The Catholic attribution of apostolicity, based on the apostolic elements, goes hand-in-hand with use of the designation "ecclesial communities" for bodies of the Protestant tradition, a terminology introduced into *De oecumenismo* in the revision of early 1964 and retained in the promulgated text in UR 19 and 22. The meaning was explained in the *Relatio* accompanying the revised text as recognizing in them "a truly ecclesial character", because of the presence and socially formative action in them of the one Church of Christ, in a true but imperfect manner. (*Acta Synodalia*, III/2, 335)

The Apostolicity of the Church

the full complement of sacramental and institutional elements, especially in its episcopal and primatial ministers, that the Catholic Church has retained, in spite of her deficiencies in faith, worship, and the mission entrusted to her. In churches whose bishops stand outside the episcopal college united with the successor of Peter, apostolicity while being genuine is also different from the apostolicity of a church in which faith, doctrine, sacraments, worship, and life are integrated by a united and collegial episcopal ministry which, in communion with the successor of Peter, continues in a unique way the ministry of the apostles. For Catholics this ministerial structure is not external to the gospel it communicates, for it mediates the gospel.

123. Parts 3 and 4 of this document will explore further the different ways our churches are apostolic, by examining our convictions and differences over ordination in episcopal succession and over teaching authority, both of which affect the way Catholic theology applies the qualification "apostolic" to the churches of the Reformation.

2.5.2 An Ecumenical Lutheran Account of the Apostolicity of the Church

The Full Dimensions of the Word of God

124. The insights of biblical theology in the last century have again reinforced for Lutherans the awareness of the gospel as God's saving word sent forth into history. The word of God is dynamic, for in it God is acting, in Christ, through the Holy Spirit. The gospel is "the power of God for salvation" (Rom 1:16), through which the Spirit gathers and sustains a new community for its corporate witness to the gospel among the nations. Through the witnessing community, as a distinctive, continuous, and embodied presence in the world, God's word is engaging historical life in an efficacious way, as Luther says in the *Large Catechism*, "The Holy Spirit continues his work without ceasing until the Last Day, and for this purpose he has appointed a community on earth, through which he speaks and does all his work."[21]

125. The word of God, to be sure, has a definite content as teaching about the Son of God and his saving work, a doctrine which must

---

[21] BSLK 659,47, 660,3; BC 439.

be attested truthfully in faithful reception of the apostolic testimony. While faith without content is void, still it is not simply assent to true statements, since God meets believers in personal encounter by engaging them in the promise of the gospel word and sacraments. Thus believers fully trust in God's promises and in faith they personally embrace true belief.

126. This awareness of the full dimensions of the word of God has implications for understanding the apostolicity of the church, the substance of which lies in the ongoing proclamation of God's saving action in Christ, through word and sacrament, in fidelity to the apostolic witness. The Holy Spirit is acting to bestow saving communion with Jesus Christ on believers living in history and to form them into a community of witness and celebration for attesting the good news to all the world. The continuity of the Spirit's saving action, taking form in the church's continuous reception and handing-on of the gospel, amid a manifold ecclesial practice centered on the gospel, is thus seen today as the depth-dimension of the apostolicity of the church.

The Elements of Apostolicity and their Configuration

127. In view of these dimensions of the gospel, as the word of God sent forth in history, apostolicity must be taken as a complex reality embracing multiple elements. A Lutheran view of ecclesial apostolicity does not simply look to the presence of these elements in the life of a community, but much more to the pattern of their configuration and to the understanding and use of them. This is of primary importance for a Lutheran account of the church's apostolic integrity. The Reformers recognized that all the elements of apostolicity were present in the late-medieval church, but the pattern of their right shape, understanding, and use had been obscured. To reform the church was to re-gather the elements of apostolicity around their proper center, so as to recover an authentically apostolic pattern of the marks of the church.

128. The center is, of course, the holy gospel that promises forgiveness and salvation given freely by God's grace, for Christ's sake, received by faith alone. The preached gospel is linked inseparably with baptism and the Lord's Supper in articulating the grace given to believers. For the good news of salvation to be communicated in

its depth and saving power, the preached gospel must be joined with the sacraments, along with the ministry of the keys. This is the vital center of the church's life, the central cluster of authentic continuity with the apostles, by which their mission continues.

129. This center does not exclude other elements of apostolicity, but their meaning becomes clear only in relation to these basic forms. Around them the witnessing community takes shape, by which the message is proclaimed and celebrated. The concern here, in Lutheran perspective, is not reduction through the exclusion of other elements, but the concentration of everything in the community on the central communication of God's life-giving forgiveness.

130. Around the central expression of the gospel in word and sacrament, the life of the community takes shape in offices and institutions, doctrines, liturgies and church orders, and an ethos and spirituality animated by the message of God's grace. Also in this account apostolicity is a gift and calling which shapes the whole life of the church as a community in history. On this basis, Lutheran theology can understand the continuity of the church with its apostolic origin in a socially embodied way, which while complex is centered on the proclamation of the gospel and celebration of the sacraments in a manner echoed by Catholic teaching in Vatican II (cf. nos. 107 and 114-116, above).

The Substance of the Gospel and its Contingent Forms

131. Today Lutheran teaching has learned that the central forms of the gospel, with the community life shaped by them, and in it the office of ministry, all come to us in historically contingent expressions. The good news of Christ comes to us in biblical texts, in a canon, and in liturgical creeds all marked by the time of their origins. The sacraments of salvation have been embedded in historically developed orders of worship and liturgical texts. The church's ministry and the office of the keys are mediated to us in contingent forms of church order and traditional pastoral care.

132. This means that the church must continuously be aware of needs for reform. But in this we cannot distill a pure gospel in abstraction from contingent forms, and we should not, for such a gospel would not be a word sent forth in history. We recognize today that the church needs, in various degrees, particular forms of apostolic con-

tinuity which are not in themselves intrinsic to the substance of the apostolic gospel. These forms serve the proclamation of the good news of Christ and bring to believers today the elements of gospel-centered apostolic continuity, while expressing as well the unity in faith between a local community and the church throughout the world and throughout the ages.

133. The widely recognized mediating forms of apostolic continuity, based on the books of the biblical canon, such as creedal formulas, catechisms, church orders, and common forms of worship, while not *necessary* in a strict sense for the gospel to be expressed with saving efficacy, are still *needed* in the church for its mission and its broader unity. Their use, however, must be continually reformed, to enable them to serve better the continuity of the church with its apostolic origin.

134. Reform must entail holding fast to and proclaiming more authentically the truth of the gospel, which in the sixteenth century led to breaking historic bonds of ecclesial communion. But today such reform should go hand-in-hand with the recollection that according to Christ's will the communion of Christians with one another is intrinsic to their witness.

Diversity and its Reconciliation

135. Historical consciousness makes us aware today of the persistence of theological diversity both throughout the history of the Christian community and today among those who receive the common apostolic legacy. Many recognize that the unity in faith and sacramental life toward which our ecumenical efforts are advancing will entail "reconciled diversity", which while leaving real diversity nonetheless shapes and orders it by what is held in common, so that differences do not entail division and opposition.

136. Reconciliation is encompassed by unity given in Christ and actualized by the Holy Spirit. It concerns that which we receive together from the apostles, in doctrine and preaching, sacramental life, mission, prayer, and ethos. The reconciling movement of communities toward each other has to attend to the confession of the apostolic faith and to doctrine. But the ground of unity in reconciled diversity is *extra nos*, outside ourselves, in the word and sacraments by which Christ is present and known to us. What reconciles is the

mutual recognition that it is the apostolic legacy which the respective churches receive in their preaching and sacramental practice. Reconciliation occurs through such shared reception of the apostolic gospel, and by finding deep common features of different receptions we draw near to a common center and enter into communion with one another.

137. In the relation between the churches, "unity in reconciled diversity" rests on recognition as a judgment that another community has authentically received the apostolic legacy, so that what it teaches agrees with the gospel's content and its communal practice communicates the good news of Christ. This leads to common confession of the apostolic faith and acknowledgment that the different ways the communities explicate the faith are open to one another in their diversity.

138. Thus a *differentiated consensus* is the form in which separated churches may come together, that is, in agreed confession with recognition that existing differences do not impede mutual recognition of the present-day continuity with Christian apostolic beginnings and do not prevent partnership in the apostolic mission.

Lutherans and the Roman Catholic Church

139. Lutherans have long held Roman Catholic teaching and practice to be discontinuous with the apostolic legacy in different respects, for instance when institutions and practices of merely human devising are considered integral to this legacy. What is essential in the life of the church has thereby been obscured. In the Lutheran view, the Roman Catholic Church has retained the substance of the apostolic legacy. It is, however, interpreted and configured in such a way that apostolicity is not properly embodied in teaching, sacramental practice and structures of governance.

140. But in the changed ecumenical situation, along with their own new insights into the implications of fundamental beliefs, Lutherans see Roman Catholics working out new understandings, for example, when they emphasize the centrality of the apostolic gospel as "the source of all saving truth and norms of practice" and interpret apostolic succession in terms of what is provided by God so that the full and living gospel might always be preserved in the church (Vatican II, DV 7).

141. While important differences remain, the discussion of apostolicity can and must proceed on the basis of the shared conviction expressed in the Malta Report of 1972: "The church is apostolic insofar as it ... abides in the apostolic faith. The church's ministry, doctrine, and order are apostolic insofar as they pass on and actualize the apostolic witness" (*The Gospel and the Church*, 52).

142. Through the signing of the *Joint Declaration on the Doctrine of Justification*, the Lutheran World Federation has acknowledged that, despite continuing differences, the teaching of the Roman Catholic Church on justification is compatible with faithful proclamation of the good news of Jesus Christ in accord with the apostolic witness. This is for Lutherans the recognition that the basic reality which makes a church apostolic is present in the Roman Catholic Church. Nevertheless, Lutherans find some doctrines and practices which they see in tension with this reality. They also see Catholics regarding some elements as integral to apostolicity, such as historical apostolic succession and papal primacy, with which they do not agree. The ecclesiological weight given to these elements prevents their giving an unrestricted recognition to the apostolicity of the Roman Catholic Church. This also shows that there are differences between the Catholic and Lutheran conceptions of the apostolicity of the church.

143. The present dialogue is thus rightly asking what we can now say together about the true apostolicity of the church, especially regarding ministry, tradition, and teaching authority in their service of the church's continuity with its apostolic origin. This will then lead to the further question of the extent of our recognition in each other of the apostolic gospel and mission in their integrity.

2.6 Conclusions on Ecclesial Apostolicity

Introduction

144. This fourth phase of the Lutheran-Catholic world-level dialogue has taken up a tension-filled complex of questions about the church, namely, the characteristic of its enduring continuity with its apostolic foundation, the apostolicity of its ordained ministry, and its means of maintaining faith and doctrine in the truth communicated by the apostles.

145. To clarify the first area, we have reviewed, compared, and probed more deeply our respective understandings of the apostolicity of the church. The initial results can be summarized here in three sections: (1) foundational convictions about ecclesial apostolicity which we share in faith; (2) shared understandings we have discovered; and (3) differences which must be examined more deeply with a view to their reconciliation and of clarifying whether they still have a church-dividing effect.

2.6.1. Shared Foundational Convictions of Faith

146. In formulating the initial results of our joint study of the apostolicity of the church, we first affirm as common convictions the central truths of the Lutheran-Catholic consensus on justification. We believe that the Triune God is working to save sinners by the incarnation, death, and resurrection of Jesus Christ. We share in the righteousness of Christ through the Holy Spirit and are accepted by God by grace alone, in faith and not because of any merit on our part. In Christ, the Holy Spirit renews our hearts and equips and calls us to good works (JDDJ, no. 15).

147. As attested in the *Joint Declaration*, we confess together faith *in* the Holy Spirit, "Lord and giver of life", who is bringing to the whole world the salvation gained by Jesus Christ. We are furthermore one in confessing the church as an essential work of that same Spirit, who created communities of believers through the gospel of Jesus Christ announced as a saving message by the apostles. We agree, as we accept the New Testament testimony, that Jesus Christ sent his apostles as authorized witnesses of his resurrection and to make disciples in the whole world and impart baptism for the forgiveness of sins. By the gospel of salvation, the apostles gathered believers into communities founded on Jesus Christ (cf. Part 1, nos. 22 and 25, above). To these communities the New Testament writings, whether composed by apostles or by evangelists, prophets, and teachers of the late apostolic period, give further apostolic instruction in faith and a manner of life worthy of the gospel of Christ.

148. By confessing that the church of every age is "apostolic" we hold that the apostolic witness is both a normative origin and an abiding foundation. The church of every age, we believe, is a work of the

Holy Spirit who makes present the apostolic gospel and makes effective the sacraments and apostolic instruction which we have been graced to receive. In faith, we accept, as individuals and communities, the call to serve the further transmission of the apostolic gospel which the Holy Spirit continues to make a *viva vox* of good news and a meaningful way of life in truth and service for men and women both of our day and in the future lying before us.

2.6.2. Shared Understandings Discovered

149. Grounded in our shared convictions of faith, our study has shown that in explicating what we believe about Christ, the Holy Spirit, and the church, which has already begun in previous documents of this dialogue, especially *Church and Justification* (1994), there are further important truths on which our two doctrinal traditions manifest a consensus.

150. This study reveals a fundamental agreement between Lutherans and Catholics that the gospel is central and decisive in the apostolic heritage. Thus we agree that the church in every age continues to be "apostolic" by reason of its faith in and witness to the gospel of Jesus Christ. This is attested by the New Testament (cf. nos. 70-81, above).

151. The pre-Reformation church understood a central component of its apostolicity to be its profession and teaching of the orthodox faith expressed in the twelve articles of the Apostles' Creed. Reformation preaching and catechesis received this legacy in a fresh manner, concentrating on the gospel of salvation as the proclamation of God's grace to sinners, a message coming from the Risen Christ and originally communicated by the apostles. By faith in this message, in every age sinners lay hold of Christ's death for our sins and his resurrection for our justification (cf. nos. 93-95, above).

152. This gospel of our salvation served as criterion in the Reformation critique of the established church of the sixteenth century and was the norm of the Lutheran constructive reshaping of church life around proclamation of and teaching on Jesus Christ as the apostolic gospel makes him present (cf. nos. 100-102, above). For the Lutheran Reformation, the gospel is a definite message about Jesus Christ in his unique role in the divine plan of salvation. As for Luther, so for modern Lutherans, the gospel is a dynamic *viva vox*

in which Christ is encountering human beings to whom he becomes present as Savior and whom he empowers by his Spirit to become believers declared and made righteous.

153. But when the Council of Trent, driven both by Reformation challenges and the intent to reform the church, probed the deeper foundations of its faith and life, it singled out the gospel of Jesus Christ, proclaimed by the apostles, as "the source of all saving truth and norms of practice". While Scripture and the apostolic traditions communicate this gospel truth and norms of living outwardly, it is the Holy Spirit who writes the same gospel interiorly on believing hearts (cf. no. 103, above).

154. Vatican II restated the centrality of the gospel, but enriched its affirmation by a christocentric and salvific account of God's word of revelation of which the gospel is the concentrated summation (cf. nos. 106-107, above). Beyond this account of the gospel as central to the church and its life, Vatican II went on to state that by the ongoing interaction of the church's living tradition of faith and life with the Scriptures, God continues to speak today and by the Holy Spirit the living word of the gospel (*viva vox evangelii*) resounds in the church and the world (DV 8.3).

155. Catholic and Lutheran teaching are also in agreement that the apostolic legacy, by which faith in Jesus Christ is instilled, nurtured, and embodied, is a manifold and many-faceted heritage. Thus, the opposition sketched at the beginning of this Part (no. 67, above) does not present the real situation.

156. In Catholic theology between Trent and Vatican II, apostolicity was narrowly conceived as continuity in papal and episcopal succession and this continuity functioned as a *nota ecclesiae* ("note of the church") in proving the legitimacy of the Roman Catholic Church. But Vatican II drew on Scripture and the Fathers to explain the apostolic tradition, in its objective sense, as an ensemble of gospel preaching, sacraments, different types of ministry, forms of worship, and the apostles' example of selfless service of the churches founded by the gospel (cf. nos. 114-115, above). The apostolic heritage, expressed in a special manner in Scripture, "comprises everything that serves to make the People of God live their lives in holiness and increase their faith" (DV 8.1). The original apostles,

formed by hearing Jesus and living with him, then instructed by the Holy Spirit, transmitted an ample basis of what the later church expresses in its doctrine, life, and worship.

157. This renewed view of apostolic tradition as unifying many components grounds the Roman Catholic approach to the churches and communities to which she is related by a true but imperfect communion. Catholic ecumenism presupposes the sincerity of faith of other Christians, but this is not properly the basis of meeting them in dialogue and striving for visible Christian unity. This rests instead on "the elements of sanctification and truth" that are present and operative in the still separated communities not in full communion. These bodies "have been by no means deprived of significance and importance in the mystery of salvation. For the Spirit of Christ has not refrained from using them as means of salvation" (UR 3).

158. In a rarely noted but remarkable correspondence with Vatican II on tradition and "the elements of sanctification and truth", Luther connected the gospel with a set of practices through which the saving message comes to individuals and gives shape to community life (cf. nos. 94-95, 100-102, above). Christ rules and works through the gospel proclaimed, but this comes to expression in baptism, the sacrament of the altar, and the ministry of the keys for the forgiveness of sins. The church is apostolic by holding to the truth of the gospel that is embodied continually in practices coming from the apostles in which the Holy Spirit continues the communication of Christ's grace. The Holy Spirit makes use of a complex of means by which believers are sanctified and church is constituted (*Large Catechism*, 3rd article of the Creed).

159. Our study has uncovered a further instance of agreement in Luther's several lists of inherited elements when he explained what the reformed churches have received from the church under the papacy (cf. no. 99, above). Consequently, gazing across the divide of separation, he insisted that a manifold Christian substance must be recognized in the Roman Catholic Church. The Reformation was not starting the church anew but instead was recovering the original significance of "elements" which it received, namely, the Scriptures, baptism, the sacrament of the altar, the keys, and the catechetical components of the Lord's Prayer, the commandments,

and the Creed with its articles of faith. For the Reformers, the use of these elements under the papacy was seriously defective as an embodiment of Christ's gospel, but the Roman Church is acknowledged as still carrying within it the principal practices by which the gospel is meant to shape the life of the church in continuity with its apostolic foundation.

160. Thus, on the apostolic tradition, both as comprising a manifold legacy of fundamental means of sanctification and as directed to shape community life by the gospel of our salvation in Christ, Lutheran and Catholic teaching and church life manifest a wide-ranging agreement. Today we therefore mutually recognize, at a fundamental level, the presence of apostolicity in our traditions. This recognition is not negated by the important differences still to be investigated.

2.6.3. Differences Calling for Further Examination

161. The fundamental mutual recognition of ecclesial apostolicity which we have set forth is presently limited on both sides by significant reservations about the doctrine and church life of the partner in dialogue.

162. A first limitation rests on differences in understanding ordination to the pastorate, ministry in apostolic succession, and the office of bishop in the church. Second, while we agree on Sacred Scripture being the norm of all preaching, teaching, and Christian life, we differ on how Scripture is to be authentically interpreted and how the teaching office serves Scripture in the latter's guidance of the church's teaching and practice.

163. This part of our study has shown the solid basis of our mutual recognition of apostolic continuity. Now we turn, in Part 3, to examine apostolic succession, the ordained ministry, and the episcopate especially in light of the experiences that were formative for our churches. Part 4 will review our respective convictions about the authority of Scripture and then examine our differences over how the teaching office is constituted and how Scripture functions as the source and apostolic criterion of all that our churches believe and teach.

164. On apostolicity as mark and attribute of the church our joint study of Scripture and history leads to a fruitful account of present-day

teaching and to agreements grounding a fundamental mutual recognition. In what follows our work aims at discovering even more commonly shared convictions and corresponding practices regarding ministry and the relation between Scripture and the teaching office. We aim at an agreement which will reduce significantly the reservations presently hindering that full communion in apostolic truth and life which is the goal of our dialogue.

Study-Document of the Lutheran-Roman Catholic Commission on Unity

PART 3
APOSTOLIC SUCCESSION AND ORDAINED MINISTRY

3.1 Introduction

165. Part 2 of this study dealt with the apostolicity of the whole church and discussed the "elements" which, by the power of the Holy Spirit, contribute to building up the church "upon the foundation of the apostles and prophets, with Christ Jesus himself as the cornerstone" (Eph 2:20). Among these elements are the Holy Scriptures, the communication of God's word in proclamation, baptism, and the Lord's Supper, the office of the keys, catechesis as transmission of the apostolic tradition, the Creeds, the Lord's Prayer, and the Ten Commandments. These elements are institutions and enactments of the communication of the word of God in which the content of the apostolic gospel becomes present to bring salvation to human beings. In doing so, they play a part in maintaining the apostolicity of the church as a whole. The apostolicity of the church is bound up with a multitude of such elements, which are of course present in our churches in different configurations.

166. Because these elements involve institutions and enactments of the communication of the word of God, human beings are an essential factor in them. There is no testimony without a witness, no sermon without a preacher, no administration of the sacraments without a minister, but also no testimony and no sermon without people who listen, no celebration of the sacraments without people who receive them. That having been said, the problem arises about how human beings take part in the communication of the word of God in such a way that the church is maintained in continuity with the apostolic tradition.

167. With respect to human beings *as hearers and recipients* of the gospel, we declare together with the *Joint Declaration on the Doctrine of Justification*: "Through Christ alone are we justified, when we receive this salvation in faith. Faith is itself God's gift through the Holy Spirit, who works through Word and Sacrament in the community of believers."[22] With respect to human beings *as co-workers*

with God in the communication of the gospel, all who have been baptized and believe are called to collaborate in the transmission of the gospel, by virtue of their sharing in the priesthood of Christ. At the same time, the church also has its ordained ministry to which some individuals are specially called. Both Catholics and Lutherans have to clarify the relation between the universal or common priesthood of all the baptized and the special ministry conferred by ordination. The answer to this question depends on the configuration of the above-mentioned elements, and then influences this configuration. The elements themselves are not independent of their particular configuration, as one sees in the relationship between ministerial office and the eucharist. So the ministry, in both its doctrinal understanding and its institutional organization, is of great significance for the apostolicity of the church.

168. A response concerning the relation between the universal priesthood of all baptized and the ordained ministry goes along with the answer to a further problem which arises here, namely, the question of a differentiation within the special ministry. This involves primarily the relation between the office of pastor or presbyter and that of bishop. The course of church history has seen this relation defined in different ways and it is understood differently by the Roman Catholic Church and the Lutheran churches. Thus these offices have a different structure in the two bodies, which affects both doctrinal understanding and church organization. For both Catholics and Lutherans the special ministry is a special service given to the apostolic gospel and thus to the apostolicity of the church. The ecumenical issue bound up with the problem of the different ways of structuring the special ministry is this: Are a *specific structure* of the pastoral office and *one specific structure* of the episcopal office, as well as a specific form of embedding the latter into a larger college of office-holders, essential to the authentic and legitimate service of the apostolic gospel? Can the one office of ministry manifest itself in different structures? What belongs to its substance and what belongs to structures of it which are, within certain limits, variable?

---

[22] JDDJ no. 16.

169. The search for answers will first be oriented by the New Testament taken in connection with the Old Testament, with the former being the primary and binding testimony of the Christian faith (Section 3.2, below). But the New Testament shows a variety of ministries and charisms, along with forms and concepts of ministry which are different while they overlap with one another. With due caution, one can distinguish lines of development within the New Testament. How this development is discerned and evaluated is of course not independent of how one assesses the later historical development of the ministry. The Early Church's structure of the threefold ministry is not attested as such in the New Testament, but it did emerge by the further development of offices referred to in the New Testament which were then brought together into a particular configuration. The development of the office of ministry in the Early Church is a specific form of the reception of New Testament testimony to ministries and charisms which were effective in the church of the apostles.

170. This Part will then sketch the historical development of ecclesial ministry in the Early Church and in the Middle Ages. This forms a part of the shared history of both the Catholic and Lutheran churches and can be encompassed in a joint description (Section 3.3, below). For both churches it is of great significance that this development led at such an early stage and with such lasting effect to a distinction between the office of presbyter and the office of bishop. It is possible to discern the reasons and motivational impulses for this distinction and to discover the inner logic of this development. To be sure, theological assessments of the normativity of this development diverge from one another, above all because the Reformers arrived at the judgment that the church of their time had in many respects become unfaithful to the apostolic gospel of God's grace, and because they saw this expressed in an understanding of the pastoral office focused on offering the sacrifice of the mass. On their side, bishops who had been convinced by their theologians of the errors of the Reformers refused to ordain Lutheran theologians. Thus Lutheran congregations which wanted reform-minded pastors were faced with the choice of either renouncing the ordination of their pastors by bishops or abandoning their conviction about justification by grace alone and by faith alone. At

that point a split occurred between two elementary aspects of apostolic succession. The examination of these questions demands a brief exposition of the development of the ordained ministry in the Lutheran Reformation and how it has been understood theologically (Section 3.4.1, below), as well as a sketch of how the Council of Trent responded to the Reformation concerning ecclesial ministry (3.4.2). This will lead to a presentation of how the Second Vatican Council both took up and developed what the Council of Trent had taught (3.5.1), followed by an overview of the current Lutheran doctrine of ministry (3.5.2).

171. Then a concluding section (3.6) will explore convergences on the subject of ministry in apostolic succession, especially when one considers the circumstances of the divergence on this topic and takes into account not only the differences but also what Catholics and Lutherans hold in common regarding the apostolicity of the church and its ministry, including both commonalities which have never been lost and those which have been rediscovered.

3.2. Biblical Orientation

172. "You are a chosen race, a royal priesthood, a holy nation, God's own people, that you may declare the mighty acts of him who called you out of darkness into his marvelous light." Thus the First Epistle of Peter (2:9) applies the content of God's address to the people of Israel in Exodus 19:5f, to the church of Christ. This designates the calling of the whole church to proclaim the word of God in the midst of the world. The Spirit leads the church on this path, makes it a witness to the gospel, enables it to read the signs of the time, and opens human hearts to belief in the gospel. Any discussion of apostolic succession and ordained ministry stands in the context of this fundamental qualification of the church.

173. In First Corinthians Paul writes, with himself in mind but characterizing the office of all the apostles, "According to the grace of God given to me, like a skilled master builder I laid a foundation, and someone else is building upon it. Each builder must choose with care how to build on it. For no one can lay any foundation other than the one that has been; that foundation is Jesus Christ" (1 Cor 3:10f). The house built on this foundation is God's temple made up of the believers forming the community: "Do you not know that

you are God's temple and that God's Spirit dwells in you?" (1 Cor 3:16). The Epistle to the Ephesians develops this image further when it says that the church is built "upon the foundation of the apostles and prophets, with Christ Jesus himself as the cornerstone" (Eph 2:20). The church can therefore only remain true to its mission to "proclaim the mighty acts of God" (1 Pet. 2:9) by constantly renewing its orientation toward the apostolic gospel. At the heart of what is later called "apostolic succession" is the transmission of the apostolic faith from generation to generation and across all boundaries of space or culture.

174. The forms in which faith is lived and the gospel is handed on are manifold and multiform. A central place of shared confession is worship, especially baptism and the eucharist. Catechesis plays a decisive role, both in leading to baptism and in deepening faith (Heb 6:1f.). Theological critique and reflection are indispensable for understanding, defending, developing, and giving ever new expression to the gospel as the word of God (cf. 1 Cor 14). The witness of deeds is part of the witness of words. Paul expresses this hope for the community at Thessalonica: "May the Lord make you increase and abound in love for one another and for all, just as we abound in love for you" (1 Thess 3:12). Because the gospel of God in Jesus Christ is the universal message of salvation and the effective word of grace, it has to influence deeply all dimensions of the life of the church and be attested and handed on in the whole diversity and fullness of the church's life of faith.

175. In 1 Cor 12-14 the Apostle Paul describes in a differentiated way the tasks within the body of Christ that are given to the manifold ministries and charisms, in order to advance in different ways the building up of the church (1 Cor 14). The diversity of charisms and ministries corresponds to the diversity of gifts which all the baptized contribute to the building up of the church (1 Cor 14) and to the variety of tasks which have to be fulfilled by the church in the world. Decisive for all charisms, ministries and instrumentalities is that they are given by one God, by one Lord, and by one Spirit, so that they benefit others and the church as a whole (cf. 1 Cor 12:4-7). The unity of their origin shapes their unity of orientation and function in building up the church. The charisms find their unity in the body of Christ (1 Cor 12:12-27; Rom 12:4f.). The vari-

ous gifts of grace make possible different services which each one should mutually accept and foster (1 Cor 12:28-30). The "way" that outshines all charisms (1 Cor 12:31) is love (1 Cor 13). Without it, all charisms are nothing (13:1-3). Only in love are they efficacious in building up the church (1 Cor 14:1-5).

176. The apostles proclaim the gospel of God as ambassadors of Jesus Christ who follow him and they entreat "on behalf of Christ" (2 Cor 5:20). The work of the apostles is, as Paul says, the "ministry of reconciliation", insofar as God calls to reconciliation through the apostles (2 Cor 5:18). The preaching of the Apostle Paul may appear feeble and lacking in wisdom, but precisely by this it calls forth a faith relying wholly on God's power (1 Cor 2:1-4). Paul sees himself as a servant of Christ and "steward of the mysteries of God" (1 Cor 4:1f.). The ministry of the apostles is invested with "authority" (2 Cor 13:10) as they proclaim Jesus Christ to build up the church. The apostles however bear the treasure of the gospel "in clay jars, so that it may be made clear that this extraordinary power belongs to God and does not come from us" (2 Cor 4:7). Because it is true of Jesus Christ that "he was crucified in weakness, but lives by the power of God" (2 Cor 13:4), therefore the apostle says, "Whenever I am weak, then I am strong" (2 Cor 12:10).

177. The apostolate should serve the expansion of the church to the ends of the earth and last until the end of time (Mt 28:20; cf. Acts 1:8). For this, the proclamation of the gospel, the administration of the sacraments, mission and catechesis, the leadership of congregations, and the fostering and coordinating of charisms must be undertaken ever anew. That this may occur requires a gift of the Holy Spirit (1 Cor 12-14; cf. Eph 4). In First Corinthians Paul strives to bring the charisms to support each other and collaborate one with the other (cf. 1 Cor 12:4-31), and he further reminds the Corinthians that "God has appointed in the church first apostles, second prophets, third teachers," before he lists at length the different gifts (1 Cor 12:28ff.). Of course the apostles must also prepare the congregations to follow the path of faith. According to Acts 14:23, Paul and Barnabas on their first missionary journey appointed presbyters in every congregation. The letters of Paul show that he had contact in each congregation with those who bore responsibilities, for example, for making his words known (1 Thess 5:27), for

taking over the diaconate as Phoebe did in Corinth or Cenchrea (Rom 16:1), or like Stephanas, the first fruit of Achaia, who put himself and his whole household at the service of the saints and deserved being recognized for this (1 Cor 16:13-17). The Epistle to the Philippians names "bishops and deacons" already in the opening address (Phil 1:1). As depicted in Part 1, Paul's co-workers, particularly Timothy and Titus, fulfill a particularly important task. Paul specifically demands that those who bear responsibility be acknowledged (1 Thess 5:12f; 1 Cor 16:16) and that his co-workers be received warmly (Rom 16:1) and be supported to the extent this is possible (1 Cor 16:10; 2 Cor 8:23f).

178. For the sake of the succession in faith, various New Testament writings speak of ecclesial ministries which serve the orientation toward the apostolic origins. The Epistle to the Ephesians names "evangelists, pastors, and teachers" (4:11); the Pastoral Epistles emphasize true doctrine through the bishop or overseer (*episkopos*); First Peter speaks of the pastoral ministry of the presbyters (5:1-11); and Hebrews refers to the "leaders" (13:7,17,24). In Acts 20:17-38, Paul admonishes the presbyters of Ephesus to lead as overseers (*episkopoi*) the church as God's flock and to maintain "the word of his grace" (20:32) even amid struggles over the true faith. According to Ephesians it is the same Spirit who raised up the apostles and prophets who also gives the "evangelists, pastors, and teachers," who are to continue building the church upon the foundation of the apostles (4:11). In the name of Paul the Pastoral Epistles demand that Timothy be acknowledged (1 Tim 4:6ff) in the ministry assigned to him by the apostle (2 Tim 4:5) because of the "grace" accorded to him (2 Tim 2:1). The presbyters who "rule well" in the community are to be given due honor (1 Tim 5:17). Similar admonitions are found in the Epistle to the Hebrews (13:17) and in First Peter (5:5). In Ephesians the ministry of the "pastors, evangelists, and teachers" (Eph 4:11) has the goal that "all of us come to the unity of the faith and of the knowledge of the Son of God" (Eph 4:13). According to First Peter the presbyters who work as pastors are admonished, "Do not lord it over those in your charge, but be examples to the flock" (1 Pet 5:3).

179. The pneumatological perspective throws light on the relation between the fundamental ministry of the apostles in laying in local

churches the foundation "which is laid, which is Jesus Christ" (1 Cor 3:11) and the work of building on this foundation by those exercising the various offices of ministry. The apostolate is differentiated from these offices insofar as Christ has made the former foundational for the church, while it is incumbent upon the ecclesial ministry, in publicly proclaiming the gospel in word and deed, to acknowledge and show to its best advantage this historically and theologically unique apostolic ministry of laying the foundation once and for all time.

180. The terminology regarding overseers and presbyters varies, but their spheres of activity seem to overlap to a large extent. One important responsibility is the leadership of the church in one place. In both Acts and the Pastoral Epistles it is the Spirit of God who inspires the apostles to institute those offices or ministries and, with the support of the whole church, to entrust them to individual Christians. Correspondingly the same Spirit enables these Christians to exercise their ministry for the church with the authority which accords with the gospel (Eph 4:7ff). Especially in the Pastoral Epistles, correct doctrine is an essential element in directing the communities, both by warding off false teaching and by constructive accounts of the content of the message of salvation. Disputes regarding the truth of the gospel cannot be excluded even among the apostles, prophets, teachers, and overseers, but must be conducted in the same Spirit of truth which keeps the whole church faithful to the gospel.

181. In the Pastoral Epistles, the laying on of hands brings about induction or ordination into the ecclesial office of the ministry. It is closely linked with the transmission of correct doctrine. Even the induction of the Seven by the Twelve takes place according to Acts 6:6 by the laying on of hands. In the Pastorals God communicates through the laying on of hands a "charism" which is then "in" those on whom hands were laid (1 Tim 4:14 cf. 2 Tim 1:6). This is a charism of ministry following the example of the Apostle Paul (1 Tim 1:18). The laying on of hands conveys "a spirit of power and of love and of self-discipline" (2 Tim 1:7). If one wishes to speak of a "grace of office" or a "charism of office," then that would refer to the grace or gift of grace that enabled Timothy and Titus to fulfil the commission given to them by Paul, namely, to follow his example in keep-

ing the church in the truth of the gospel (cf. 1 Tim 1:16ff. and 2 Tim 1:6ff. in its context).

182. Timothy is told, "Do not lay hands on anyone hastily" (1 Tim 5:22), possibly in reference to the installation of presbyters or overseers. The evidence in these letters does not describe a unified rite, for according to 1 Tim 4:14 it was the presbyters who laid hands on Timothy, while according to 2 Tim 1:6 it was the apostle. The relationship between the two rites is not fully clear. Exegesis has given divergent answers to the question of whether it is permissible in view of 1 Tim 5:22 to speak of a "chain" of laying on of hands. Protestant theology places greater emphasis on the open-ended and diverse nature of biblical witness. When Catholic theology views the succession of the laying on of hands as a sign of connection with Christ, of continuity of gospel proclamation effected by the Spirit, and of the unity of the church over time, it bases itself on the Pastoral Epistles. But in this it does not isolate the laying on of hands from the life of the church, but perceives it as an essential form by which the *successio apostolica*, which is necessary for the sake of *successio fidei*, becomes efficacious through the power of the Spirit. By the practice of ordination, understood from the New Testament, the church does not set itself up as lord over the gospel but submits to it. The authority accorded to the ecclesial office of ministry through the Spirit serves the freedom of all believers in the truth of the gospel. The laying on of hands is a sign for the whole church that it lives by listening to the gospel as a word that she does not enunciate to herself, but which is spoken to her by God through human beings in a human manner.

183. Paul challenges his congregations to imitate his example as he imitates that of Christ (1 Cor 4:16, 11:1; Phil 3:17, 4:9; 1 Thess 1:6). According to 2 Tim 1:13, Timothy should take the "sound teaching", which he heard from Paul as his example, in order to remain constant "in the faith and love that are in Christ Jesus". This is presupposed when 2 Tim 3:10 speaks of Timothy having observed "my teaching, my conduct, my aim in life, my faith, my patience, my love, my steadfastness, my persecutions and sufferings" (cf. also 1 Tim 4:6). In this sense succession does not mean simply the continuation of Paul's work but the ongoing orientation toward the example of the apostle who according to 1 Tim 1:16 is in turn the

example for all, insofar as he has "received mercy." In the New Testament "apostolic succession" takes place within the horizon of following Jesus Christ. It unites all Christians, including the apostles, with their Lord and with one another. The disciples of Jesus knew that they were called to be followers even to the cross (Mark 8:34-38 par.), so that they would have communion with Christ even in his mission entailing suffering. Despite their failures they are called once more to discipleship by Jesus, who will go ahead of them to Galilee (Mark 14:28; 16:7; cf. 10:32ff.). In speaking of "apostolic succession" regarding the ecclesial office of ministry, one has to include how those sharing in this have to orient themselves to the apostles – to their discipleship, their proclamation, their practice and their ministry – and allow themselves to be molded by this. Understood in this way, "apostolic succession" maintains the uniqueness proper to the ministry of the apostles while mediating it, within the horizon of the following of Jesus Christ, to an ongoing ministry for building up the church on the foundation of Jesus Christ which the apostles once laid.

3.3. Ordained Ministry in the Early Church and the Middle Ages

184. Some New Testament writings, and in particular the Pastoral Epistles, express the conviction that the apostles provided for the offices of leadership in the congregations which they founded, and a close connection is established between the office of leadership and the transmission of the "teaching" of the apostles, the "treasure entrusted" to the disciples of the apostles (cf. 2 Tim 1:13f.). But only with the First Letter of Clement (A.D. 96) does the concept of a succession of the apostles appear, understood as a single line of commission from God through Christ to the apostles and "their first-fruits" whom, "after prior examination in the spirit" they "appointed . . . to be bishops and deacons of those who should afterwards believe." Shortly after, we read: "Our apostles also knew through the Lord Jesus Christ that there would be strife on account of the office of the episcopate (*peri tou onomatos tes episkopes*). For this reason, therefore, inasmuch as they had obtained a perfect foreknowledge of this, they appointed those already mentioned and afterwards gave instructions, that when these should fall asleep,

The Apostolicity of the Church

other approved men should succeed them in their ministry."[23] Along with bishops, mention is made of instituted and appointed presbyters in nos. 44,5, 47,6, 54,2, and 57,1, since disregard for them had caused the letter to the church in Corinth to be written.

185. In the transitional phase from the apostolic to the post-apostolic period the ministerial structure began to evolve which provides for a bishop as overseer of the local church, with a college of presbyters and deacons at his side, and this gradually prevailed as the only model. The letters of Ignatius of Antioch (ca. 110) give the first unambiguous testimony to the existence of a single bishop surrounded by a college of presbyters and deacons. He speaks of the presbyterate as the independent hierarchical level between bishop and deacon. He frequently mentions the triad of the bishop (always in the singular), the presbyterium or the presbyters, and the deacons. This three-fold hierarchy is a reflection of the heavenly one, with God the Father, Christ and the apostles.[24] Nothing that concerns the church can be done without the bishop: "Let that be deemed a proper eucharist which is administered either by the bishop or by one to whom he has entrusted it. Wherever the bishop shall appear, there let the multitude also be; even as, wherever Jesus Christ may be, there is the Catholic Church. It is not lawful without the bishop either to baptize or to celebrate a love-feast."[25]

186. The consecration and ordination formulae found in the *Traditio apostolica* of Hippolytus of Rome (ca. 215) for the ordination of the bishop, presbyters and deacons show clearly that by the beginning of the third century this structure of ministry was quite firmly established. During the Sunday assembly of the congregation and the presbyterium, the new bishop who has been elected and confirmed by all, receives the laying on of hands from all the bishops who are present. The presbyterium does not take part in this laying-on of hands. All keep silent and pray in their hearts for the Holy Spirit to descend. One of the bishops present, at the request of all, lays his hands on the ordinand and says the consecration

---

[23] First Epistle of Clement, 42,1-4, 44,1-3, in A. Roberts and J. Donaldson, eds., *The Ante-Nicene Fathers* (Reprint, Grand Rapids, 1977), 16-17.

[24] Epistle of Ignatius to the Magnesians, 6,1, in *Ante-Nicene Fathers*, 1, 61.

[25] Epistle of Ignatius to the Smyrnaeans, 8,1f, in *Ante-Nicene Fathers*, 1, 89-90.

prayer. This is followed by the celebration of the eucharist. At the ordination of a presbyter the bishop lays on hands and says the consecration prayer, while the priests who are present also touch the ordinand, i.e. also lay on their hands. At the ordination of a deacon, only the bishop lays his hands on the ordinand and says the consecration prayer. He is not ordained as a priest, but "for service."[26] According to the order enshrined in the *Traditio apostolica,* the ordained ministry since the beginning of the third century consisted of bishop, presbyter and deacon.

187. Because of the controversial questions which emerged in the second century concerning the authentic content of the gospel message, emphasis fell on the link between the word and the person of the witness to such an extent that the continuity of bishops in one local church became the criterion for recognizing the continuity of the public mediation of apostolic teaching. Irenaeus wrote in this context about "the tradition of the apostles manifested throughout the whole world; as we are in a position to reckon up those who were by the apostles instituted bishops in the churches and to demonstrate the succession of these men to our own time."[27] According to Irenaeus one must seek true teaching in the tradition which the bishops and the presbyters instituted by them received from the apostles, and which they in their turn passed on to their successors down to the present time. In third century North Africa, Tertullian and Cyprian took up the concept of the apostolic tradition corresponding to the succession of bishops, and this later became the teaching of the Fathers of the fourth and fifth centuries.

188. The process leading to the development of a unified ministerial structure with the episcopate at its head reflects an ongoing task by which, in very difficult situations, a binding witness has to be made to preserve the unity of the church and protect the integrity of the faith. Especially in the battle against gnosticism, the personal criterion of succession among the witnesses of apostolic tradition evolved alongside the substantive criterion of faithfulness to the biblical testimony and to the *regula fidei,* and succession continued to grow in importance. Within the ecclesial process

---

[26] *The Apostolic Tradition of St. Hippolytus of Rome*, ed. Gregory Dix (London, 2nd ed., 1968), 15.

[27] Irenaeus, *Adversus Haereses*, III, 3, 1, in *Ante-Nicene Fathers*, 1, 415.

of transmitting the gospel, which is borne by all members of the congregation in forms which encompass the totality of the Christian witness, a distinct level became discernible, which is the level of those who hold the ministry of leadership and oversight and who are regarded as the criterion for orientation in conflict situations.

189. Around this central function of the episcopate and the ordained ministry, which serves the continuity of apostolic proclamation, several functions were grouped which concern oversight over the whole of church life and have the purpose of safeguarding unity. The role and authority which the bishops gradually assumed within the church depended on the close link between the oversight of the inviolate nature of the apostolic tradition and the ministry of the unity of the church. For the unity of the church there can be no other criterion than the apostolic gospel which is accepted in faith, celebrated in the sacraments, and attested through the word and works of love.

190. In the course of the fourth century, a second step of great importance was taken regarding the structuring of the episcopate and presbyterate. Following the spread of Christianity beyond the urban areas, new congregations were formed and entrusted to the pastoral care of the presbyters. While initially they had formed a college which assisted the bishop, they were now entrusted with the tasks of administering baptism and presiding at the celebration of the eucharist, which means that they assumed functions which had previously been the typical functions of the bishop. When the office of presbyter assumed "episcopal" characteristics, the office of bishop lost its distinctive feature of a ministry presiding over congregations present in one particular place, and became an office with a regional character. This ministry in which the administrative and juridical functions now predominated gave expression to the unity between the various eucharistic congregations. It is striking that, during this transitional period in the development of the life of the church and of the structures of its mission, the number of bishops did not increase, which would have been in keeping with the principle which provided for a bishop for every local church, but instead a further "specialization" of the ministries of bishop and presbyter evolved. Both ministries, in different ways and on

different levels, were in the service of the local church while remaining closely linked with one another, as is demonstrated by the principle of the dependence of the presbyter on the bishop.

191. If one were to describe the ecclesiology of the Early Church, as it evolved in the life and consciousness of the church itself, the concept of communion (*koinonia*) comes to mind. Every ecclesial community is a *koinonia*. More precisely, one could describe it as the *communio* of faith and of the sacraments which the bishop serves, above all in the celebration of the eucharist and in proclaiming the faith which he teaches and protects, but also by his care for preserving the unity of the whole church. Every church which is a *koinonia* is also in communion with the other churches and therefore the bishop is understood not only as an individual but as one in communion with the other bishops. This collegial structure of the episcopate becomes very clear in the ordination of a bishop, as laid down for instance in Canon 4 of the Council of Nicaea, which states that every bishop should "at best" be ordained by all the bishops of the province, and in cases of emergency only at least three bishops should gather for the ordination. The confirmation of the process for each province however is the duty of the Metropolitan.[30] Canon 6 furthermore forbids that a bishop should be instituted without the agreement of the Metropolitan and mentions the precedence of Alexandria, Rome and Antioch. Canon 7 ascribes a "precedence of honor" to Jerusalem, the "mother of all churches."[31] Constantinople is added to this list of precedence as the "new Rome" following the Council of Constantinople (381).[32] The Synods and Councils themselves testify to the *koinonia* of the churches and their bishops. This laid the foundation for a structure which extended beyond the local churches, and which evolved into church provinces and patriarchates. For the episcopal office this means that it is exercised not only in personal contact with the congregation (personal dimension), in which it is essentially rooted (communal dimension),

---

[30] Tanner, 7.
[31] This designation occurs in the "Letter of the Bishops gathered in Constantinople" of the Synod of 383 (Tanner, 30) which is a summary of what happened at the Council of 381, including the deposition of Maximus and ordination of Nectarius as Bishop of Constantinople.
[32] Canons 2-3 of the Council of Constantinople. Tanner, 31-32.

but also requires communion with the other bishops (collegial dimension).

192. The reflections on the ordained ministry which developed in the Middle Ages, particularly by Peter Lombard, largely follow the thought of Jerome in his emphasis on the equality between presbyters and bishops, while taking account of the fact that the theological definition of the ministry originated in presidency at the eucharist. Subsequently the priestly ministry came to predominate as the focal point for the understanding of the ministry of the church. This corresponded to a difficulty in the theology of the episcopate, concerning whether or not its special status was due to the sacrament of ordination. But the tendency prevailed to define the episcopate almost exclusively in juridical terms.

193. However, the opposite tendencies also existed, most clearly in Thomas Aquinas, who describes the difference between priest and bishop regarding authority – with reference to the church as the *corpus Christi mysticum* – in the sense of a higher episcopal authority, which is an "apostolic priesthood". The bishop receives this spiritual authority through consecration.[33] Thomas however embeds this authority for building up the church as the body of Christ in his concept of the mediation of grace and salvation by Christ, the head of the church, and in the idea of the instrumental causality of Christ's humanity. His theology of grace led him to see Christ above all as the one who mediates grace, and on the basis of his theology of the *lex nova* he can even consign institutional matters to the second rank of ecclesiology.

3.4. The Ordained Ministry in the Lutheran Reformation and the Council of Trent

3.4.1. The Lutheran Reformation

194. In the area of the 16th century Lutheran Reformation, the ministerial office developed amid a complex set of problems. There were differing and sometimes contradictory theological interpretations of the ministry, for example, giving rise to criticism of understand-

---

[33] *In IV Sent*, 24, 3,,2 qu 2 ad 3: "Omnis potestas spiritualis datur eum aliqua consecratione".

ing ministry from offering the sacrifice of the mass. Differing, sometimes contradictory, concepts of grace and justification prompted the bishops to refuse to ordain Lutheran theologians. Among non-theological factors, the constitution of the German Empire included the institution of prince-bishops, whose mingling of secular and spiritual power evoked sharp criticism from the Reformers. There was an interplay of action and reaction, theological criticism and counter-criticism, and institutional measures in church and state. The Reformers wanted to shape the church but had limited means for doing this, while the princes strove to extend state power over the church. The ministry and its theological understanding evolved within this tangle of extremely heterogeneous factors. Only part of this complex can be discussed in the following sections.

195. For the Lutheran Reformation, ministry and ordination are among the visible signs of the church, especially in their relation of service to preaching and the sacraments, as Luther states in *On the Councils and the Church*. "Fifth, the church is recognized externally by the fact that it consecrates or calls ministers, or has offices that it is to administer. There must be bishops, pastors, or preachers, who publicly and privately give, administer, and use the aforementioned four things or holy possessions [the word of God, the sacraments of baptism and the supper, the public use of the keys] on behalf of and in the name of the church, or rather by reason of their institution by Christ. ... Wherever you see this done, be assured that God's people, the holy Christian people, is present."[34]

The Priesthood of All the Baptized

196. According to Luther, "priest", in the original and strict sense of the word, is Christ alone. Christians are priests only by sharing in Christ in faith, according to the logic of the "happy exchange": "Now just as Christ by his birthright obtained these two prerogatives, so he imparts them to and shares them with everyone who believes in him according to the law of the above-mentioned marriage, according to which the wife owns whatever belongs to the husband. Hence all of us who believe in Christ are priests and kings in Christ, as 1 Pet 2:9 says: 'You are a royal priesthood and a priestly kingdom.'"[35]

---

[34] WA 50, 632, 35 - 633, 11; LW 41, 154.
[35] WA 7, 27, 17-21 (*Freedom of a Christian*, 1520); LW 31, 354.

Christians become priests not through ordination but through a new birth, the spiritual birth of baptism. They are not made priests, they are born priests.[36] "Accordingly we are all consecrated as priests through baptism."[37]

197. The priesthood of each baptized person, as sharing in the priesthood of Christ, is according to Luther lived out or realized in priestly action, when a person offers sacrifice to God on behalf of all and teaches them about God, so as to bring their concerns before God and God's concerns to them.[38] The first occurs in prayer and dedication to God, especially in suffering, the second in proclaiming the gospel. Every Christian prays in Christ and so comes before God.

198. Since the priesthood of all the baptized has its foundation in baptism and is lived out in faith in Christ's promise, therefore before God all Christians are equal, that is, equal as priests (*sacerdotes*). The difference between a pastor and a Christian who is not a pastor is a difference of office. Regarding their state of grace and in view of salvation, there is no difference between those who are ordained and those who are not ordained. "All Christians are truly of the spiritual estate. And there is no difference among them, except that of office."[39] Christians, as Christians, are not office-holders. "It is true that all Christians are priests, but not all are pastors. To be a pastor one must not only be a Christian and a priest but must have an office and a field of work committed to him. The call and command make pastors and preachers."[40]

199. The doctrine of the universal priesthood removed the theological foundation of the social and legal division of Christendom into clergy and laity, based on Gratian's dictum, "Christians are of two kinds".[41] together with the medieval concept of a hierarchy of estates in which the spiritual estate ranked above the secular.

---

[36] Cf. WA 12, 178, 9f and 179, 15-21 (*De instituendis ministris Ecclesiae*, 1523); LW 40, 18 and 20.

[37] WA 6, 407, 22-23 (*To the Christian Nobility of the German Nation*; 1520); LW 44, 127.

[38] Cf. WA 8, 422, 20-22 (*De abroganda missa privata*, 1521); LW 36, 139.

[39] *To the Christian Nobility.* WA 6, 407, 13-15; LW 44, 127.

[40] WA 31/I, 211, 17-20 (*Exposition of Psalm 82*, 1530); LW 13, 65.

[41] "*Duo sunt genera christianorum.*" Decretum, Pars II, C.XII, q. 1 c. 7. *Corpus iuris canonici*, ed. E. Friedberg (Leipzig 1879-81), I, 678.

Apostolic Succession and Ordained Ministry

The Relation between the Priesthood of All the Baptized and the Ordained Ministry

200. Luther as a rule calls the pastor *minister*. This shows the general trend of his understanding of the pastorate: while in his time the sacrament of ordination did not of itself place the ordained in the service of a congregation, according to Luther ecclesial office has to be an office of ministry (*ministerium*), namely that of publicly proclaiming the gospel in word and sacrament in the congregation. Now if every baptized Christian has certain duties toward God and humankind as a priest, in prayer and proclamation of the gospel, then the question arises about the basis and understanding of the special ecclesial ministry, since the proclamation of the gospel is also an essential element of this ministry. There has been for some time considerable debate on this question.

201. In many passages Luther speaks explicitly of the divine institution of ordained ministry. For example in *To the Christian Nobility of the German Nation* (1520): "I want to speak only of the ministry which God has instituted, the responsibility of which is to minister word and sacrament to a congregation, among whom they reside."[42] And: "I hope, indeed, that believers, those who want to be called Christians, know very well that the spiritual estate has been established and instituted by God, not with gold or silver but with the precious blood and bitter death of his only Son, our Lord Jesus Christ. From his wounds indeed flow the sacraments, as they used to depict this on broadsides. He paid dearly that men might everywhere have this office of preaching, baptizing, loosing, binding, giving the sacrament, comforting, warning, and exhorting with God's word, and whatever else belongs to the pastoral office. . . . I am not thinking, however, of the spiritual estate as we know it today in the monastic houses and foundations. . . . The estate I am thinking of is rather one which has the office of preaching and the service of the word and sacraments and which imparts the Spirit and salvation."[43] The Lutheran con-

---

[42] *To the Christian Nobility*. WA 6, 441, 24f ; LW 44, 176.
[43] *A Serman on Keeping Children in School*. WA 30/II,526, 34 - 527, 8 and 528, 1-2.8-10.

fessional writings state unequivocally: "The ministry of the word has the command of God and has magnificent promises," and "The church has the mandate to appoint ministers."[44]

202. Luther's treatise for the Bohemians, *De instituendis ministris Ecclesiae* (1523),[45] is one of the texts cited to prove that according to Luther the ordained ministry is derived from the priesthood of all the baptized. But, in fact, this work does not even discuss the basis of the ministry, for its title refers to appointing ministers (*ministri*), not to instituting ministries (*ministerii*) in the church. What it discusses is whether appointment to ministerial office is only possible through the act of a bishop, or whether, in an emergency, as when the Roman bishops refuse to appoint ministers of the word,[46] the assembled congregation can choose from amid its ranks one or several suitable persons and, with prayer and the laying-on of hands, commend and confirm them to the whole church. Here Luther presupposes, first, that a church cannot be without God's word, and, second, as the implicit premise, that there can be no proper proclamation of God's word in the church if there are no special ministers of the divine word (*ministri verbi divini*). The alternative which Luther sees here can only be understood in the following way. If the bishops do not agree to institute any ministers of the word worthy of this name, there are only two alternatives: either the church will perish because it lacks the word of God, or else the ministers of the word will be appointed to their office in another way than through episcopal ordination. Luther conceives the ordained ministry as necessary to the church, and this necessity rests, as other texts show, on the institution of the office through Christ.

203. For Luther, this office is fundamentally related to the universal priesthood because the precise task of the ministry is to enable and keep alive the priesthood of all Christians. The reason for this is that the baptized are priests in Christ alone, but they are in Christ only by faith in the word of God. Public proclamation and the essentially public administration of the sacraments are required for

---

[44] *Apology of the Augsburg Confession*, Art. XIII, 10f. BSLK 293, 40-42.50-51. BC 220.
[45] WA 12, 169-195; LW 40, 7-44.
[46] "*Episcopi papales nolint dare verbi ministros.*" WA 12, 191, 19f; LW 40, 37.

Apostolic Succession and Ordained Ministry

the word of God to be present *universally* to all, to awaken and preserve faith, and for that the spiritual office is required.

204. Ordained ministry and the priesthood of all the baptized exist therefore in an indissoluble correlation. The special ministry has its purpose in service to the universal priesthood. Inversely, the general priesthood of all the baptized bears the fundamental capacity for enabling the ordained ministry and also the responsibility for appointing to this ministry. As far as the latter is concerned, this does not contest the bishops' right and duty to ordain ministers of the word of God. Luther argues that, regarding ordination, the church normally has the capacity to act through the bishops. "Therefore, when a bishop consecrates it is nothing else than that in the place and stead of the whole community, . . . he takes and charges him to exercise this power on behalf of others."[47] The bishop acts "in the person" of the *whole* church. Normally, it is through the bishop that the church is the acting subject in ordination. But if the bishops do not perform the ordination of evangelical pastors, a church or congregation which needs a pastor must regain its lost ability to act, through an assembly reaching a "common agreement of the faithful, those who believe and confess the gospel"[48] and appoint a pastor on that basis.[49]

205. In this emergency situation, the priesthood of all the baptized is called upon in the following way regarding the office-holder: baptism represents the fundamental qualification for the office of minister, and therefore members of the community who are suitable for the ministry, who have been duly chosen and "confirmed" with prayer and the laying-on of hands before the gathered congregation, are rightful bishops and priests in this emergency situation, even if ordination by a bishop represents the normal procedure. Referring to Mt 18,19f, Luther says that in such a case there can be no doubt that an ordination taking place in this way has been accomplished by God. In the calling and induction into office it is God who is actually at work.[50]

---

[47] WA 6, 407, 29f (*To the Christian Nobility*); LW 44, 128.
[48] "*Conventu facto communibus suffragis ...*" WA 12, 191, 26f; LW 40, 37.
[49] Cf. also Melanchthon's *Tractatus de potestate papae*, 66-70. BSLK 491, ...1-492,6; Cf. BC 340f.
[50] Cf. WA 12, 191, 25f: "*indubitata fide credendo, a deo gestum et factum esse.*" LW 40, 37.

206. According to Luther, bishops, pastors and preachers who preach in public and distribute the sacraments act "in the name of the church, or rather, by reason of their institution by Christ".[51] The church calls the office-holders, and to that extent they act in its name. What they do in their ministry, however, they do by force of Christ's institution, because the gospel is *not* the word of believers but instead the word of Christ. The institution of the office by Christ enables and has the purpose of making the word of the gospel come to all people as the word of Christ.

The Authority of the Ministry

207. From the perspective of the tradition handed down to Luther, the acts of evangelical ministers could be considered as insufficient, since the office according to Lutheran thinking does not have any "indelible character" and its specific power has not been passed on by a bishop who was consecrated by another bishop. However the following is clear in Lutheran understanding: "Nor does this detract from the efficacy of the sacraments when they are distributed by the unworthy, because they represent the person of Christ on account of the call of the church and do not represent their own persons, as Christ himself testifies 'Whoever listens to you listens to me' (Luke 10:16). When they offer the word of Christ or the sacraments, they offer them in the stead and place of Christ. The words of Christ teach us this so that we may not be offended by the unworthiness of ministers."[52] More precisely, this is to be understood as follows.

208. In *The Babylonian Captivity of the Church*, Luther writes about baptism: "Hence we ought to receive baptism at human hands just as if Christ himself, indeed, God himself, were baptizing us with his own hands. For it is not man's baptism, but Christ's and God's baptism, which we receive by the hand of man. Therefore beware of making any distinction in baptism by ascribing the outward part to man and the inward part to God. Ascribe both to God alone, and look upon the person administering it as simply the vicarious instrument of God, by which the Lord sitting in heaven thrusts you

---

[51] WA 50, 633, 3; LW 41, 154.

[52] *Apology,* Art. VII/VIII, 28. BSLK 240, 40-47; BC 178, translating the Latin text of September 1531.

under the water with his own hands, and promises you forgiveness of your sins, speaking to you upon earth with a human voice by the mouth of his minister."[53]

209. The two aspects belong together, namely, highest esteem for what the pastor does, for his hands in baptism are God's hands, his voice is God's voice, and low esteem for him as God's "vicarious instrument". Each determines the other reciprocally, for only if and insofar as the pastor acts purely as an instrument, vicariously for God, can his action be said to be at the same time God's action. That the pastor can and must preach, baptize, and administer the Lord's Supper presupposes a mandate from Christ for these actions and a promise regarding them. That is why the institution of the sacraments is so important for the Reformers. Only by appealing to Christ's command and in trust in his promise can a pastor dare to act in the name and in the stead of Christ. That he or she can be called before the whole congregation in response to Christ's command and promise and thus act in the name of Christ, presupposes his or her calling and ordination to the office and to its public enactments. The ordained minister has the right and the duty, through the authority of the command and promise of Christ, to proclaim the gospel in public and to administer the sacraments. And because the pastor is instituted as minister of the word of God, the question of his authority is the question of his calling to his ministry and the question of the authority of the word which he is to serve.

210. In a famous remark at table, Luther rejected the following distinction which he called a metaphysical one: "Men preach, the Spirit works; the pastor baptizes, absolves, but God cleanses and forgives. Not in the least! Rather we conclude: God preaches, baptizes, absolves".[54] This does not blur the distinction between God and man, between divine actions and human actions. Rather he has in mind an *effective unity* between the action of the Holy Spirit and the specific act of the pastor, a unity decisive for the actions of proclamation and administration of the sacraments being efficacious for human salvation. "Good God! What consolation can a weak con-

---

[53] WA 6, 530, 22-31; LW 36, 62f.
[54] "*Homo praedicat, Spiritus operatur, minister baptisat, absolvit, Deus autem mundat et remittit etc. Nequaquam! Sed concludimus: Deus praedicat, baptisat, absolvit.*" WA TR 3; 671, 10-11; No. 3868.

science receive from a preacher if it does not believe that *these very words* are *God's* consolation, *God's* word, *God's* judgment?"[55]

The Problematic of the Episcopate at the Time of the Reformation, and the Reaction of the Reformers

211. Regarding the episcopal office, historical factors which the Reformers encountered but had no power to change played an important role. The bishops and archbishops of the Holy Roman Empire of the German Nation were at the same time secular princes and as such had a firm place in the institutions of the Empire. Bishops had seats and votes in the Diet, while three archbishops were even prince electors, with places among the seven princes who chose the emperor. Careful consideration of the historical parameters of the episcopal office in the sixteenth century is of great significance for the Lutheran churches as well as for the Roman Catholic Church: for the former, so that they do not remain fixated on one specific historical constellation in their position regarding the episcopate; for the latter, to help in reaching an appropriate assessment of the decisions made by the Reformation churches regarding their leadership.

212. The combination of heterogeneous tasks in the office of bishop led to conflicts between their various duties. The secular power was sometimes used for spiritual ends in a questionable way and *vice versa*, while the duty of spiritual leadership was neglected. Often, the holders of episcopal office were unfit for their spiritual duties and they appointed other persons to represent them. The Reformers severely criticized the intermingling of the two powers in the one person of the bishop, as in Art. 28 of the *Augsburg Confession*. They emphasized that "the first and only duty of all bishops is to see that the people learn about the gospel and love of Christ."[56] It seemed to the Reformers that the imperial bishops neither gave to God what was God's, nor to Caesar, the Emperor, what was Caesar's.

213. More significant and more problematic for the Reformation, however, was the fact that most of the bishops adhering to the traditional faith did not allow evangelical preaching, but instead put

---

[55] From the same remark as in the previous note: "*Optime Deus, quam consolationem potest a praedicatore recipere infirma conscientia, nisi credit* haec ipsa verba *consolationemesse* Dei, *verbum* Dei, *sententiam* Dei?" Emphasis added.

[56] WA Br 1, 111, 39-41 (Letter to Abp. Albrecht of Mainz, October 31, 1517); LW 48, 47.

obstacles in the way of priests and preachers who turned to the Reformation or even persecuted them, and refused to ordain reform-minded theologians. Melanchthon writes in the Apology to the Augsburg Confession: "The bishops compel our priests . . . to reject and to condemn the kind of doctrine that we have confessed. This keeps our priests from acknowledging such bishops. . . . We have clear consciences on this matter since we know that our confession is true, godly, and catholic. For this reason, we dare not approve the cruelty of those who persecute this doctrine. We know the church exists among those who rightly teach the word of God and rightly administer the sacraments."[57] As a consequence, a conflict developed for the Reformation between faithfulness to the apostolic tradition, that is, the gospel, or adherence to the traditional forms of transmission of office and of its integration into the hierarchically structured community of the church.

The Theological Definition of the Relationship between the Pastorate and the Episcopate

214. As the ministry of proclaiming the gospel in word and sacrament, the office of ministry is essentially *one* office, just as the gospel is one, even if for practical reasons specific tasks (e.g. *episkopé*) are delegated to individual ministries. Luther relates the office originally to the local congregation which can in principle assemble at one place for divine worship. The fundamental principle of his theology, that the Holy Spirit effects faith and salvation through the external word, has as a consequence the primary identification of church and worshipping congregation. With his understanding of the congregation assembled for worship as the primary point of reference for the office, Luther's position is very close to that of the Church Fathers for whom the eucharistic community was the focus of reflection on the church.

215. Luther refers back to New Testament language (Titus 1:5.7; 1 Tim 3:1-7; Acts 20:17.28) where *episkopos* and *presbyteros* are used interchangeably. For Luther this shows that the ministry is one but that different terms are used for it. Luther finds the same in the Church Father Jerome who wrote to the presbyter Evangelus that

---

[57] *Apology*, Art. XIV,2-4. BSLK 297, 11-19; BC 222f.

at the time of the apostles "presbyter" and "overseer" (*episkopos*) meant the same. Only later was one from among the group of presbyters chosen and given a superior position, with the title *episkopos*, in order to prevent divisions in faith.[58] Luther points out that this letter by Jerome was included in canon law and thus has the approval of the Roman Church.[59] Furthermore, in holding that the original ministry was the presbyterate, Luther is in line with a tradition which was widespread, if not predominant, during the Middle Ages. He could read in the *Sentences* of Peter Lombard, the basic textbook for theological studies in the high and late Middle Ages, that the canons know of only two sacred ordinations, the diaconate and the presbyterate, because it was said that the Early Church had only these and we had a command given by the apostle for them alone.[60] This means that within the priestly *ordo* the bishop has a special office and a particular rank, but the episcopal office does not constitute an *ordo* of its own, nor does episcopal consecration convey a specific sacramental character. This tradition is of great significance for the evaluation by the Reformers of what they undertook in the question of ordination.

216. Luther often takes his orientation from the situation in the town congregations of the Early Church, for example when he designates Augustine as the town pastor of Hippo.[61] But he also considers that a regional episcopate is the normal case. In *De instituendis ministris*, the urban bishops, i.e. the pastors, can choose from among themselves one or several clerics who will then be called "archbishops", who are to visit the bishops and churches. The episcopate arises out of the necessary task of visitation, for oversee-

---

[58] Jerome, Letter CXLVI to Evangelus; Migne, *Patrologia Latina* XXII, 1192-1195, and M. Luther, *Resolutio Lutherana super propositione sua decima tertia de potestate papae* (WA 2, 227-230). Cf. also WA 50, 65-89, especially 84f, and Melanchthon, *Treatise on the Power and Primacy of the Pope*, 62. BSLK 489,43-490,20; BC 340).

[59] Cf. *Decretum*, Pars I, Dist. XCII, c. 24. *Corpus iuris canonici*, ed. E. Friedberg (Leipzig 1879-81), I, 327-329. Referred to by Luther at WA 2, 230, 17-19.

[60] Lombard, *Sentences* IV, dist. 24, cap. 12. Lombard refers to Can.1 of the Synod of Benevento (DS 703). The sentence is found in Gratian's *Decretum*, Pars I, Dist. LX, c.4 (ed. Friedberg. I.227).

[61] Cf. *The Private Mass and the Consecration*, 1533. WA 38, 237, 25-238, 10; LW 38, 196-197. Cf. also *To the Christian Nobility*: "According to the institution of Christ and the Apostles, every city should have a priest or bishop, as Paul says clearly in Titus 1, 5." WA 6, 440, 21f; also 6, 440, 30-36; LW 44, 175.

ing in several congregations the purity of the proclamation of the gospel which creates faith and the church, along with ordaining office-holders and examining them as to their suitability for office. Melanchthon writes: "In the church regents are necessary, who examine and ordain those called to the church's ministries, who preside in church courts, and who exercise a ministry of oversight over the teaching of the priests. And if there were no bishops, one would have to create them."[62]

217. What is to be preached in the different congregations is not something specific to them, but is the *one* gospel. However, the correct preaching of the one gospel everywhere cannot be taken for granted, because erroneous teaching is always possible and indeed a reality. Therefore a supra-parochial ministry of oversight is not merely optional. Melanchthon continues: "So that there may be one church sharing in a consensus, God has always spread abroad the same gospel through the Fathers and the prophets and later through Christ and the apostles. And Christ has instituted one office that should remain until the end of the world. ... That is, he has preserved the gospel and intends that, after the apostles, shepherds be called forth in all the churches, that is, those whom he calls to administer the office of teaching the gospel. Although they differ in gifts, they nevertheless provide the same service. The unity of the church consists therefore in this association under one head through the same gospel and the same office. ... But so that everything in the church happens in an orderly manner according to the rule of Paul, and so that the shepherds would yield to one another and be concerned for each other and avoid differences of opinion and divisions, a useful order was added, namely, that out of many presbyters one was chosen as bishop to guide the church by teaching the gospel, taking care for discipline, and being himself head of the presbyters. . . . These orders are useful in preserving the unity of the church, if those who are the heads fulfill their office."[63]

218. According to Lutheran understanding, the special tasks of bishops, beside the preaching of the gospel, are the following: the examination and ordination of those who are to be called to the ministry of

---

[62] *Consilium de moderandis controversiis religionis* (1535), CR 2, 745f.
[63] Melanchthon, CR 4, 367f., from his formulation of the Wittenberg theologians' reactions to the *Regensburg Book*.

the word, the visitation of pastors and their congregations, examination of doctrine, the naming and rejection of heresy, and the implementation of excommunication. Even though in areas of the Lutheran Reformation in Germany the development of a genuine episcopate was impeded for centuries, in part by the fact that bishops in Germany occupied secular positions defined by imperial law, reference must be made to the competent system of superintendents which did arise. Also Melanchthon's judgment in the *Apology* should be borne in mind: "We have frequently testified . . . that it is our greatest desire to retain the order of the church (*politia ecclesiastica*) and the ranks in the church - even though they were established by human authority. We know that church discipline in the manner described by the ancient canons was instituted by the Fathers for a good and useful purpose."[64]

Ordination and "Apostolic Succession"

219. The Early Church's concept of the apostolic succession was unknown in the Middle Ages even though ordination practice remained by and large in continuity with the order of the Early Church. During the Reformation era, the concept of "apostolic succession" appeared first in the work *Enchiridion christianae institutionis* (1538) of the Catholic theologian Johannes Gropper, who refers to Cyprian, Augustine, and especially to Irenaeus in *Adversus haereses*, Books III and IV. This principal work of the Bishop of Lyons became known in the West through the edition of Erasmus (1526), while earlier Peter Lombard and the *Decree* of Gratian did not know it. Gropper says about 1 Tim 4:14, that "in order to preserve the unity of the church it is extremely necessary to practice ordination as it had been instituted by Christ, later practiced by the apostles, and handed down to us in continuous succession."[65] Gropper appeals to Irenaeus when he rejects the opinion that succession in faith is sufficient. "One must believe only the priests who stand in succession from the apostles

---

[64] *Apology*, Art. XIV, 1. BSLK 296, 14 - 297,1; BC 222.

[65] Johannes Gropper, *Enchiridion Christianae institutionis*, 1538, fol. 67v, quoted from G. Kretschmar, "Die Wiederentdeckung des Konzepts der 'Apostolischen Sukzession' im Umkreis der Reformation," in *Das bischöfliche Amt. Kirchengeschichtliche und ökumenische Studien zur Frage des kirchlichen Amtes* (Göttingen 1999), 317, n. 29.

Apostolic Succession and Ordained Ministry

and who with succession in the office of bishop have received the certain charism of truth, according to the will of the Father."[66]

220. As early as 1539, in his work, *The Church and the Authority of God's Word*, Melanchthon rejected these opinions which tie church "to the orderly succession of bishops, just as empires exist through the orderly succession of their rulers. But it is different in the church. It is an assembly which is not tied to an orderly succession but to the word of God."[67] Gropper's ideas were to play no constructive role in the unity colloquy of 1541 at Regensburg.

221. Regarding ordination, which normally is administered by an ordained person, Luther can speak quite openly about succession as a fact: "God calls in two ways, either by means or without means. Today he calls all of us into the ministry of the word by a mediated call, that is, one that comes through means, namely, through man. But the apostles were called immediately by Christ Himself, just as prophets in the Old Testament had been called by God Himself. Afterwards the apostles called their disciples, as Paul called Timothy, Titus, etc. These men were called bishops, as Titus 1 says, and the bishops called their successors down to our own time, and so on to the end of the world. This is a mediated calling, since it is done by man. Nevertheless, it is divine."[68] "Now if the apostles, evangelists, and prophets are no longer living, others must have replaced them and will replace them until the end of the world, for the church shall last until the end of the world, and so apostles, evangelists, and prophets must therefore remain, no matter what their name, to promote God's word and work."[69]

222. The Reformers' desire to maintain the catholicity and apostolicity of the ministry is very clear from the available Wittenberg ordination certificates.[70] Beginning in 1535 in the Electorate of Saxony and on orders of the Elector, the examination and ordination of new clergy was undertaken by the Wittenberg theological faculty.

---

[66] Gropper, *Enchiridion*, fol. 67r, citing *Adversus haereses*, IV, 63, quoted from G. Kretschmar, as in n. 42.

[67] *Melanchthon's Werke in Auswahl*, Vol.1, ed. R. Stupperich (Gütersloh, 1951), 330,19-23.

[68] On Gal 1:1, in the printed text. WA 40/1, 59, 16-23; LW 26, 17.

[69] *On the Councils and the Church*, 1539. WA 50, 634, 11-15. LW 41, 155.

[70] Cf. WA Br 12, 447-485.

The faculty had the mandate to ordain but the person who actually ordained was Bugenhagen who, although a member of the faculty, functioned as town pastor of Wittenberg and as regional bishop. This made it clear that ordination is not an academic but a church matter. Before the ordination, the faculty examined the competence and doctrinal correctness of the candidate who had received the call (*vocatio*) from a congregation. "With particular emphasis repeated reference is made to the doctrinal agreement between 'our church' and the 'catholic church of Christ'. Luther understood the latter, appealing to the Apostles' Creed, as the whole Christian church. After 1542 the certificates reinforce this agreement in one spirit and one voice with the catholic church of Christ. In the same way reference is made to the condemnation of fanatical opinions by the judgment of the catholic church of Christ. The same trend is evident when after Summer 1542 an explicit reference is constantly added that it is according to apostolic teaching (above all, Tit 1:5 and Eph 4:8.11) that the office of teaching and administration of the sacraments be passed on to the ordinand through public ordination."[71] However, the succession in teaching is not understood as something that takes place in isolation from the human practices of transmitting doctrine. Maintaining doctrine requires persons who pass it on and it needs human actions in which this occurs and is also examined. The ordination certificates, which the ordained pastors took with them to their congregations, always state that the doctrine of the ordinand has been examined.

223. It is also noteworthy that the ordinations did not take place in the individual congregations which had issued the call but in Wittenberg, which was in total disregard of Bugenhagen's objections. This, again, was to show that ordination was not simply an installation as pastor but took place as ordination to ministry in the church as a whole. This also is clear from repeated references to Canon 4 of Nicaea, according to which a bishop has to be consecrated by neighboring bishops.[72] Thus the apostolicity and catholicity of the ministry are to be ensured by including other ordained persons in the ordination. The Bible readings at the Wittenberg ordination service also speak of the office of a bishop, namely 1 Tim. 3:1-7 and Acts 20:28-31.

---

[71] *Ibid.*, 448, from the Editor's Introduction.
[72] *Ibid.*, 456, 7-15. Cf. Tanner, 7.

224. Ordination takes place with the constitutive elements of prayer and the laying-on of hands. It is really God who acts in ordination, as shown by the opening prayer which asks him to send laborers into his harvest (Mt 9:38), as well as by the prayer for the Holy Spirit. Through ordination, God's call claims the ordinand's whole person.[73] Trusting that these prayers are heard, the commissioning is carried out with 1 Peter 5:2-4. An ordination administered in this way corresponds to an understanding of ministry which is expressed in this way in one version of the ordination formula: "The ministry of the church is most important and necessary for all churches and is given and preserved by God alone."[74]

3.4.2 The Threefold Ordained Ministry of Bishop, Priest, and Deacon according to the Council of Trent (1545-1563)

225. The Council of Trent is a decisive point of reference in stating the Roman Catholic understanding of the ordained ministry and its threefold articulation. At Trent the Fathers' main concern was to hold to the apostolic tradition as it had been handed on and practiced through the centuries. Over against the doctrines of the Reformation, and deliberately defining the differences, they strove to formulate the Catholic faith's common understanding of central and now controverted topics, such as Scripture and tradition, original sin and justification, and the sacraments. In so doing Trent avoided settling issues on which the schools (*viae*) of Catholic theology advanced different positions. Trent also initiated the needed reform of the church. But on ordained ministry, the Council was not able to integrate its teaching into a coherent ecclesiological framework.

226. The doctrine and canons of Trent's Decree on the Sacrament of Order (*sacramentum ordinis*) were determined by the policy of demarcation against the Reformation. Its teaching is derived from the doctrine that there is in the New Covenant a sacrifice, namely, "the holy sacrifice of the Eucharist", and for that reason Christ instituted a new "visible and external" priesthood (*sacerdotium*).

---

[73] WA 38, 425, 1-17; LW 53, 125.
[74] "*Res maxima et necessaria est omnibus ecclesiis ministerium ecclesiae et a deo solo datum et conservatum.*" WA 38, 423, 21-25; LW 53, 124, with note 1.

The power necessary for this was given "to the Apostles and their successors in the priesthood" (DS 1764; Tanner, 742). This priesthood has the "power to consecrate and offer the true body and blood of the Lord, and to forgive and retain sins." In this way it is explicitly differentiated from the "ministry . . . and mere service of proclaiming the gospel" (DS 1771; Tanner, 743). Trent retains "other ordinations, for higher or lower orders" (DS 1772; Tanner, 743) and defines that "Order (*ordo*) or holy ordination" is a sacrament instituted by Christ and not solely a "rite for choosing ministers of the word of God and of the sacraments" (DS 1773; Tanner, 743). The Council holds to a conferral of the Spirit on the ordinand and to the sacramental character by virtue of which the person once ordained remains a priest for ever (DS 1774; Tanner, 744).

227. The Tridentine discussion shows the decisive role played by the concept of priesthood in preserving the traditional teaching on church ministry. Because of the key function ascribed to priesthood by the patristic and medieval tradition for the understanding of church ministry, the Fathers of the Council of Trent judged Luther's criticism of using this theological category to designate the ordained ministry and his application of it to every Christian believer to be a reversal of the basic structure of the church ministry. They stressed therefore that a priesthood oriented toward the celebration of the eucharist belongs to the Catholic tradition, but they did not adequately develop the ecclesiological framework for understanding of church ministry. The dogmatic doctrine of the Council of Trent thus focused on the sacramentality of ordination and on the specific character of the priesthood conferred through ordination in differentiation from the priesthood of all believers.

228. The task of preaching entrusted to those ordained to the ministry was certainly present in the mind of the Tridentine Fathers, even if the topic was not explicitly integrated into their dogmatic teaching, but was instead developed in the decrees that give directives for reforming clerical life and pastoral care. Recent studies have however brought out the complexity of Tridentine doctrine on ordained ministry, while showing the impact of teaching about the pastoral aspects of ministry on the theology of the episcopal office. The concern of the Council was, first of all, to assert the

sacramentality of the Sacrament of Order. But no less important was the intention of renewing the life of the clergy, with the main goal of the desired reforms being a more effective pastoral ministry. For that reason the bishop must examine and choose suitable ordination candidates and bishops and priests were both reminded of their duty to preach. While the dogmatic canons focus on priesthood, that is, its authority and power to celebrate the eucharist, the reform canons on the Sacrament of Order bring to the forefront norms for the appointment and promotion of clerics, for their ordination, and for visitations. In this regard the bishop, not the priest, both ordains and defines the practice of ministry. The bishop decides who is to be ordained and in his visitation he determines how the priest is to exercise his ministry.

229. Because Trent's concept of "visible and external priesthood" marked the difference between ordained ministry and the "invisible internal priesthood" of all believers, it also left open the question of the inner structure of ministry and the hierarchical relationship between bishops, presbyters and deacons. The need to clarify the last question produced a shift of perspective in dealing with the dogmatic side of teaching on church ministry. During the early stages of the Council, Order was treated within the context of the Decree on the Sacrifice of the Mass, so that offering sacrifice and priesthood were the points of reference for the Sacrament of Order. But the third and last session (1562-63) relativized priesthood as the starting-point for the Sacrament of Order and moved toward clarifying the ecclesial setting both of the ordained ministry and of the relationship between the different ministries. The result of this effort is summarized in Canon 6, which after debate at the Council received its present form: "Excluded shall be anyone who denies that there exists in the Catholic Church a hierarchy consisting of bishops, priests, and ministers, instituted by divine appointment" (DS 1776; Tanner, 744). The priesthood is thus understood as a structure which includes different degrees of spiritual authority. Priesthood therefore entails internal diversity and the diversity of grades must be applied to the sacramental hierarchy, at least to presbyters and bishops.

230. Regarding the inner structure of the ordained ministry, a noteworthy aspect is the expression "by divine appointment" (*divina*

ordinatione), which is weaker than the technical expression "of divine right" (*iure divino*). This shows that while the inner differentiation of ministry corresponds to the will of God and to his plan for the church, still one cannot exclude a certain degree of historical contingency.

231. The hierarchical structure of ministry also includes the relation between the bishops and the bishop of Rome. But the Tridentine discussion was not able to work out the needed clarification of the thorny issue of the foundation of episcopal authority and it left open the question of the relation between order and jurisdiction. As the question of jurisdiction was excluded due to earlier debates on the powers of bishops and their relation to the authority of the pope (delegated or direct), the hierarchy was treated within the framework of the Sacrament of Order in a more narrow sense, i.e. with respect to the sacramental grades of Order. The canonist Paleotti, who was responsible for the final version of Canon 6, wrote in his notes on 6 July 1563, the day of the vote: "Bishops perform all the sacramental actions just like the Pope. In this area therefore they do not stand under the Pope. For there exists a double hierarchy, one on the level of holy actions, the other in the area of church leadership. The former belongs to the Sacrament of Order, which we are treating here, and in it the highest grade is that of bishops."[75] In addition, Paleotti understands the episcopate as a pastoral ministry, endowed with a sacramentally based jurisdiction, which is responsible for "grazing the flock" (*pascere*) and which is distinct from the task of leadership (*regere*).

232. On one hand the Council of Trent took as central the category of priesthood, but at the same time it enlarged the concept so as to include pastoral tasks. Thus Order is no longer exclusively understood on the basis of priesthood, while priesthood must be understood on the basis of Order with its manifold pastoral tasks, so that the concrete church becomes the comprehensive framework for Order. By assigning the position of pre-eminence to the bishop, Canon 6 represents a basic change of direction in the understanding of the Sacrament of Order, moving away from the eucharistic body toward the ecclesial body of Christ and its members. This

---

[75] CT III/1, 684

change becomes even clearer and easier to grasp in the Reform Decrees which use the model of shepherd and pastor to describe the bishop.

233. Trent's doctrine on church ministry and its reform decrees contain two theologies of ordained ministry. The first has priesthood as its basic concept, while the second centers on the episcopate. The second perspective could not prevail everywhere because it was difficult to clarify the relation between episcopate and primacy, but it gave a differentiated shape to a teaching originally oriented to priesthood. It made possible the retention of a sacramental difference between bishop and presbyter, against St. Jerome's idea of the sacramental identity between bishop and priest based on their common relation to the eucharist. However, the view that the priesthood has to be understood on the basis of Order and not *vice versa*, did not prevail in the following centuries. One part of the Catholic understanding of the ministry, priesthood, was later emphasized so much that it was sometimes taken to be the whole of ordained ministry. Only with Vatican II was this narrow conception of the Counter-Reformation overcome.

234. The lack of agreement on the relationship between *ordo* and jurisdiction was also the reason why the Council omitted a discussion of apostolic succession, especially during and after the second session. It was clear to the Council participants that bishops were successors of the apostles and the Pope successor of the Apostle Peter. But this initial idea was not developed from this basis into a theological explanation of the episcopate. The Council wanted to avoid the question of the relation between apostolic and Petrine succession regarding jurisdiction. The theme of apostolic succession in the episcopate was not abandoned, but was simply stated in a subordinate clause: "the bishops, who have succeeded to the place of the Apostles" (*episcopos, qui in Apostolorum locum successerunt*; DS 1768; Tanner, 743, Latin text) and so lost its function of providing the basis for the bishop's eminent position and specific authority. The episcopal functions in which the superiority of the bishops finds its expression are then simply listed: "they are higher than priests and are able to confer the sacrament of confirmation, to ordain the ministers of the church and to fulfill many other functions, whereas those of lower order have no power to perform any

of these acts" (DS 1768; Tanner, 743.). But the Decree gave no indication of the foundation of these roles.

3.5 The Ordained Ministry according to Vatican II and in Lutheran Teaching Today

3.5.1 Vatican II on the Ordained Ministry

235. While the Council of Trent gave a direct response to issues raised by the Reformation, the Second Vatican Council (1962-65) sought to treat the same questions in a more balanced manner, taking account both of a broader ecclesiological setting and of the new awareness, fostered by the ecumenical movement, of a shared heritage of faith. Vatican II saw the other Christian churches and ecclesial communities in the fresh perspective of emphasis on Christian elements shared in common. Vatican II did not depart from or minimalize the binding doctrine of Trent, but it drew on a wider church tradition and introduced new accents in its presentation of the church.

The Common Priesthood of All the Baptized

236. The Council of Trent did not work out a doctrine of the common priesthood of all believers but in its treatment of the Sacrament of Order and the other sacraments it neither excluded nor denied it. It was concerned with the *ordo* of the church and with the Sacrament of Order because it considered both to have been endangered and denied by the Reformation. Medieval theology knew the doctrine of the sharing of the baptized in Christ's priesthood, based sacramentally in baptism. Thomas Aquinas for instance speaks of a "priesthood of the life of grace", and of a "sacramental priesthood" given by baptism and confirmation which enables the faithful to receive and celebrate the sacraments, while differing from the priesthood of ordained ministers.[76]

237. The doctrine of the priesthood of all the baptized was mentioned in older manuals of Catholic dogmatic theology, but magisterial statements about it first appear in the twentieth century, in the wake of the liturgical movement, for instance, in the Encyclical of Pius XII *Mediator Dei* (1947), on the liturgy, in which a central idea

---

[76] Cf. *Summa theologiae*, III, q. 63, arts. 3 and 5.

is *actuosa participatio,* the active participation in worship of the whole priestly people of God. But Vatican II recaptures the biblical, patristic and medieval approaches to the common priesthood and makes them central concepts of its ecclesiology (cf. LG 10f, 34; SC; AA 3; PO 2). Drawing on the classic New Testament texts on the priestly character of the people of God, especially 1 Peter 2:4-10, the Council describes in the *Lumen gentium* (LG 10) the common priesthood, while distinguishing it from the ministerial or hierarchical priesthood exercised by the ordained ministry. Speaking of the eucharist, LG 11 says of believers, "Taking part in the eucharistic sacrifice, the source and summit of the Christian life, they offer the divine victim to God and offer themselves along with him. And so it is that, both in offering (*oblation*) and in Holy Communion (*communion*), in their separate ways, though not of course indiscriminately, all have their own part to play in the liturgical action."

238. The phrase "in their separate ways" refers to the distinction already stated between the common and the hierarchical priesthood, which LG 10 describes as differing "essentially and not only in degree (*essentia et non gradu tantum*)". This means that "church ministry cannot be derived from the congregation, but it is also not an enhancement of the common priesthood, and the minister as such is not a Christian to a greater degree."[77] The priesthood of all believers and the ordained ministry are both grounded in the priesthood of Christ, but they belong to different areas, because the first expresses the basic Christian identity of every member of the people of God while the second characterizes the capacity to exercise the pastoral ministry, as is necessary for building up the people of God. The specific character of priestly service is described in LG 10 with reference to the liturgy: the officiating priest "in the person of Christ ... brings about the eucharistic sacrifice and offers it to God in the name of all the people. The faithful, indeed, by virtue of their royal priesthood, share in the offering of the Eucharist." LG 34 describes in greater detail the common priesthood of all believers and their participation in the worship of the church, but also the priestly service of their whole lives. It emphasizes once again the associa-

---

[77] Roman Catholic - Lutheran Joint Commission, *The Ministry in the Church* (Geneva 1982), 9 (no. 20, note 23).

tion and interaction between the common priesthood of all believers and the ordained priesthood. One is unthinkable without the other but both are special and different ways of participating in Christ's priesthood, that is, in ways which cannot be derived from each other.

Apostolic Mission and Church Ministry

239. The rediscovery by the Second Vatican Council of the doctrine of the common priesthood of all baptized and the ecclesiological role given to this doctrine in Chapter 2 ("The People of God") of the Dogmatic Constitution on the Church, *Lumen gentium,* has an impact also on the doctrine of the ordained ministry. The concept of priesthood (*sacerdotium*) can no longer serve as the only appropriate and immediate description of the nature of church ministry. Without denying the legitimacy of the concept, Vatican II follows a different path in explaining the foundation and the specific character of ordained ministry and places the priestly-liturgical dimension of it within the framework of the mission coming from Christ. "This divine mission, which was committed by Christ to the apostles, is destined to last until the end of the world (see Mt 28:20), since the Gospel they are obliged to hand on is the principle of all the Church's life for all time" (LG 20). The apostles can be considered from two different points of view according to the Decree *Ad Gentes*: they "were both the seeds (*germina*) of the New Israel and the beginning (*origo*) of the sacred hierarchy" (AG 5). The task of proclaiming the gospel is given to the whole church so that all those who belong to the people of God "have been made sharers in their own way in the priestly, prophetic, and kingly office of Christ and play their part in carrying out the mission of the whole Christian people in the church and in the world" (LG 31). Within the mission entrusted to all the people of God, there is a specific apostolic mission entrusted to the episcopal college. This college continues the work of those appointed by the apostles who "ruled that on their death, other approved men should take over their ministry" (LG 20). The theme of succession in the apostolic mission and apostolic ministry has thus a central place in the theology of the ordained ministry worked out by Vatican II.

Apostolic Succession and Ordained Ministry

The Episcopal Office

240. The new perspective from which *Lumen gentium* deals with church ministry explains both the central place given to the episcopate, contrasting with Trent's focus on the priesthood, and the importance of the theme of apostolic succession. Without denying the doctrinal, missionary and existential dimension of the apostolic succession, Chapter 3 of *Lumen gentium* speaks primarily on its ministerial aspect: "the sacred synod consequently teaches that bishops have by divine institution taken the place of the apostles as pastors of the church in such wise that whoever hears them hears Christ and whoever rejects them rejects Christ and him who sent Christ" (LG 20; cf. Lk 10:16). The bishops are "transmitters of the apostolic seed" and "the apostolic tradition is manifested and preserved throughout the world by those whom the apostles made bishops and by their successors down to our own time" (LG 20).

241. Succession in ministry for service of the apostolic tradition going back to the origins is therefore according to Vatican II the foundation of the episcopate. "The order of bishops is the successor to the college of the apostles in their role as teachers and pastors, and in it the apostolic college is perpetuated. Together with its head, the Supreme Pontiff, and never apart from him, it is the subject of supreme and full authority over the universal Church" (LG 22). The special place and the authority of the bishop of Rome within the episcopal college have their foundation in the succession of Peter (cf. LG 20). For Vatican II the episcopate thus becomes the basic form of ordained ministry and the point of departure for the theological interpretation of church ministry. Thus it completes and brings to conclusion the development already begun at the Council of Trent. It consistently takes the pastoral perspective and includes not only the liturgical task but also the office of preaching and leadership, as the theological framework for understanding ordained ministry and presents the episcopal office as the fundamental, primordial and full form of this ministry.

242. The Council then describes the substance and functions of episcopal ministry in terms of the "three offices" (*munera*), those of teacher, priest and shepherd. The proclamation of the gospel takes pride of place over the other "principal duties of bishops" (LG 25). One could say that the proclamation of the gospel and the celebration of the

sacraments are the means by which the bishops as shepherds "pasture" the people of God entrusted to their leadership.

243. The sacrament of ordination is the path that gives access to the episcopal ministry and to the bishops' college: "The holy synod teaches, moreover, that the fullness of the Sacrament of Orders is conferred by Episcopal consecration . . . [which] confers, together with the office of sanctifying, the offices also of teaching and ruling, which, however, of their very nature can be exercised only in hierarchical communion with the head and the members of the college" (LG 21). This account of episcopal ordination emphasizes two aspects: the sacramental origin of the episcopal ministry and its collegial character. The gift of the Spirit by the sacrament makes the bishop capable of performing the tasks of preaching, presiding over the liturgy, and governing the church. At the same time, the sacrament makes him a member of a college, which is "the subject of supreme and full authority over the universal Church" (LG 22). Because of the collegial structure of the episcopate, "it is for bishops to admit newly elected members into the episcopal body by means of the sacrament of Orders" (LG 21).

244. The essentially collegial structure and nature of the episcopate means also that the bishop is incorporated into the college of bishops in which the communion of the churches (*communio ecclesiarum*) expresses itself as communion among the bishops (*communio episcoporum*). On the basis of this correspondence between the college of bishops and the communion of the churches, Vatican II formulated as well the basic statement of its ecclesiology, which therefore can be called a *communio*-ecclesiology. "Individual bishops are the visible source and foundation of unity in their own particular churches, which are modeled on the universal church; it is in and from these that the one and unique Catholic Church exists (*in quibus et ex quibus una et unica Ecclesia catholica exsistit*). And for that reason each bishop represents his own church, whereas all of them together and with the Pope represent the whole Church in the bond of peace, love, and unity" (LG 23).

Presbyters and Deacons

245. Vatican II also considers the other ordained ministries of presbyter and deacon within the preceding framework of the mission of the

apostles and their successors, the bishops. In order to keep the historic question of the inner structuring and differentiation of the ordained ministry as open as possible, the Council formulated very cautiously the text of *Lumen gentium* on the ministry of presbyters, saying that the bishops "duly entrusted in varying degrees (*vario gradu*) various members of the church with the office of ministry (*munus ministerii*)" (LG 28). And, conscious of the time it took for the terminology of ministry to establish itself in the first two centuries and of the problems raised by the attempt to define precisely the relationship between the episcopal ministry and the presbyterate, the Council speaks just as carefully: "Thus the divinely instituted (*divinitus institutum*) ecclesiastical ministry is exercised in different degrees (*diversis ordinibus*) by those who even from ancient times (*iam ab antiquo*) have been called bishops, priests and deacons" (LG 28).

246. About the ministry of the presbyters it is said that "while they do not have the supreme degree of the pontifical office and depend on the bishops for the exercise of their power, priests are for all that associated with them by reason of their priestly dignity (*sacerdotali honore*). By virtue of the sacrament of Orders, they are consecrated . . . to preach the gospel and shepherd the faithful as well as to celebrate divine worship as true priests of the New Testament" (LG 28). This repeats what Trent had set forth, but the starting-point is not, as after Trent, the sacerdotal dimension, but instead the pattern of the threefold office from which theology of the presbyterate develops.

247. Vatican II's Decree on Priests (*Presbyterorum Ordinis*) locates the origin of this ministry in the proclamation of the gospel, in a manner similar to the Council's theology of the episcopate. The priestly ministry starts with the preaching of the gospel. "The people of God is formed into one in the first place by the word of the living God, which is quite rightly expected from the mouth of priests. For since nobody can be saved who has not first believed, it is the first task of priests as co-workers of the bishops to preach the gospel of God to all" (PO 4). Vatican II is no longer concerned with only a part of priestly ministry but with the whole of it. After preaching, there follows a description of the liturgical ministry of the priest, and the eucharist is described as "the source and the summit of all

preaching of the gospel," and "the center of the assembly of the faithful" (PO 5). Reflections on the pastoral ministry then round off the whole. These include the key work of priests being "instructors of the people in the faith" who have to see to it "that all the believers are led in the Holy Spirit to the full development of their vocation in accordance with the gospel teaching, and to sincere and active charity and the liberty with which Christ has set us free" (PO 6). It becomes clear that the particular dimensions of priestly ministry are seen as closely connected with each other, and that only the sum-total of these tasks constitutes the ordained ministry.

248. It is worth noting the similarity between the descriptions of the ministerial functions of presbyters and of bishops. The same pattern of the threefold office – preaching, liturgy, leadership – is used for bishops and presbyters, and in the concrete life of the church precisely the latter carry out the ordinary exercise of these functions through which the church is built up, while the bishops have oversight over teaching and care for the communion among local communities. However the presbyters exercise their ministry in subordination to the bishops and in communion with them. The sacramental origin and hierarchical relation to the episcopate are therefore the two characteristic features of the office of presbyters. On one hand their mission and authority rest on the gift of the Spirit conferred by the sacrament of ordination, while on the other hand they exercise their ministry under the bishops, and through them are within a structured church communion.

249. The Decree on Priests also mentions explicitly the ecclesial integration of presbyters into the priestly people of God. All members of the church share in Jesus' anointing by the Holy Spirit. In him "all the faithful are made a holy and kingly priesthood, they offer spiritual sacrifices to God through Jesus Christ, and they proclaim the mighty acts of him who has called them out of darkness into his marvelous light (cf. 1 Pet 2:5.9). Therefore, there is no such thing as a member who does not have a share in the mission of the whole body. Rather, all of the members ought to revere Jesus in their hearts (see 1 Pet 3:15) and by the spirit of prophecy give testimony to Jesus" (PO 2). The building-up of the body of Christ is seen as the basis and the goal of the priestly ministry. About these

ordained ministers the Decree says: "These men held in the community of the faithful the sacred power of order, that of offering sacrifice and forgiving sins, and exercised the priestly office publicly on behalf of men and women in the name of Christ" (PO 2). As Trent had done, Vatican II mentions the power to offer sacrifice and to forgive sins, but goes on to speak of the public dimension of ministerial office.

250. In the Western church, the diaconate always existed as a grade of ordination, but only in a stunted form as a transitional stage to the presbyterate. It had already lost its function as an independent ministry before the end of the first millennium. Only with the Second Vatican Council has the permanent diaconate really been revived. Concerning deacons, the Council used a formulation from the liturgies of the Early Church and says that they receive the laying-on of hands "not for the priesthood but for a ministry of service (*non ad sacerdotium sed ad ministerium*)" (LG 29). For the rest this rediscovered ordained ministry of the permanent diaconate in the Catholic Church is a quite open ministry employed in various services in the church. Furthermore the diaconate shows that even an ordained ministry can be without function or place for centuries, and that the ministerial practice of the Catholic Church has undergone far-reaching changes.

251. To sum up this survey on the ordained ministry, one could say that Trent is constantly present in Vatican II but that new accents were placed by the latter which are not entirely foreign to the Lutheran theology of ministry, such as, the connection with and embedding of the ministry in the common priesthood of all the baptized, the public nature of the ordained ministry, and especially the emphasis on the proclamation of the gospel as the main task of the ordained ministry in general. Viewed in this way, Vatican II really represents an answer to the Reformation and its attempts to retain the ordained ministry on the basis of the center of the faith, that is, the proclamation of the gospel in word and sacrament. On the other hand, when Vatican II emphasizes the episcopate as the basic form of church ministry, it gives prominence to a difference from the Lutheran understanding of ministry, which is fully realized in the public service of word and sacrament in the local community.

3.5.2. The Ordained Ministry in Lutheran Teaching Today

The Ordained Ministry and the Priesthood of all the Baptized

252. The ministry of communicating the gospel to the whole world has been entrusted to the people of God as a whole and to each individual member of it. From the Lutheran perspective, ordained ministry has to be seen in the framework of the priesthood of all the baptized precisely because the task of passing on the message of the gospel has been given to both. But the foundation for the one is characteristically quite different from the foundation for the other. It is precisely in this differentiation that they are related to each other.

253. All those who are baptized in the name of the Triune God receive in baptism a share in his priesthood which they live out in faith in Christ. Part of this priesthood is, first, that those who are baptized will bear witness before others to Christ with whom they are linked in faith and whose qualities, such as justice, holiness, wisdom, are bestowed on them by virtue of faith, and they thus pass on the gospel. Second, it is part of their priesthood that they become a Christ for others in as far as they share in bearing their burdens (Gal 6:2), especially their sins, and they bring others before God in prayer. This is the communication of the gospel through the witness of faith and life in the various everyday circumstances of life.

254. The ordained ministry, as a special ministry, rests on divine institution. This ministry is not obtained by baptism but by a special vocation and ordination. Among the most important characteristics of this ministry are its public nature and its ordered institutionality. Its specific task is the *public* proclamation of the gospel in word and sacrament. The administration of the sacraments is one of its specific tasks because, by their nature, sacraments are public enactments. This ministry is directed to *all*. For that reason one of its essential tasks is fostering the unity of all those who are priests by the priesthood of all the baptized. Within the one task of the whole people of God, which is to communicate the gospel to the whole world, there is therefore a differentiated referential relationship between the specific tasks of the general priesthood of all the baptized and of the ordained ministry.

255. The institution of the ordained ministry by God corresponds to the externality of the word of God which stands apart from the congregation because the congregation lives by this word. Because, and in as far as, the ministry has its basis and criterion in the task of communicating the gospel to the *whole* congregation in such a compelling way that assurance of faith is awakened and made possible, the ordained minister also stands apart from the congregation - precisely for the sake of the general priesthood. A *particular* ministry is required so that this priesthood may be *general* and *one* while the *general* priesthood is realized in the *particular* everyday situations in which Christians live.

256. If, like Luther, one takes the ordained ministry to be a divine institution, this does not mean a seizure of power by the clergy as is often supposed. On the contrary! If the particular ministry has the duty of preaching the external word of the gospel to all in a binding way, this means that the ministers are required, as far as possible, to renounce their own will in order to make room for the word of God, and to put aside all partisanship which is necessarily linked with power struggles. It is precisely the nature of their task that obliges them to do so. It would be quite different if the office-bearer were simply a functionary of the will of the congregation. This obligation remains even if reality often seems to contradict it.

257. The ministry has the task of proclaiming the gospel in such a way that the believers become familiar with Christ's voice and thus become "the lambs that hear the voice of their shepherd."[78] This process of education itself is the presupposition for the congregation's ability to evaluate doctrine and the proclamation of the office-holders. This competence derives from the fact that believers are guided by the external word, and therefore have the capacity to interpret Scripture. This means, first, that it is the congregation's duty to evaluate the ministerial performance of their male and female pastors, from the viewpoint of ensuring that it really is the gospel, as distinct from the law but still in relation to it, that is proclaimed. Secondly it means that office-bearers cannot expect approval of their doctrine or preaching simply by virtue of formal reference to the authority of their ministry, but only by

---

[78] Luther, *Smalkald Articles*, III, 12, citing Jn 10:3. BSLK 459, 22; BC 324f.

giving reasons which are directly or indirectly linked with Holy Scripture. Third, however, it means that inversely the judgment of the members of the congregation also requires the same scriptural substantiation, so that both, congregation and ministers, meet within the medium of scriptural exegesis in the widest sense, and that they there deal with conflicts and seek consensus. Only when this occurs can one speak of the exercise of the ordained ministry and the general priesthood.

258. The priesthood of all the baptized is not primarily a legal entitlement to share in decision-making in the church, but means above all being enabled and commissioned to become Christ for others, because the believers live by Christ's gospel and are united with him in faith. But this also means that representing Christ cannot be limited to the incumbents of the ordained ministry unless this representation is understood in a specific sense. Lutheran churches consider themselves empowered and obligated to call women too to the ordained ministry.

259. The authority and power of the ministry are basically grounded in the authority and power of the word of God which the ministry serves. Ministers act in reference to the word of God and its authority, for instance, when they pronounce the words of institution at the celebration of Holy Communion. These acts essentially take place publicly and for all. Therefore no individual can simply take up office, but an external call is a prerequisite. However, induction into the ministry cannot be simply a calling, for it must also be an authorization, because the incumbent of the ministry is a witness to the gospel. All testimony is influenced by the individuality and the perspectives of the witness. And yet the witness, man or woman, has to testify to the Christ event and therefore speak of something other than himself or herself, as in 2 Cor 4:5, "We do not preach ourselves, but Jesus Christ who is our Lord." This requires authorization through the promise that the Holy Spirit will constantly support the ministers in the exercise of their ministry.

260. Credible, in the strict sense of the word, is the word of God alone, not the life of the minister. Nevertheless the testimony of these witnesses is either enhanced or weakened by their lives, because Christ as the Lord lays claim to the whole of their life for himself. The list of requirements for the overseer in 1 Tim. 3:1-7, and also

in 1 Peter 5:2f, is proof of the significance of the life of the minister for his or her ministry. On the basis of this calling and authorization, ministers can be assured that the Holy Spirit will use their acts as his instruments to bring fruit and they can trust that in the power of the Holy Spirit they can properly obtain a hearing and a place for the word of God. This authorization helps them not to be broken by or to fail in the task to which they have been called, despite their insufficiency and sin. It also gives them freedom to admit mistakes, because the call and the authorization are conferred without a time limit. Therefore Lutheran churches should also be open to the hope for the specific gift of grace related to ministry being conferred through prayer and laying on of hands in ordination, as spoken of in 1 Tim 4:14 and 2 Tim 1:6. This however does not change the office-holder's state of grace before God.

261. Ordination as induction into office is performed with prayer and the laying-on of hands. It is both prayer for the Holy Spirit and reliable promise of the support of the Holy Spirit and thus authorization for the ministry. It therefore can be said about the *presbyteroi* that the Holy Spirit has instituted them to be *episkopoi*, to shepherd God's congregation (Acts 20:17.28). Ordination is the call to ministry in the *whole* church; it is not repeated on the occasion of a change of placement or after a temporary interruption of service in the church. It is a *lifelong* call and claims the whole person for the service of God.

Differentiation of the Ministry

262. Because the proclamation of the word of God and the administration of the sacraments awakens and maintains faith and thus builds up the church, the basic unit of the church is the congregation gathered in worship around word and sacrament. The ordained ministry primarily relates to this congregation. However, every Christian and every congregation is linked with all other Christians and congregations believing in the same Lord. This spiritual reality, like every spiritual reality, needs to find concrete expression in people and practices which as instruments of the Holy Spirit in turn maintain and strengthen the bonds within the church. This corresponds to the factual logic of the external word which the Holy Spirit uses as his instrument. It is not sufficient to simply affirm each worshipping congregation's link with the universal

church; the link requires a deliberate and institutionalized structuring if it is not to wither away and damage the unity between the congregations. These spiritual bonds must be discerned and fostered by a ministry and by people especially called to it.

263. As we noted above, the task of the incumbent of ministry is to preach the message of the gospel to the whole congregation, and to distribute it to all in the sacraments. Experience teaches that the incumbents of the ministry by no means always do this correctly, that is, that in different congregations the gospel is preached in different and sometimes even contradictory ways and that the sacraments are by no means always rightly administered. But the truth of the gospel cannot be one truth in one congregation and another truth in another. Therefore a ministry is required that exercises oversight over congregations and their pastors. This derives *necessarily* from the interplay of the following factors: first, the fact that the church is only found where the gospel is properly preached and the sacraments administered according to their institution; second, the fallibility and sinfulness of office-holders in the exercise of their ministry, particularly in the preaching of the gospel and the administration of the sacraments; third, the common bond between all Christians and Christian congregations; and fourth, the need to give a concrete institutionalized form to the spiritual reality of the bond between all Christians and Christian congregations.

264. In order that the church may be *one* beyond the bounds of the individual congregation, it requires a supra-congregational ministry. This ministry has the task of both ensuring the unity of the church and at the same time of keeping the church faithful to its apostolic origins. Indeed, this ministry can only ensure the unity of the church by insisting that in their life and teaching all Christian congregations remain in agreement with their apostolic foundation. This task is no different from the task of the presbyterial office, but in the supra-local ministry the area of responsibility is wider, and certain additional tasks and responsibilities arise. From these derive the special rights and duties of a bishop.

265. In terms of its fundamental duties, therefore, the ministry is *one* even if internal differentiation is necessary for the unity of the church. This does not, however, determine what form the supra-local oversight will take in any individual case. This cannot be con-

strued on the basis of a principle, for the experiences the church has undergone play a decisive role. This means that one has to expect a diversity of forms, because those experiences are not always and everywhere the same. Clearly the Lutheran Reformation in Germany wanted to retain the episcopate despite its criticism of the institution of prince-bishops. Within the German Empire, in contrast to the Nordic countries, this was not possible, in part for constitutional reasons. Nevertheless there have always been supra-local ministries.

266. When, after the breakdown of the monarchy in 1918 the Lutheran Church in Germany also had to be re-organized, the episcopate was gradually reinstated almost everywhere. It was however aligned to the synod in its supra-local tasks of supervision, in accordance with the principle that all non-ordained members of the church share the responsibility for the church on the basis of the general priesthood. Non-ordained members are therefore also included in the ministries of church leadership on various levels. However, many questions arise at this point concerning both the theological basis and matters of detail in the organization of the relationship. Not all of these questions have so far been answered satisfactorily. The issue of the internal structuring of ministry concentrates here on the question of pastoral and episcopal office, because the question of apostolic succession relates primarily to this issue. It should be pointed out as well that in many Lutheran churches an intensive discussion is taking place concerning the diaconate and its relationship to ordained ministry.

267. If ordination is induction into the ministry of the *whole* church, it is logical that the ordaining person is the office-bearer who represents the whole regional church, who is as a rule the bishop. On the basis of the unity of the ministry a presbyteral ordination is possible in principle; however, according to the intention of the episcopal ministry, ordination by a bishop should be the normal practice. Since however the local congregation, that is, the worshipping congregation, is the fundamental unit of the church and the ordained ministry is intended for it, congregational participation in the ordination must also have its place.

268. Thus a bishop has to care for the unity of a local church. Just as in the relationship between individual congregations, the problem of

The Apostolicity of the Church

the unity of the church recurs in the relationship between dioceses. For the sake of the unity of the church extending beyond the diocese, it is appropriate that the episcopate be exercised in a collegial manner. In Lutheran churches this does in fact occur on the national level to a certain extent through the bishops' conferences and joint synods. But since, in the theological sense, nations are not or should not be relevant factors for the reality of the church, the continued development of collegiality among Lutheran bishops beyond the national framework remains a challenge. In recent years the Lutheran World Federation has begun holding regional and global meetings of bishops and presidents of Lutheran churches. But until now, such meetings do not have a formalized role within the Lutheran Communion. And the role of the episcopal ministry in expressing and safeguarding the unity in the whole church remains an issue of discussion among Lutherans.

269. The historic episcopate, which has been the subject of regional ecumenical agreements between Anglicans and Lutherans, is recognized by Lutherans as a sign of the apostolicity of the church. It is not understood as a guarantee of apostolicity but as a sign which commits the whole church, and within it the bishops in particular, to care for this apostolicity. The Porvoo document says: "The use of the sign of the historic episcopal succession does not by itself guarantee the fidelity of the church to every aspect of the apostolic faith, life and mission. There have been schisms in the history of churches using the sign of historic succession. Nor does the sign guarantee the personal faithfulness of the bishops. Nonetheless, the retention of the sign remains a permanent challenge to fidelity and to unity, a summons to witness to, and a commission to realize more fully, the permanent characteristics of the Church of the apostles."[79] Since a bishop is both responsible for the unity among the congregations at one time synchronically and, through ordination, stands for the unity and apostolicity of the church through the ages diachronically, it is appropriate to express the temporal dimension of apostolicity in the sign of the historic succession: it is

---

[79] *The Porvoo Common Statement* (1993), no. 51, cited from *Together in Mission and Ministry. The Porvoo Common Statement with Essays on Mission and Ministry in Northern Europe* (London 1993), p. 27.

the continuity of the church, wrought by the Holy Spirit. Under the Spirit's guidance and help, the bishop can be the servant of the continuity and apostolicity of the church.

3.6 Conclusions: Apostolic Succession and Ordained Ministry

270. The ordained ministry belongs to the essential elements which, through the power of the Holy Spirit, contribute to the church being and remaining apostolic, while they in turn express the church's apostolicity. To fulfill that task, the ministry itself must be ministry in apostolic succession. What this means, and under what conditions ministry is rightly called apostolic has been a matter of dispute between Catholics and Lutherans since the beginning of the Reformation. At present the relationship is asymmetrical insofar as Lutherans recognize the ministry of the Catholic Church as apostolic, while the reverse is not the case from the Catholic side. But the expositions of this Part have brought to light important agreements as well as important differences between the Roman Catholic Church and the Lutheran churches regarding both the institutional reality and the doctrinal understanding of ministry. From this, new perspectives open up concerning the recognition of ministries.

3.6.1 Agreements

271. Together, Catholics and Lutherans affirm: The church is apostolic on the basis of the apostolic gospel and in its faithfulness to it. This gospel is continually prior to the church, as Paul says, "God was ... entrusting the message of reconciliation to us. So we are ambassadors for Christ, since God is making his appeal through us; we entreat you on behalf of Christ, be reconciled to God" (2 Cor 5:19c-20). The apostles who were called to be witnesses of the Risen Jesus Christ are the first and normative witnesses of the gospel. In the characteristic of being eye-witnesses they have no successors, but their testimony remains foundational for the church of all times. The church can be apostolic solely by agreeing with the witness of the apostles.

272. In their proclamation and in their deeds the apostles are ambassadors for Christ, which is their human activity. But it is God himself who actually speaks in their proclamation. God is the true subject of this appeal: "Be reconciled to God." God makes himself present

The Apostolicity of the Church

to human beings in the human words of proclamation and physical words of the sacraments. Lutherans and Catholics agree in the conviction that Christ, the one sent by the Father, gives himself to human beings in the audible words of proclamation and in the physical words of the sacraments. This takes place by the power of the Holy Spirit and is to be grasped and held in faith. The working of the Holy Spirit is the context of the theological discussion of the ministry.

273. Catholics and Lutherans are in agreement that all the baptized who believe in Christ share in the priesthood of Christ and are thus commissioned to "proclaim the mighty acts of him who called you out of darkness into his marvelous light" (1 Pet 2:9). Hence no member lacks a part to play in the mission of the whole body. "All the members ought to reverence Jesus in their hearts and by the spirit of prophecy give testimony to Jesus" (PO 2).

274. Ordained ministers have a special task within the mission of the church as a whole. Lutherans say that the ministers are commissioned for public proclamation of God's word and for the administration of the sacraments. "The gospel bestows on those who preside over the churches the commission to proclaim the gospel, forgive sins, and administer the sacraments."[80] Catholics also declare that it is the task of ordained ministers to gather the people of God together by the word of God and to proclaim this to all so that they may believe. Priests are also "made sharers in a special way in Christ's priesthood and, by carrying out sacred functions, act as ministers of him who through his Spirit continually exercises his priestly role for our benefit in the liturgy" (PO 5). Thus priests are commissioned to administer the sacraments, which "are bound up with the Eucharist and are directed toward it," for it is "the source and summit of all preaching of the Gospel" (PO 5). Thus for both Catholics and Lutherans the fundamental duty and intention of ordained ministry is public service of the word of God, the gospel of Jesus Christ, which the Triune God has commissioned the church to proclaim to all the world. Every office and every office-holder must be measured against this obligation.

---

[80] Melanchthon, *Treatise on the Power and Primacy of the Pope*, no. 60. BSLK, 489, 30-35; BC 340. Melanchthon says explicitly that this refers to what was already affirmed in Art. 28 of both the *Augsburg Confession* and the *Apology*.

Apostolic Succession and Ordained Ministry

275. For both Catholics and Lutherans, the common priesthood of all the baptized and the special, ordained ministry do not compete with each other. Instead, the special ministry is precisely service to the common priesthood of all. Office-holders have the task of passing on the gospel correctly to all, so that the faithful can, each in his or her own place, be priests in the sense of the universal priesthood and fulfill the mission of the church in that place. Thus ministers act for the unity of believers in one faith in the one Lord, so that they are "one body and one spirit" (Eph 4:4). As service to the word of God this ministry stands over against the congregation, while at the same time the minister also belongs to the congregation.

276. Catholics and Lutherans affirm together that God instituted the ministry and that it is necessary for the being of the church, since the word of God and its public proclamation in word and sacrament are necessary for faith in Jesus Christ to arise and be preserved and together with this for the church to come into being and be preserved as believers who make up the body of Christ in the unity of faith.

277. Induction into this ministry takes place by ordination, in which a Christian is called and commissioned, by prayer and the laying on of hands, for the ministry of public preaching of the gospel in word and sacrament. That prayer is a plea for the Holy Spirit and the Spirit's gifts, made in the certainty that it will be heard. Christ himself acts in the human rite of ordination, promising and giving the ordinand the Holy Spirit for his or her ministry. That does not alter the justifying grace of ordained ministers before God, but their ministry is to take place in the power and with the support of the Holy Spirit. Ordination is essentially induction into the ministry of the whole church, even though the present divisions of the churches prevent this from being fully realized. Through their call and commission, the ordained are claimed for lifelong service of the gospel. To this extent Catholics and Lutherans agree in their understanding of ordination.

278. Ministry is service to the gospel, which has two interrelated implications. On the one hand, the gospel is not at the disposal of the office. Ministry, if it is to fulfill its intention, can have no other purpose than to serve the gospel and assist it to prevail. On the other hand, the gospel encounters human beings in a concrete way

in preaching and in the sacraments of the church. Both facets belong together, because it is the Holy Spirit who makes Jesus Christ and his deed of reconciliation of the whole world present in a saving way to all human beings through human words and actions.

279. The differentiation of the ministry into a more local and a more regional office arises of necessity out of the intention and task of the ministry to be a ministry of unity in faith. The congregation gathered for worship is the place where human beings hear and receive the word of God by word and sacrament. Thus faith is awakened, nurtured and renewed, and believers are gathered and unified in faith in Christ. But there are many such congregations gathered for worship. In order that they may be one in faith in the one gospel and have communion with each other, there must be a ministry which takes responsibility for this unity. Particularly from the fourth century onwards the task of regional leadership developed, which was increasingly entrusted to bishops, while presbyters became the leaders of local congregations. The supra-local visitations of the Reformation era did not happen by chance but emerged out of inner necessity. Thus Lutheran churches too have always been episcopally ordered in the sense of having a ministry which bears responsibility for the communion in faith of individual local congregations. How this ministry is structured in detail remains open, as does the relationship of this ministry to the office of pastor. But differentiation within the ministry is itself necessary. The supra-local ministry of oversight in Lutheran churches today is carried out both by individuals and by synods in which both the ordained and non-ordained work together.

280. The document *The Ministry in the Church* states: "*If* both churches acknowledge that for faith this historical development of the one apostolic ministry into a more local and a more regional ministry has taken place with the help of the Holy Spirit and to this degree constitutes something essential for the church, then a *high degree of* agreement has been reached."[81] When one considers what has been shown above about the objective necessity of a differentiation within ministerial office, which is effectively present in the Lutheran

---

[81] Roman Catholic - Lutheran Joint Commission, *The Ministry in the Church* (Geneva, 1982), no. 49.

churches and is recognized as such, then the hypothetical wording of this sentence can be changed into an affirmation. Catholics and Lutherans say together that the *episcopé* of ministry must be exercised at two different levels, that is, both locally in the congregation and regionally.

3.6.2 Differences

281. Catholic doctrine holds the divine institution of the hierarchy consisting of bishops, priests and deacons in the church.[82] Today, Catholic theology for the most part does not understand this as referring back to a single institutional act by Jesus. For matters of divine right (*ius divinum*) can well come into being through historical developments during the apostolic age or later, but these are in accord with the gospel and have ongoing importance for its communication. What results from such a process expresses the true structure of the church, while bearing features of historic contingency. Because the Holy Spirit guides the church along its way, Catholics are convinced that the very early and lasting development of the threefold ministry must be understood as the formation of a basic structure which, having once evolved, is from then on irreversible and belongs to the fullness of the nature of the church.

282. Lutherans teach the continuity of the church and emphasize "that at all times there must be and remain one holy, Christian church."[83] Therefore the history of the ministry from the time of the New Testament onwards is also part of their history, which as the history of the church is unthinkable without the Holy Spirit. Lutherans, to be sure, want it to be taken into account that their forebears in the sixteenth century could not perceive or experience the office of bishop as an office of unity in faith, but that they were instead faced with a choice between fidelity to the gospel and submission to the bishops, which constrained them to give precedence to the former over the latter. Precisely because they held ministerial office to be essential for the existence of the church, they had to practice presbyterial ordination because the Catholic bishops refused to ordain

---

[82] "*[D]ivina ordinatione institutam*," Council of Trent, Canon 6 on the Sacrament of Order (DS 1776; Tanner, 744).

[83] *Augsburg Confession*, Art. VII BSLK 61.2-4; BC 42.

Lutheran theologians. They did so while being conscious that the office is essentially one, and being certain that the Holy Spirit is at work in their ordinations. It is almost universally the practice in Lutheran churches today that the responsibility for ordaining pastors is assigned to persons who hold supra-local office. Thus, it is not a matter of controversy between Lutherans and Catholics that bishops (or other supra-local office holders in Lutheran churches) are those who perform ordinations.

283. What is in dispute between Lutherans and Catholics is neither the differentiation nor the distinction between a more local and a more regional ministry, nor that ordination belongs to the regional ministry. The controversy is instead over what makes a person a rightful holder of a regional ministry and what grounds the power to ordain. At issue is apostolic succession in episcopal office. What is the significance of prayer and the laying on of hands by other bishops and of incorporation into the Roman Catholic episcopal college of bishops in communion with the Pope? It is Catholic doctrine that the practice and doctrine of apostolic succession in the episcopate is, together with the threefold ministry, part of the complete structure of the church. This succession is realized in a corporate manner as bishops are taken into the college of Catholic bishops and thereby have the power to ordain. Therefore it is also Catholic doctrine that in Lutheran churches the sacramental sign of ordination is not fully present because those who ordain do not act in communion with the Catholic episcopal college.[84] Therefore the Second Vatican Council speaks of a *defectus sacramenti ordinis* (UR 22) in these churches.

284. A further difference is connected with the preceding one. "For Lutherans the local congregation is church in the full sense, for Catholics it is the local church led by a bishop."[85] The special importance accorded to the bishop according to Catholic doctrine derives from his special task of ensuring the unity of the eucharistic congregations in his local church and the unity of his local church with other local churches. He is the connecting link between the local,

---

[84] See above, no. 243.
[85] Lutheran–Roman Catholic Joint Commission, *Church and Justification* (Geneva, 1994), no. 84.

Apostolic Succession and Ordained Ministry

the regional and the universal levels of the church. He holds that function of course only as a member of the college of bishops under the head of this college, the Pope. According to Catholic teaching the legitimacy and the authenticity of the ministry depend on this visible and physical mediation of catholicity. Consequently, ordination by a member of the college of bishops is the efficacious sacramental sign that the office is characterized in its origins by an essential association with the apostolic tradition and the universal church.

285. When Lutherans say that the local church is church in the full sense, they presuppose that the congregation assembled for worship stands in an essential relation to the universal church. This is so because the local church is not the whole church although it is wholly church. This relation to the universal church is not something secondary, subsequently added to the worshipping congregation, but is already always intrinsic to it. So this is not the point at which Lutheran and Catholic conceptions diverge. But they answer differently the question of how this relation with the universal church is mediated personally and institutionally. According to Lutheran understanding, a spiritual reality cannot be without a physical, perceptible dimension, because the Holy Spirit creates and maintains faith and the church by making use of the physical word of proclamation and sacraments as means.

286. Lutherans hold that the universal church is perceptibly present in the congregation at worship through those elements which were treated in Part 2 of this study: that is, through Holy Scripture, which is the authoritative witness to the gospel of Jesus Christ; through the creeds of the Early Church, in which one confesses a shared understanding of the gospel; through baptism by which individuals are taken into the body of Christ; through the common prayers, such as the Lord's Prayer, the Psalms, along with the *Benedictus*, *Magnificat* and *Nunc dimittis*; through the Ten Commandments and the double commandment of love as principles of living; and through ordination, which is indeed performed in an individual church but is in its intention ordination to ministry in the one church, which is understood as God-given. The differentiation and alignment of individual congregations and the local church or diocese is taken for granted in Lutheran churches. Where size

permits, bishops or the agencies of church leadership of the regional churches meet within a larger, mostly national, framework.

287. The communion of Lutheran churches in a worldwide framework is less developed. The competency of leadership bodies above the level of the individual churches and the binding force of their decisions for these churches is variously regulated and insufficiently clarified. Lutherans have different views with regard to whether there ought to be an institutional exercise of a universal ministry of unity and, in such a case, how such a ministry should be structured. But there is no controversy between Lutherans and Catholics concerning the essential relation between each worshipping congregation and the universal church; nor do we differ over this relation being perceptibly represented and mediated in diverse ways. But there is a dispute about what intensity and what structure this relation to the universal church must have for the worshipping congregations and individual to be in accord with their apostolic mission.

3.6.3 An Ecumenical Perspective on These Differences

288. For apostolic succession, succession in faith is the essential aspect. Without this, succession in office would lack all value. The ministry is service to the apostolic gospel. But now, the *Joint Declaration on the Doctrine of Justification* has ascertained the existence of a "consensus in basic truths of the doctrine of justification" between the Catholic Church and Lutheran churches. This shows a high degree of agreement in faith, that is, in that which represents the heart of apostolic succession. According to the *Joint Declaration*, the doctrine of justification is "the measure and touchstone for the Christian faith", of which it is said, "No teaching may contradict this criterion."[86] The Catholic view of the ministry of the Lutheran churches, along with the Lutheran view of ministry in the Roman Catholic Church, cannot remain untouched by the *Joint Declaration*. For, even if preserving correct doctrine is not the task of the ordained ministry alone, it is still its specific task to teach and proclaim the gospel publicly. The signing of the *Joint Declaration* therefore implies the acknowledgement that the ordained ministry in both churches has by the power of the Holy Spirit fulfilled

---

[86] JDDJ, *Annex to the Official Common Statement*, no. 3.

Apostolic Succession and Ordained Ministry

its service of maintaining fidelity to the apostolic gospel regarding the central questions of faith set forth in the Declaration.

289. The relation between the offices of priest and bishop has been defined in different ways in the history of the Catholic Church. Hence it is of great importance that what happened at the time of the Reformation be judged today by Catholics in an historically differentiated manner. According to the Second Vatican Council, "the function of the bishops' ministry was handed over in a subordinate degree to priests" (PO 2). The fullness of ministerial office is present in the bishop's office, with the consecration of bishops being understood sacramentally. In medieval times, this was not the case, at least for a very broad spectrum. Instead, following Jerome, the bishop's office was fundamentally equated with the pastoral office, while certain functions reserved to the bishop were matters of canon law. Since this conception was cited in Gratian's *Decree*, the Reformers could not regard presbyterial ordination as a break with tradition, especially since they wished to retain the episcopal office in the church, as they asserted repeatedly.[87] But, as was shown above, they faced a situation in which for them the elements of apostolicity of ministry, that is, fidelity to the apostolic gospel and canonical ordination by a bishop, had come into conflict with one another, so that they had to make a decision. They opted for fidelity to the apostolic tradition, as they understood it. This should be taken into consideration when Catholics assess the development of the ministry in Lutheran churches.

290. In the course of nearly 2000 years of history, the ministries of the Catholic Church have undergone far-reaching structural changes, while retaining the same names. These have been sketched earlier in this Part. While for Ignatius of Antioch the bishop had to preside over the worship of a community, from the fourth century onwards the bishop became increasingly the holder of a regional office charged with care of communion between congregations celebrating the eucharist. This is a major difference. Since that time an essential factor in the distinction between the presbyterial and episcopal office has been the difference between local and regional

---

[87] *Augsburg Confession*, Art. XXVIII; *Apology*, Art. XVI, 1. BC 102, 222.

The Apostolicity of the Church

leadership responsibilities. In almost 2000 years of church history a variety of transformations have occurred in the structure of the ministries of bishops and priests, corresponding to very different contexts. This grounds a distinction between a fundamental form or elementary task of this office and the structures within which it is exercised. Nor are the different interpretations of the office in theological and ecclesial doctrine merely external, but they involve its lived reality. Catholic theology emphasizes that the fundamental form of the office has persisted throughout these structural changes. But since the historical structural changes are not judged to entail a contradiction of the fundamental form of the threefold ministry, the question arises whether the structure of ministry in Lutheran churches, because of the substantial commonalities described above, and after they have emerged in different contexts parallel with the Catholic Church, may not be recognized as valid forms of the public ministry of word and sacrament.

291. It is Catholic doctrine that an individual bishop is *not* in apostolic succession by his being part of a historically verifiable and uninterrupted chain of imposition of hands through his predecessors to one of the apostles. It is instead essential that he be in communion with the whole order of bishops which as a whole succeeds the apostolic college and its mission. Thus the consensus of the bishops among themselves is the decisive sign of the apostolicity of their teaching. Catholicity is the means and expression of apostolicity. If catholicity is a sign of apostolicity, then apostolicity is a condition for catholicity. Thus fidelity to the apostolic gospel has priority in the interplay of *traditio*, *successio* and *communio*. The internal order of those three aspects of apostolic succession is of great significance. From this point it becomes once more clear how important is the expressed and confessed agreement in the fundamental truths of the doctrine of justification. The Roman Catholic Church recognizes a priestly ministry and true sacraments, by apostolic succession, in certain churches even though the bishops of those churches are not in communion with "the bishops with Peter's successor at their head."[88] But there are now many individuals at many locations in Christendom who exercise the office of supervi-

---

[88] UR 15, for the recognition, and UR 2, for the phrase cited.

Apostolic Succession and Ordained Ministry

sion which in the Roman Catholic Church is performed by bishops. These others bear a special responsibility for the apostolicity of doctrine in their churches, and they can do justice to this responsibility, as the Catholic Church recognizes in the *Joint Declaration*. They preside over churches and ecclesial communities, about which the Second Vatican Council asserts "that the Spirit of Christ has not refrained from using them as means of salvation" (UR 3). But if the consensus of bishops is the definitive sign of apostolicity of their doctrine, then Catholics cannot exclude these other *episkopoi* from the circle of those whose consensus is according to the Catholic view the sign of apostolicity of doctrine.

292. What has been said makes clear that regarding ministry it is not right to look for a simple either-or between this or that understanding of ministry or between this or that institutional structure of the ministry. But then one has to ask whether a differentiated consensus is not possible as well in the doctrine of the ministry or ministries. For we agree that the church is apostolic on the basis of fidelity to the apostolic gospel, that all the baptized who believe in Christ share in his priestly office, that the ordained ministry is essential in the church for the public proclamation of the gospel in word and sacrament, and that this ministry for its service of unity in faith is differentiated into local and regional forms. To be sure, on ministry the situation is different from that of the doctrine of justification in that we are dealing here not only with different forms of doctrine, but with different structures of ministries, therefore with institutionally ordered realities which are, of course, never without an accompanying theological interpretation. Therefore the issue is both the possibility of a differentiated consensus on the doctrine of the ministry and an approach to the differing forms of ministry, in which one discovers so much common ground that reciprocal recognition of ministries would be possible.

293. Such a differentiated consensus can appeal to the agreements in understanding the ordained ministry that are set forth above, namely that the ministry's fundamental task is to serve the apostolic gospel which is prior to the church. This service is performed in the power of the Holy Spirit, who is the true subject who proclaims the gospel and distributes the sacraments. In human actions, the Holy Spirit makes Christ present to human beings, awak-

ens their faith, and gives them salvation. We believe that the Holy Spirit is present in these actions in such a way that human beings can be assured that Christ encounters them here in a concrete way. Nevertheless, the action of the Holy Spirit is greater than the specific forms in which a given church realizes its service to the apostolic gospel. Thus a spiritual judgement is possible that "some, and even very many, of the significant elements and endowments which together go to build up and give life to the church itself" (UR 3) do exist in other churches outside one's own church. One can go further to state about the other churches, that "the Spirit of Christ has not refrained from using them as means of salvation" (UR 3). That is a spiritual judgment. A comparable spiritual judgment regarding the ministry could be possible, if one deliberately follows the path of a differentiated consensus, as was taken by the *Joint Declaration*, that is, by accepting the possibility of differing structures of ministry which realize and serve the fundamental intention of ministerial office. Such a spiritual judgment would have to build on theological insights such as those given here, but would also go beyond them. It is a risk to be taken while trusting in the support of the Holy Spirit.

Study-Document of the Lutheran-Roman Catholic Commission on Unity

PART 4
CHURCH TEACHING THAT REMAINS IN THE TRUTH

4.1 Introduction

294. This study has shown a notable degree of Lutheran-Catholic agreement on the gospel that makes the church apostolic and keeps it such (Part 2) and on the fundamental role in the church of the ordained ministry of word and sacrament (Part 3). The present Part takes up issues concerning how church teaching remains in the truth revealed in the gospel of Jesus Christ.

295. Two major topics now come to the fore: the Scriptures of the Old and New Testament in their canonical authority in the church and the church's ministry of official teaching. Lutherans and Catholics agree that the church has the essential basis of its teaching in the canonical Scriptures, which witness to the history of God's saving deeds in Israel and to the gospel of Jesus Christ, so that the world may hear a message that becomes effective in the power of the Holy Spirit. By the same Spirit God has promised to keep the church constantly in the truth, which comes about by church teaching that lives from God's word witnessed in Scripture, a word which by proclamation creates and builds up the church as a communion in the truth.

296. From the time of the Early Church, official teaching ministries have existed to preserve and communicate the message and doctrine of the apostles, principally by interpreting the authoritative Scriptures. But notable differences have existed since the Reformation, and even more since the First Vatican Council, over the structuring of these ministries which constitute the church's teaching office and over their functioning in relation to the authoritative Scriptures to maintain the church in the truth of God's saving revelation.

297. While Lutherans and Catholics agree that the church lives by the word of God, to which Holy Scripture is the original witness, we have differed over the way in which the canonicity of Scripture is grounded and made certain and over the way in which Scripture is

authentically interpreted in binding doctrines. But the participants in this dialogue remain confident that a methodical re-examination of our history and doctrines can bring progress toward agreement on these questions.

298. The following sections offer first a New Testament orientation to the truth of doctrine, to teaching ministries, and to the resolving of doctrinal conflicts (Section 4.2). Then follow early and medieval developments regarding teaching in accord with the transmitted faith, the establishment of the biblical canon, and methods and instances of biblical interpretation in the church (4.3). Then our perspectives on Scripture, doctrine, and teaching ministries will be presented as they emerged from the Lutheran Reformation (4.4) and from Roman Catholic developments from Trent to Vatican II (4.5). A final section (4.6) will state the nature and degree of our ecumenical agreement on teaching which preserves the church in the truth of our salvation in Christ.

4.2 Biblical Orientation

299. According to John 18:37, Jesus says before Pilate, "For this I was born, and for this I came into the world, to testify to the truth." The Fourth Gospel emphasizes throughout that Jesus came to serve the truth. His whole life was so uncompromisingly committed to the truth and this truth was so much God's revelation of himself in Christ, that he said to his disciples in the farewell discourse, "I am the way, the truth, and the life" (Jn 14:6). While no one has ever seen God, God's only-born Son, "has made him known" (Jn 1:18). Jesus is *the* witness to the truth, the only one in whom the witness and what is witnessed are identical (Jn 5:31-38). Jesus brings truth to the world, by giving believers a share in God's life and opening for them the way to God. Concerning this truth, Jesus says, "the truth will make you free" (Jn 8:32). This means freedom from sin and death, which is freedom to believe and to love, given by the Spirit. Church teaching that remains in the truth speaks of nothing else than the truth of God that Jesus revealed in the Spirit for the salvation of the world.

300. In the Synoptic tradition, Jesus is the teacher who speaks the truth, as the scribe acknowledged after Jesus answered him with the double commandment of love (Mk 12:28-34). Jesus alone deserves

to be called "teacher" in the full sense: "You are not to be called rabbi, for you have one teacher" (Mt 23:8). Church teaching maintained in the truth recognizes the primacy of Jesus as teacher, aiming to fulfill his mission mandate of "teaching them to obey everything that I have commanded you" (Mt 28:20).

301. According to Acts, the risen Christ addressed to the eleven the commission, "you will be my witnesses ..." (Acts 1:8). They carried out this mission along with other heralds of faith after the Spirit had come upon the whole church gathered at Pentecost and filled everyone (Acts 2:1-13). Stephen, Philip, Barnabas and Paul, along with many unnamed witnesses empowered by the Spirit, shared with the twelve apostles the founding mission of the church. In Acts 13:47 Paul says about Barnabas and himself, "So the Lord has commanded us, saying 'I have set you to be a light for the Gentiles, so that you may bring salvation to the ends of the earth.'" But the apostles and all other Easter-witnesses sense their bond in the Spirit with the Old Testament prophets (cf. Rom 1:1-4). But in the church, they are the first, but not the only ones, who serve the gospel by their witness in the following of Jesus Christ.

302. In Paul's letter to the Romans, the gospel of Jesus Christ (cf. 1:9), preached by the apostle (1:1), is the saving power of God for everyone who has faith, because the gospel reveals the righteousness of God (Rom 1:16f). This is the inherent truth of the apostolic gospel. For this "truth of the gospel" (Gal 2:5.14) Paul intervened at the apostles' council in order to show the universality of the righteousness of faith imparted by Christ (Gal 2:1-10). Paul underscored that in the controversy over the mission to the gentiles the Jerusalem leaders recognized that he had been entrusted with the "gospel for the uncircumcised," just as Peter had been entrusted with the "gospel for the circumcised" (2:7). He therefore emphasized as well that "James and Cephas and John, who were acknowledged pillars, . . . gave to Barnabas and me the right hand of fellowship" (2:9).

303. Witness must be given to the truth of the gospel for the sake of the uniqueness of God and of the promise the gospel brings. Any other "gospel" falsifies the true gospel of Jesus Christ. Consequently, already in Paul we find an "anathema!" (Gal 1:6-9). Paul saw as most important the shared struggle concerning the truth and the search for deeper understanding of the truth. Remaining in the

Church Teaching that Remains in the Truth

truth is, to be sure, a question of correct teaching and right understanding, but it is much more a question of the following of Christ and of a faith in the gospel that works through love (Gal 5:6). No human authority can guarantee possession of the truth, but still Jesus promised that the "Spirit of truth" would remain both "with" and "in" his disciples (Jn 14:17).

304. Paul as apostle was also teacher of his congregations and he names "teachers" among those to whom God has given charismatic ministries in the church (1 Cor 12:28). Paul was remembered in the church as a "teacher of the Gentiles in faith and truth" (1 Tim 2:7). Ephesians sees teachers as Christians who, together with the evangelists and pastors, perform a special service, on the foundation of the apostles and prophets, for the growth of the body of Christ (Eph 4:11).

305. In the Pastoral Letters the public teaching of the gospel in the church appears to be the special task of the *episkopos* (overseer), along with the *presbyteroi* (elders). As teacher, the *episkopos* has to speak out to correct teaching deviating from the gospel. This task of teaching is essential to the church, as appears in the connection of this ministry and its exercise with the apostolic gospel. Those whom the Spirit has made teachers in the church are called to teach the gospel publicly so that the unity of the church grows in the truth. Fulfilling their ministry, they stand in the church, which as a whole and in its individual members shares in the prophetic mission of Jesus Christ to give witness to the truth.

306. The New Testament shows that disputes over the gospel broke out even among the apostles and teachers. At issue was the correct understanding of the faith and its practice. This was the case in the conflict between Paul and Peter at Antioch described by Paul in Gal 2:11-14. This follows the account of the apostles' council (2:1-10), at which recognition of Paul, the missionary to the gentiles, as an apostle was sealed by a handshake. But when Paul was in Antioch he withdrew from common meals with the entile Christians, in which Paul saw "hypocrisy" and a contradiction of the "truth of the gospel" (Gal 2:14) and of the freedom given by the gospel (cf. Gal 2:4). Paul opposed Peter "to his face" (2:11). Holding to the basic principle of justification by faith (Gal 2:15f), he assumes that Peter as well holds this, as he speaks of "we" in what follows. Paul sees

his ecclesial fellowship with Peter as not broken by Peter's conduct and he struggles to keep it intact.

307. All through his letter to the Galatians, the Apostle Paul makes an impassioned effort to maintain the bonds of church communion. He links the argument of the moment with a basic determination: "I am astounded that you are so quickly deserting the one who called you in the grace of Christ and are turning to a different gospel – not that there is another gospel, but there are some who are confusing you and want to pervert the gospel of Christ. But even if we or an angel from heaven should proclaim to you a gospel contrary to what we proclaimed to you, let that one be accursed!" (Gal 1:6-8). Such conflicts are for Paul a threat to church fellowship and so the conflict over "another gospel" called for clarifications, both concerning Paul's mission as apostle of the gentiles (Gal 1:15f) and on justification by faith without works of the Law (Gal 2:16-20).

308. For Paul, certain notions of the gospel show that ecclesial fellowship is no longer intact, as was the case with the "false believers" who slipped into the apostles' council (Gal 2:4), along with the somewhat different conflicts with those who deceitfully disguised themselves as apostles in Corinth (2 Cor 11:13; cf. 11:5 and 12:11) and with the "dogs" who teach evil in Philippi (Phil 3:2). Throughout, the issue is justification by faith which grounds both the mission to the gentiles and the unity of the church, in which "There is no longer Jew or Greek, slave or free, male and female; for all of you are one in Christ Jesus" (Gal 3:28). Paul is the New Testament author who shows that disputes over the truth are a way to grasp this truth, defend it, and testify to it. Conflict became necessary, to keep human considerations and plausible ideas from replacing the apostolic witness to the truth in the power of the Spirit.

309. Acts and the Catholic Letters show that disputes broke out in the early communities, even among church teachers, over basic tenets of christology and eschatology. In his Miletus discourse in Acts 20:17-38, Paul warns the presbyters of Ephesus, whom he addresses as *episkopoi*: "Some even from your own group will come distorting the truth in order to entice the disciples to follow them" (Acts 20:30). So Paul exhorts them to follow his example of dedicated ministry and above all to hold to what he preached and taught. In the Pastorals the bishops must especially be firm in "sound teaching"

(1 Tim 1:10; 2 Tim 1:13; 4:3; cf. 1 Tim 4:6; 6:3), which is central in the example and doctrine of the apostle. The Letters of John, Jude, and 2 Peter make clear that early communities were also torn over teaching departing from faith in Jesus' divine sonship and denying the credibility of his message of the reign and kingdom of God. In such cases, 1 John points to the decisive need to hold to what is fundamental, namely, the saving work of Jesus Christ and the witness of those who first experienced this: "We declare to you what was from the beginning, what we have heard, what we have seen with our eyes, what we have looked at and touched with our hands, concerning the word of life" (1 Jn 1:1).

310. Teaching must serve the truth of the gospel and thereby the building up of the church and ultimately human salvation. In the New Testament, the resolution of disputes is decided by objective agreement with the original apostolic witness. Even Paul demanded that prophecy should be in agreement with faith (cf. Rom 12:6). This must be decided by the quality of better arguments, but also by the effects of the teaching: consolation for those in sorrow, faith for those who doubt, love by those who hope, and the building up of the church. The subject of this knowledge in faith is the whole church, but for the individual Christian the voice of conscience is decisive, however weak it may be (1 Cor 8-10).

311. In accord with this New Testament perspective, the church in later times takes as the basic testimonies of its doctrine the recollections of Jesus recorded in the gospels, the early creedal formulas (for example, Rom 10:9f.), the baptismal confessions, the first communities' liturgy, prophecy and catechesis, the letters of the first communities, the letters of the apostles, and not least of all the Holy Scriptures of Israel (Rom 1:2). Thus the fundamental document for church teaching is the Bible of the Old and New Testaments, which forms the canon, criterion, and yardstick of the church's teaching for all time.

312. God's truth presents itself to believers in the power of the Spirit, for the same Spirit who empowers witnesses to the gospel also makes it possible for others to hear and understand. Faith confessing the truth is both insight into and affirmation of this truth, along with the trust making it possible to commit one's whole life to this truth (Rom 10:9). But knowledge, for the duration of time,

is affected by human limitations and errors, which will only be overcome in that consummation of seeing God "face to face" (1 Cor 13:12). But even now we are, in a manner effective for our salvation, known by God, which is mediated by knowing God in faith (Gal 4:9). This then is the faith that with hope and love "abides" (1 Cor 13:13), even though it is lived out by persons whose spirit is willing but flesh is weak (Mk 14:38).

313. According to John, the risen Christ breathed upon his disciples (Jn 20:22) to give them life, much as God breathed into Adam the breath of life (Gen 2:7). In this Spirit they are sent, as Jesus was sent by the Father (Jn 20:21). The Spirit, "which believers in him were to receive" (7:39), is the "Spirit of truth" (14:17; 15:26). This is the Paraclete, the advocate, supporter, exhorter, and comforter, who will abide "forever" with Jesus' disciples (14:16), who "will teach them everything" and remind them of all that Jesus had said to them (14:26). The Spirit will witness on Jesus' behalf (15:26). In his farewell discourse, Jesus states the promise that will accompany the disciples on their mission: "When the Spirit of truth comes, he will guide you into all the truth" (16:13).

4.3 Doctrine and Apostolic Truth in Early and Medieval Developments

314. This section identifies multiple components of church teaching and indicates how they witnessed in the church to the truth of God's word during the centuries before the outbreak of controversy in the Reformation era.

4.3.1 Early Testimonies to the Gospel, Doctrine, Teachers, and Scripture

315. In connection with the emerging canon of New Testament books, the Apostolic Fathers refer in varied contexts to the components of gospel, teaching, ministers, and the inherited Scriptures of Israel. *First Clement*'s call to restore order in Corinth has a gospel background, as seen in references to the blood of Christ poured out to bring repentance and redemption by the Holy Spirit abundantly given (12,7, 21,6, 49,6, 2,2, 8,1) and to Jesus Christ as the highpriest in whom believers are called to justification not by holy deeds but by faith effected by God (36, 32,4). Ignatius of Antioch spoke of the new life opened in Christ, "who for our sakes suffered death that you might believe in his death and so escape dying yourselves.

He is our hope, and if we live in union with him now, we shall gain eternal life" (*Trallians* 2,1-2).

316. In *Didache*, chs.1-6, sound teaching is a catechesis on walking in the "way of life" while avoiding "the way of death". Ignatius knows that the Ephesians closed their ears to an alien "evil doctrine" (*Ephesians* 9,1). Against error Ignatius responds by insisting that Jesus "was really born, ... really crucified and died, ... was really raised from the dead" (*Trallians* 9).

317. The *Didache* speaks of itinerant teachers, apostles, and prophets, whose way of life should be examined before they may stay in the community (11,1-8, 13,1-7), where teachers instruct on the "two ways" (7,1). For Ignatius, the bishop serves by witnessing publicly to the gospel. At the martyrdom of Polycarp, bishop of Smyrna, a mob cried out, "This is the teacher of Asia, the father of Christians, the destroyer of our gods, who teaches many not to sacrifice nor to worship" (*Mart. of Polycarp* 12,2).

318. First Clement assumes that the inspired Scriptures are well known (45,2, 53,1, 62,3), and cites them frequently. Ignatius insisted that Scripture be interpreted in the light of Christ's cross, death, and resurrection (*Philadelphians* 8,2; *Smyrnians* 7,2).

319. On the basis of the gospel, doctrine, teachers, and the Scriptures, the Roman Church took action ca. 140 A.D. against Marcion. Justin tells of Marcion's heretical teaching on a God greater than the Creator and Father of Jesus (*First Apology* 26, 58), for which Marcion had been expelled in order to protect the truth of apostolic and scriptural teaching. This action of doctrinal *episcopé* was a watershed that clarified orthodox teaching and ensured for later ages, against Marcion's reduction, the two-part canon of Scripture including the four canonical gospels, Acts, and apostolic letters.

4.3.2 The Rule of Faith

320. Works of the late second and early third century indicate a form of "sound doctrine" which serves as a central means in keeping the churches in the truth of God's revelation. Irenaeus of Lyons, Tertullian, Clement of Alexandria, and Origen present the "canon of truth" or "rule of faith" (*regula fidei*), that is, a set framework and content of faith, now professed and taught in the churches as coming from the apostles. The rule is to believe in God, the Father

Almighty, who created all that is; in Jesus Christ, the Son who became incarnate for our salvation; and in the Holy Spirit, who spoke through the prophets of Christ's birth, passion, resurrection, and ascension, of the future resurrection and coming manifestation of Christ in glory as just judge of all (Irenaeus, *Adversus haereses* I, 10, 1-2). In the rule of faith, Christian tradition received an early but very clear formulation.

321. The rule was not verbally fixed, but it gave structure to the transmission of the gospel and basic doctrine to catechumens, before their baptism when they came under this norm of belief. The rule expressed faith's trinitarian structure which protected the unity of creation, redemption, sanctification, and revelation. Adaptation was possible, when errors made it necessary to emphasize particular points, as in formulations of the unity of the two testaments against Marcion and the reality of the Son of God's entry into the flesh of our humanity against strains of gnosticism.

322. The rule was not applied to the prophetic and apostolic books as an ecclesiastical principle external to them. For the rule expressed Scripture's meaning, which teachers were publicly transmitting in the churches to foster an ordered understanding of God's saving works. The rule was a formulation, but, as Irenaeus said, it corresponded to the salvation written in believers' hearts by the Holy Spirit who had anointed them (*Adversus haereses* III, 4, 2).

4.3.3 Creeds for Professing the Apostolic Faith

323. Early formulations for professing the apostolic faith are known in the New Testament, as in the concentrated declaration, "Jesus is Lord" (1 Cor 12:3) or, as Paul expands this, to "confess with your mouth that Jesus is Lord and believe in your heart that God raised him from the dead" (Rom 10:9). Around 200 A.D., in North Africa, the one being baptized first renounced Satan and then professed faith in response to three set questions about belief in Father, Son, and Holy Spirit (Tertullian, *De corona* 3; also Hippolytus, *Apostolic Tradition*, 21). The earliest baptismal creed involved a dialogue with answers of "I believe" to questions about the work of Father, Son, and Holy Spirit.

324. Many fourth century creeds served in the catechumenate, in which the handing over of the church's creed (*traditio symboli*) marked a

passage in preparation for baptism. After instructions on the contents, candidates publicly recited the creed before the assembled community (*reditio symboli*; cf. Augustine, *Confessions*, VIII, 2,5). These declarative creeds formulated the core of God's revelation of himself and the work of salvation in Christ. In the creeds the doctrinal component of Christian tradition became explicit regarding the central contents of the transmitted faith.

325. The Council of Nicaea in 325 A.D. began a new development with its declarative creed for the whole church (DS 125; Tanner, 5), expressing the faith in a form that excluded error about Jesus Christ. This dogmatic creed protected the apostolic faith, while prohibiting an erroneous biblical interpretation and securing the understanding of salvation as God's own work in his divine Son. In church life, the Nicene Creed was not used in the catechumenate for the expression of personal faith by individual believers, but was professed by the people in many eucharistic liturgies and served bishops and teachers working publicly as a criterion of communion between the churches and as a norm of orthodoxy.

326. As public professions, creeds derive from the preaching of Christ's apostles and are used under the supervision of those who expound and guard the transmitted word in the churches. But in personal profession of the creed an individual allows God's good news to reach its intended term in giving new life in the Triune God. Consequently, Thomas Aquinas stated the principle: "The act of the believer does not reach its term in the formula but in the reality expressed" (*Actus autem credentis non terminatur ad enuntiabilem sed ad rem. Summa theologiue*, II-II, q. 1, art. 2 ad 2). The creed expresses the truth of revelation, but the text is not the ultimate object. Professing a creed is, by the work of God's Spirit, a moment in movement toward union with God in saving communion.

4.3.4 The Canon of Scripture

327. Contemporaneous with growing clarity on doctrine, by the rule of faith and creeds, the churches also arrived at greater certainty about the biblical writings received from Israel and from the apostolic generation. A few decades after Nicaea, the limits of the canonical Christian Bible, whose central content was already clear, was more precisely defined. Here the term "canon" has two over-

lapping meanings. It is first the catalogue of the books making up the Bible of the church. But as the "canonical" Scriptures, the Bible is the normative criterion of the life and teaching of the church.

328. In Judaism down to ca. 100 A.D. the Torah and Prophets were essentially closed collections while the Writings, even with the singular authority of the Psalms, varied in extension in the traditions of different groups. But in the reconstitution of Judaism after the destruction of the Temple, the rabbinical conception eventually prevailed, by which absolute authority for synagogue teaching was ascribed to the canon of twenty-two books originating in Hebrew, to the exclusion of additional works included in the Septuagint Greek Bible of diaspora Jews.

329. From the beginning, the Scriptures of Israel, later called the "Old Testament", constituted the Bible of Christians, as the first part of Holy Scripture. Consequently, it was of central importance when the church rejected Marcion's denial of any role for Christians of the Scriptures of Israel. This led to a campaign in catechetics and theology (as in Irenaeus and Origen), which accentuated the essential contribution of the Old Testament's witness to faith in the one God who is Creator of all and Father of Jesus Christ.

330. But soon, differences emerged over the status of the Septuagint books not included in the Jewish canon, Tobit, Judith, 1-2 Maccabees, Wisdom, Sirach, Baruch, and parts of Esther (chs. 11-16) and Daniel (3:25-90, chs. 13-14). In the East, Athanasius and Cyril of Jerusalem, joined by Jerome, saw these books as giving useful instruction for life but not as canonical authorities for faith. But in the West, Augustine defended these books as proven in usefulness in the liturgy and in their contribution to both doctrine and piety. The regional councils of Hippo in 393 A.D. and Carthage in 397 A.D. sanctioned the more extensive canon, which Pope Innocent I confirmed in 405 A.D. (DS 213). These actions insured the presence of the "deuterocanonical" books in the Vulgate Bible of Western Christianity.

331. The canon of New Testament books emerged by the continuous use of the four gospels and apostolic writings, while other early Christian works were not received by the whole church as canoni-

cal. Two factors led to the clarity widely attained in the third and fourth centuries. Marcion had reduced the authoritative texts to ten Pauline letters and an edited text of Luke. Gnostic teachers featured further books of alleged origin from Jesus and the apostles. In reaction, writers in the great churches, like Irenaeus, criticized both views, especially by applying the *regula fidei*, so as to go well beyond Marcion's reduction, while rejecting works of Gnostic provenance as being infected with error.

332. Early in the fourth century Eusebius told of a broad consensus over four gospels, Acts, the Pauline corpus, and 1 John, but also related that differences exist over James, 1-2 Peter, Jude, and 2-3 John, while the standing of Revelation is debated (*Ecclesiastical History*, III, 25). The earliest list corresponding to our New Testament canon is Athanasius's Festal Letter of 367 A.D., which imposed uniformity on the lectionaries of Egypt and ruled out Gnostic gospels and apocalypses. The Western canons of Hippo, Carthage, and Pope Innocent agreed in listing the twenty-seven books that exclusively make up the New Testament canon of the Christian churches.

333. Numerous individuals contributed to giving the Christian biblical canon its shape and content. Bishops, alone or in synods, took important actions to regulate public liturgical reading of Scripture. For this, a principal criterion of judgment was the coherence of the received books with the transmitted faith, as is evident in the rejection of Gnostic "gospels" which lacked accounts of the passion, death, and resurrection of Jesus. The transmitted faith conveyed the central contents of early and uncontested gospels and letters. All the received New Testament books had connections with apostles of Jesus, so as to bring their readers into nearness to Jesus and to the church-founding ministries of the apostles and their close associates.

334. The books of the canon serve to keep the church in every age "apostolic", as the creed professes that it is and will remain. The canon gives all Christians the list of the books they read and interpret on a daily basis in order to deepen the authenticity of their faith and to take guidance from God's word of truth in the changing circumstances of their lives.[89]

---

[89] Below, Sections 4.4 (Lutheran) and 4.5 (Catholic) will treat the traditional arguments and differences over the canon and the Conclusion (4.6) will examine the degree to which they are open to ecumenical reconciliation.

335. The establishment of the canon leads to two further questions. First, how did the canonical Scripture contribute to the dogmatic tradition that emerged in the teaching of general councils? Second, how did early and medieval teachers interpret the biblical books to make their communication of the truth of revelation formative of the faith and lives of believers?

4.3.5 The Councils of the First Eight Centuries

336. The service rendered to the truth of faith and to its public profession by the Council of Nicaea (cf. no. 325, above) had ample precedent in regional synods of bishops beginning in the second century, such as those that condemned the Montanist "new prophets" (after 160 A.D.). Major synods of bishops meeting at Antioch in the third century condemned the adoptionist christology of Paul of Samosata, whose errors were detailed in the synods' letters to other regions of the church. Norms of penitential practice were laid down in synods at Elvira (Spain) in 306, Arles (Gaul) in 314, and Ancyra (Asia Minor and Syria) also in 314. In 320, ca. 100 bishops of Egypt and Libya gathered in Alexandria to judge Arius' teaching as contrary to the gospel teaching on the Word (*Logos*) who was from the beginning and by whom all things were made. Bishop Alexander of Alexandria sent out encyclical letters to other bishops to warn them against receiving followers of Arius, because they opposed the apostolic doctrine of piety.

337. The Council of Nicaea, in 325, raised synodical practice to the level of all the churches of the Empire. Its Creed was gradually received as expressing and protecting the orthodox faith and subsequent councils, both regional and ecumenical, made it the authoritative starting point of their doctrinal deliberations. At Ephesus in 431, the reading of the doctrinal texts of Nestorius and Cyril of Alexandria was preceded by the Nicene Creed, which was to serve as the norm for judging the doctrines of the two disputants as orthodox or deviant.

338. The *acta* of the Council of Chalcedon refer frequently to the previous Councils of Nicaea, Constantinople, and Ephesus, assuming that they have taught the truth concerning God and Christ. Gregory the Great revered the first four general Councils on a par

with the four gospels, since the Councils are a foundation on which rises the edifice of the church's faith.[90]

339. In conciliar teaching, bishops gave testimony to the faith of the church that should be held inviolately, in binding decisions about what should and should not be preached and taught publicly and about how Scripture should and should not be interpreted.

340. At the great councils, deliberations took place before an open book of the gospels, placed on a chair to indicate that Christ was presiding. But while later theological writers defended conciliar teaching by amassing Scripture texts in expounding doctrines, councils themselves judged controverted doctrines by their agreement or disagreement with the teaching of earlier councils and works of recognized orthodox teachers. When synodical letters communicated the decisions of councils, as after Ephesus in 431, the basis given was the "faith of Nicaea" taken as the epitome of biblical doctrine.

341. At Second Nicaea in 787 A.D., the Council document approving the veneration of images began with four biblical texts, but then gave a long list of patristic texts in evidence of the tradition of honoring images. Earlier creeds and Church Fathers were decisive in councils because in doctrinal controversy both sides appealed to Scripture, as in the Arian appeal to texts subordinating the Son to the Father. Later Councils deliberated in the presence of the open gospels, but the doctrines that they taught served to renew for their time what they received from their predecessors in the conciliar tradition.

4.3.6 Interpreting the Truth of Scripture for the Church: Early and Medieval Approaches

342. While Christians of every age have heard from Scripture God's authoritative word, they also know what the Ethiopian eunuch said about the reader of Scripture needing guidance (Acts 8:30-31). Interpretation is, thus, a constant activity, in which, however, different methods have been employed. Writers of Late Antiquity dis-

---

[90] *Epistle* I, 25; PL 77, 478, which was later well known through its citation in Gratian's *Decretum*, Dist. XV, c. 2.

cussed the ways and means of an interpretation which recovers for the church the binding truth of God's revelation from its attestation throughout the Bible.

343. Jesus cited Israel's Scriptures as authoritative and inspired (Mk 2:25, 11:17, 12:36), while indicating that their center was love of God and neighbor (Mk 12:29-31). The apostolic preaching of Jesus' death and resurrection declared these events to be "according to the Scriptures" (1 Cor 15:3-4), while the same Scriptures were central in apostolic pastoral teaching, "for whatever was written in former days was written for our instruction, so that by steadfastness and by the encouragement of the Scriptures we might have hope" (Rom 15:4). The Letter to the Hebrews solidified the church's hold on the inherited Scriptures by typological readings of the Israelite Scriptures applied to Jesus, while the evangelist Matthew reflected Christian assurance that Jesus' coming and life "fulfilled what had been spoken by the Lord through the prophet" (Mt 1:22, etc.). In John 5:39, Jesus asserts that the Scriptures testify on his behalf, while the Gospel of Luke ends with the risen Jesus assuring the disciples "that everything written about me in the law of Moses, the prophets, and the Psalms must be fulfilled" (Lk 24:44). Apostolic practice in searching the inherited Scriptures is sketched in Paul's defense that he was "saying nothing but what the prophets and Moses said would take place: that the Messiah must suffer, and that, by being the first to rise from the dead, he would proclaim light both to our people and to the Gentiles" (Acts 26:22-23).

344. A notable second-century approach to Scripture is Justin's amassing of Old Testament testimonies predicting what took place in Christ and in the spread of Christianity. Irenaeus insisted that the *regula fidei* conveys in summary form the biblical message relevant for faith. The *regula* is accepted by patristic interpreters as a norm with which interpretation must be consistent. In it a doctrinal authority came upon the scene, expressing an aspect of tradition and applied publicly by teachers in the church to guide reading and interpretation of Scripture.

345. In the milieu of cultured Alexandria, Clement and Origen adopted Hellenistic traditions of allegorical interpretation, in order to find in Scripture a total meaning. Paul used the methods of allegory (Gal 4:24) and typology (1 Cor 10) for interpreting the Scriptures of

Israel as pointing to Christ. This developed in the Early Church in complex ways, to give a biblical basis for doctrine and conduct, for learned accounts of the world and human nature, and for mystical instruction. Faith in inspiration instilled the expectation of finding in the texts, beyond the surface of the letter, many meanings given by God's Spirit to instruct and nourish life and prayer, in interpretation that expressed in practice the sufficiency of Scripture for faith and conduct.

346. The school of Antioch, represented by Theodore of Mopsuestia and John Chrysostom, insisted that events narrated in Scripture had for the authors and their first readers a meaning which interpretation must respect and set forth with sober attention to the plain sense of the texts. The Antiochenes saw prophecies and types of Christ in the Old Testament, but far fewer than what was offered by the spiritual reading of the Alexandrines. Antiochene interpretation, privileging a single original meaning, suffered by its association with Nestorius, but was well exemplified by Augustine's close reading of Paul in his anti-Pelagian works. It fostered detailed, textual study and was received in the medieval principle that in debate the original, literal sense of Scripture was alone probative of "sacred doctrine" (Thomas Aquinas, *Summa theologiae.*, I, q. 1, art. 10 ad 1).

347. Augustine made the famous affirmation that the authority of the church moved him to believe the gospel (*Contra ep. Fundamenti*, 5, 6), but also said that the canonical books provide all that is needed for faith and for life in hope and charity (*De doctrina christiana*, 2, 9, 14). The biblical authors have never erred, but they also left texts difficult to grasp, and so interpretation must turn for guidance to the rule of faith, received from clear passages of Scripture and from the church's authority (*Ibid.*, 3, 2, 2). But all of Scripture must in the end be related to its purpose, namely, fostering the love of God and neighbor, as Scripture itself testified (*Ibid.*, 1, 36, 40).

348. After Augustine's death, Vincent of Lerins gave the famous rule for understanding rightly the divine and authoritative word of Scripture, that is, "to hold fast to what has been believed everywhere, always, and by all" (*ut id teneamus quod ubique, quod semper, quod ab omnibus creditum est* [*Commonitorium*, 2, 5]). Tradition thus

conveys the true meaning of Scripture for the church, but this tradition develops, without substantially changing, to bring forth further understanding in the church (*Ibid.*, 23, 1ff.). Vincent sought to explain an authentic doctrinal interpretation of Scripture, which however is in itself a perfect witness to truth "in itself for all things more than sufficient" (*cum ... ad omnia satis superque sufficiat* [*Ibid.*, 2, 2; also 29, 3]).

349. For Vincent the problem is that interpretations of Scripture vary with the variety of interpreters (*Ibid.*, 2, 3-4), and many heretics offer scriptural warrants for their doctrines (*Ibid.*, 25, 3). When this happens, appeal must be made to the agreed teachings of the forebears in the catholic communion (*Ibid.*, 28, 5), especially to the decrees issued by bishops gathered in council (*Ibid.*, 23, 18 and 29, 5), as at Ephesus where Nestorious was judged to be at odds with the Catholic faith transmitted by authentic witnesses in the whole known world (*Ibid.*, 29-30). Scholarship is not agreed on Vincent's precise intent, but it is clear that for him the tradition expressed in the Fathers and Councils is not another source beside Scripture, but is instead the very truth of Scripture as this is articulated in the church.

350. But for some Fathers tradition had another sense beyond the transmitted truth of Scripture, namely, certain practices passed on orally from the apostles, as held, for example, by Tertullian (*De corona*, 3-4) and Augustine (*De baptismo*, 2, 7, 11). Basil of Caesarea listed such apostolic traditions not recorded in Scripture which are observed in liturgical prayer and sacramental rites (*De Spiritu Sancto*, 27), in a text given an extended afterlife in the *Decretum* of Gratian (Dist. XI, c. 5). In Basil, Scripture is not being supplemented by orally transmitted doctrines of faith, but instead the church is consolidating its worship and life in forms which loyal Christians will follow in practice.

351. In the twelfth century, Master Gratian contributed to our question by recognizing, along with official conciliar and papal teaching, the interpretation of Scripture by others, namely commentators who combine spiritual gifts, learning, and a sound use of reason. While those holding jurisdiction in the church have pre-eminence "in deciding cases", including doctrinal disputes, in the exposition of Scripture the commentators come first (*Decretum*, Dictum ante Dist.

XX, c. 1). A century later, St. Thomas spoke similarly of the two chairs, which differ in their task and competence: the "magisterial chair" from which teachers communicate acquired learning concerning the faith, and the "pontifical or episcopal chair" from which prelates make binding decisions as shepherds of Christ's flock (*Quaestiones quodlibetales*, III, 4, 1). The Thomist ecclesiologist Juan Torquemada, O.P. (d. 1468), distinguished between scholars who show what the biblical text means, which does not require the assent of believers, and the Pope who determines in a binding way the meaning of Scripture to be held in the church (*Summa de ecclesia*, II, 107). Thus, medieval teachers of unquestioned authority know well a plurality of ecclesial agents who serve revealed truth.

352. For Thomas Aquinas the truth of faith is transmitted and professed in the creeds of the church, which are several in answer to successive heretical attacks (*Summa theologiae.*, II-II, 1, 9 ad 2). Creeds have been issued by general councils, but when error makes it necessary the Pope, in virtue of the mandate of Lk 22:32 and his service of unity in faith, can also ascertain what is of faith and formulate this in an updated creed (*Ibid.,* q. 1, art. 10).

353. For Aquinas and the teachers of the high Middle Ages, magisterial actions clarify the meaning of the prophets and apostles who mediate God's word to us in Scripture. Scripture is the materially sufficient source of sacred doctrine, with the meaning also being inherent in tradition.[91] But late-medieval accounts of the sources of Catholic truth grew ever more refined, and in polemical defenses against Marsilius of Padua and John Wycliffe, novelties emerged, such as deriving the authority of Scripture from the church that authoritatively fixed the canon (Guido Terreni, O. Carm., d. 1342) and expanding Basil's unwritten traditions of practice to include binding tenets of faith going back to Christ, not given in Scripture but instead transmitted orally until formulated in writing and approved by the church, e.g., on the sacrament of confirmation (Thomas Netter, O. Carm., d. 1430; Gabriel Biel, d. 1495).

354. Early sixteenth-century Europe was a place of rising expectations of better preaching, Christian instruction, and pastoral care. Calls

---

[91] See Yves Congar, *Tradition and Traditions* (London, 1963), 107-118 (Ch. 3, Excursus A), "The Sufficiency of Scripture according to the Fathers and the Medieval Theologians."

for reform had been heard with some frequency (cf. Part 2, no. 92, above). When printing made Scripture newly accessible, soon in editions in the original Hebrew and Greek, new possibilities opened for reform based on the pre-eminent source of faith and life. Glossed bibles surrounding the text with blocks of early Christian commentary soon lost their appeal. When the Reformation translated calls for reform into action, numerous questions became urgent for which previous centuries offered no agreed answers. How does Scripture ground authentic doctrine, e.g., for catechesis? In the manifold contents of Scripture, what is the center that should control interpretation? In interpreting God's word, what is the proper interrelation between previous traditions, creeds, councils and the Pope, and textually based theological proposals?

4.4 The Church Maintained in the Truth According to the Lutheran Reformation

4.4.1 Canon, Interpretation of Scripture, and Teaching in the Lutheran Reformation

355. For the Reformers, a close connection linked the issue of the church being maintained in the truth with the certainty, "that at all times there must be and remain one holy, Christian church."[92] They understood this church as "the assembly of all believers among whom the gospel is purely preached and the holy sacraments are administered according to the gospel."[93] Thus for the church to remain church, being maintained in the truth of the gospel is essential. The promise that the church will continue to exist pertains to the church as a whole. However, in the era of the Reformation divisions broke out precisely over the question of truth and error in doctrine and over preaching and the administration of the sacraments. These divisions made it questionable for those in one part of Christianity whether those who taught differently were remaining in the truth. On certain issues, groups came to contest in a definitive manner the validity of teaching by others.

356. Initially the controversy broke out over questions of dogmatic content, regarding both indulgences, in doctrine and practice, and the

---

[92] Augsburg Confession, Art. VII. BC 42.
[93] *Ibid.*

certainty of faith by which a penitent should in confession rely on the word of absolution. But when Luther was accused of heresy and the Pope censured a list of his teachings as heretical or offensive or false,[94] this immediately raised new questions, first, about the authorities to which one could appeal in deciding for or against such a judgment and, second, about the proper instances of judgment which were competent and relevant in such a case. Between 1517 and 1521 the controversy escalated in intensity with startling rapidity.

357. As the controversy began, Luther repeatedly named the authorities that had to be heard in a doctrinal controversy, namely, Holy Scripture, the Church Fathers, and the canonical decretals, and he did this in the assumption that they would be in agreement, with Holy Scripture having the leading role.[95] But in the course of the dispute Luther became more and more convinced that several positions cited against him from canon law were not convincingly based in Scripture and that this deficit was being covered by appeals to the authority of the teaching office. With this, the traditional ordering of the authorities became questionable for Luther and thereby the competent instances of teaching became themselves an issue of controversy. In 1518 at Augsburg Luther met a representative of the magisterium in the person of Cardinal Cajetan and during his exchange with him Luther appealed from the poorly informed Pope to one better informed, doing this in the expectation that in the eventual decision of the Pope he would hear Christ speaking.[96] But shortly after, when Luther saw the letter with the Pope's instructions to Cardinal Cajetan,[97] he also appealed to an-

---

[94] The complete list of censured propositions is given in DS 1492.

[95] He repeatedly charged that the Pope had issued a doctrine without giving the grounds in Scripture, the Fathers, the canons, or even arguments from reason. *Ad dialogum Silvestri Prieratis de potestate papae responsio* (1518), WA 1, 647,32f, 648,19f, and 648,35. In his appeal to the Pope, Luther declared that he wanted to hold and say nothing which could not be proven from Scripture, the Fathers, and the sacred canons (*Appellatio M. Lutheri a Caietano ad Papam* [1518]), claiming that his *Explanations of the Ninety-Five Theses* had done just this. WA 2, 32,28f.

[96] Luther, *Appellatio a Caietano*. WA 2, 32,25-27.

[97] Luther, *Acta Augustana*. WA 2, 23–25,4.

other instance, one in which the whole church, which does not err, would speak, namely, a Council.[98]

358. Shortly after Luther's Augsburg hearing before Cajetan, the Pope made an authoritative clarification on indulgences.[99] But because the text gave no biblical or other arguments, Luther did not hear in it either the voice of Christ or of the church. Soon after, Luther began raising exegetical objections against the biblical grounding of papal primacy and questioned the way in which his opponents were presenting papal authority, even though this was not authoritatively defined. And so when the Pope's bull of 1520 demanded that he recant his teachings, Luther responded by calling the Pope "the Antichrist" and based this on the charge that the Pope was putting himself above the word of God and creating new articles of faith.[100]

359. For Luther the further appeal to another instance remained in force, namely, to a Council. But during the Leipzig Disputation of 1519, he took the position that the Council of Constance had erred in condemning certain propositions of Jan Hus, which led Luther inevitably to deny the inerrancy of Councils. Therefore Luther concluded that he could submit to a conciliar decision only after testing its validity on the basis of Holy Scripture. With this, Luther seemed to be an individual opposing the church, that is, the instances that traditionally were competent to speak for the church, namely, the Pope who had already censured many of his teachings, and the council that he could not unreservedly acknowledge as a final judge. On the other hand, Luther was really not alone but was leading a growing movement, because more and more people were being convinced by his notion of the gospel and by the arguments he was presenting.

360. At the time, Luther's dispute quickly reached a stage beyond any easy solution, although in retrospect after study of the sources, one can certainly imagine another outcome. There was at that

---

[98] Luther, *Appellatio F. Martini Luther ad Concilium* (28 November 1518). WA 2, 36-40.
[99] Decree "Cum postquam" (9 November 1518). DS 1447-49.
[100] The bull in which Pope Leo X called for Luther's recantation is "Exsurge Domine" (15 June 1520), given in DS 1451-92. Luther's "Antichrist" accusation, we note, has in the interim been explicitly revoked by Lutherans.

time no unanimity over the systematic ordering of Christian norms. The plurality of possible conceptions left a larger area for maneuvering than the actual course of events would suggest. Appearances, in this case, can deceive, for both sides were to an extent facing the same problems and tasks, while the area of agreement between them was more extensive than many would suppose today.

361. Both Luther and his opponents agreed that Holy Scripture is normative for church teaching. The dispute however was about the precise relationship between the church and Scripture, as became clear at the Leipzig Disputation between Luther and Johann Eck (1519), where conflict about the canon broke out over the question of the biblical basis of the doctrine of purgatory.[101] Luther denied the possibility of grounding purgatory in Scripture, because the text cited for this, 2 Maccabees 12:46, was from a book not belonging to the canon and so was for Luther not a suitable proof against denials of purgatory. Regarding canonical validity, Luther made a clear distinction between the books of the Hebrew canon and books transmitted only in the Septuagint. Johann Eck offered the counter-argument that even though 1-2 Maccabees was not in the Hebrew canon the church had nonetheless, with an appeal to St. Augustine, received it as canonical.[102] To this Luther responded that the church was not able to ascribe more authority to a book than the book had in itself.[103]

362. Eck then framed his objection to Luther's idea of Scripture with a general principle, "It is by the authority of the church that Scripture is authentic."[104] This pertains first to canonicity, with books of Scripture being canonical on the basis of their being recognized by the church. Second, as a consequence, the church is capable of giving binding interpretations of Scripture and is obliged to do this. The basis for this was the often cited statement of Augustine, "I would not believe the gospel, if the authority of the church did not

---

[101] *Disputatio inter Ioannem Eccium et Martinum Lutherum* (1519). WA 59, 525,2866–549,3655.

[102] WA 59, 528,2958-2963. Cf. Augustine, *The City of God*, XVIII, 36 (CSEL 40/2, 326).

[103] WA 59, 529,2985f.

[104] J. Eck, *Enchiridion locorum communium adversos Lutheranos*, ed. P. Fraenkel, Corpus Catholicorum 34 (Münster 1979), 27.

bring me to do this."[105] Luther's opposing position is that interventions of the church regarding the extent of the canon mean to be judgments in which the church ascertains that certain books have shown themselves to her as the word of God and because of this, the church has declared the books canonical.

363. The Lutheran Reformation declined to issue a complete list of canonical books of Scripture, a fact all the more remarkable in light of the emphatic opening statement of the *Formula of Concord*, "that the only rule and guiding principle according to which all teachings and teachers are to be evaluated and judged are the prophetic and apostolic writings of the Old and New Testaments alone."[106] The Lutheran option rests on Luther's view that for recognizing the canonical and apostolic standing of a book, its apostolic authorship was less important than its content. The books of Scripture are brought together to form a unity by their central content, Jesus Christ. Luther stated, "Take Christ out of the Scriptures, and what will you find left in them?"[107] Everything in Scripture points to Christ, and because the apostles' office is to preach Christ, consequently the touchstone for the apostolic standing of particular books is whether or not they "inculcate Christ."[108] This is not verified in the Letter of James, who also interprets Abraham in a manner contrary to Paul's doctrine of justification.[109] But one should note the fact that Luther did not act on his very critical comments on James by excluding the Letter from the canon. He only changed the order of the last nine New Testament books, placing James toward the end.

364. The reformers needed no special justification for holding that the Scriptures were normative in their two original languages. "For it was not without purpose that God caused his Scriptures to be set down in these two languages alone – the Old Testament in Hebrew, the New in Greek. Now if God did not despise them but chose

---

[105] *Contra epistulam Manichaei quam vocant fundamenti*, no. 5 (CSEL 25/1, 197). Cf. no. 347, above.
[106] *The Epitome*, no. 1. BC 486.
[107] *The Bondage of the Will* (1525), WA 18, 606,29; LW 33, 26.
[108] *Preface to the Epistles of St. James and St. Jude* (1522). LW 35, 396; WADB 7, 384,27.
[109] *Ibid.*, WADB 7, 384,9-18.

them above all others for his word, then we too ought to honor them above all others."[110] "Although the Gospel came and still comes to us through the Holy Spirit alone, we cannot deny that it came through the medium of language, was spread abroad by that means, and must be preserved by the same means."[111] This explains many of the obscurities that people find in Scripture, so that "they have held that God's word is by its very nature obscure and employs a peculiar style of speech. But they fail to realize that the whole trouble lies in the languages. If we understood the languages nothing clearer would ever have been spoken than God's word."[112] Theology should learn its way of speaking about God from the words that God himself used, and for this, knowledge of the original languages is needed, along with familiarity with the original biblical text.

365. The biblical writings are externally clear in a meaning that everyone can grasp. One can clarify obscure passages in Scripture in the light of clear passages. For this one must know the languages and be able to apply all the requisite philological methods. But Scripture is really understood by the heart taking hold of its inner clarity, which is beyond the ability of a person whose heart is darkened. For this one needs the Holy Spirit, since the Spirit is the one who opens to us Holy Scripture as God's word, preserves it, and makes it credible. By reason of its clarity, Scripture can be grasped through itself and in its own spirit. It should not be interpreted according to peculiar ideas of the reader and according to one's own spirit. "Note that the strength of the Scripture is this, that it is not changed into the one who studies it, but that it transforms one who loves it into itself and its own strengths."[113] Scripture alone should reign, for which it must be its own interpreter.[114]

366. For Scripture to interpret itself means that formally one understands and explains particular texts by other texts. Regarding content, this means that the Letter to the Romans throws light on the

---

[110] *To the Councilmen of All Cities in Germany That They Establish and Maintain Christian Schools* (1524), LW 45, 359; original at WA 15, 37,18-22.

[111] *Ibid.*, LW 45, 358; WA 15, 37,4-6.

[112] *Ibid.*, LW 45, 364-365; WA 15, 41,3-5.

[113] *Lectures on the Psalter* (1513-15), on Ps 68,14; LW 10, 332; original at WA 3, 397,9-11.

[114] *Assertio omnium articolorum.* WA 7, 98,40 – 99,2.

whole of Scripture of which it is the *summa*, being "really the chief part of the New Testament and is truly the purest gospel."[115] To do this is for Luther the working out of what he grasped by his reformation insight.[116] At issue was the right interpretation of Romans 1:16f and in particular the meaning of "the righteousness of God." Laboring in search of understanding, Luther sought the meaning of that phrase, "meditating day and night," until by God's grace he was given a philological discovery, "attending to the connection between the words." The outward clarity he thereby found in the text led him to inner clarity and with this to a new relation to God, so that the whole Scripture took on a new appearance. This overpowering experience of discovering meaning, in which Scripture became by God's Spirit an acting subject, points to what Luther means by the clarity and self-interpretation of the Scripture.

367. The communication of the scripturally-attested gospel (as distinguised from the Law) occurs both in a worshipping assembly and in personal experience of an individual, by the transmission of "the main doctrine of Christianity", that is, "Christ for me (*pro me*)."[117] The office of preaching is thus a teaching office and correlatively "teaching" is for the reformers both proclamation and doctrine. When one preaches in the name of the Triune God, God makes himself present for human salvation, granting knowledge of himself together with trust in his word. God's word is doctrine, because it brings to those who hear and believe it a definite content which then fundamentally marks them. Faith as reliance on God's address and as taking hold of Christ entails as well the essential dimension of assent to the articles of faith.[118] Faith as trust and as assent are not contrary to each other but are intrinsically related, because the articles of faith always contain the *pro me* and so draw the believer beyond himself or herself into relation with God. But this relation needs the articles of faith to insure that it is with the true God and not with a false God. The reformers hold that doctrine is so important that, "as one's doctrine is, so is one's faith as well. If the doctrine is

---

[115] *Preface to the Epistle of St. Paul to the Romans.* LW 35, 365; WADB 7, 2,3-4.
[116] Cf. WA 54, 185,12–186,24; LW 34, 336-339.
[117] *Lectures on Galatians* (1535), on Gal 2:4-5. LW 26, 91 (translating WA 40I, 168,20-27).
[118] *Ibid.*, on Gal 5:5. LW 27, 33 (WA 40II, 27,14-16).

correct, then one's faith is right, but false doctrine is poison that makes faith false and dead."[119] Consequently one holding pastoral office not only has to "graze" but also to protect, as takes place when one points out heretical errors.[120]

368. For the church to remain in the truth, the individual has to have daily contact with Holy Scripture, for which Luther names three steps which show the right way to study theology, namely, prayer, meditation, and temptation.[121] Since Scripture teaches about eternal life, it opens itself to the knowledge of the heart only by the Holy Spirit's enlightenment and guidance. Consequently the believer always begs for the Holy Spirit in prayer before beginning attentive and repeated reading in meditation on Scripture. But what we read is often contrary to what we meet in life and experience, and so we meet temptation by what seems to refute Scripture. But precisely these experiences of guilt and sin, under accusation by God's law, of God's hiddenness amid opposition posed by life in the world lead the believer to understand Scripture more deeply and to experience the reliability of God's word. Amid such biblical meditation, believers not only experience that they interpret Scripture but that Scripture itself becomes the active subject of interpretation. Scripture interprets its interpreter. This is the interpretation that gives rise to doctrine that is not our own but God's doctrine.

369. Every church doctrine setting forth the content of faith in a proper linguistic form, as in the catechism, in confession, or in theological proposals, has to be grounded directly or indirectly in Holy Scripture. Luther is emphatic on this: "Doctrine has to be pure Scripture."[122] We see this exemplified in the catechism. The three components of the Creed, the Our Father, and the Ten Commandments represent "all that Scripture contains and should be always preached, all that a Christian has to know, and they express this both in its basics and its richness."[123] The contents of the cat-

---

[119] Sermon on Gen 9 (1527). WA 24, 207,21-23.
[120] *Lectures on the Epistles to Titus and Philemon* (1527). WA 25, 29,1f.
[121] Preface to Vol. 1 of the Wittenberg Edition of Luther's German Writings (1539). WA 50, 658,29–660,30.
[122] *Church Postil* (1522), on the Epiphany. WA 10/I/1, 605,7f.
[123] From Luther's catechetical work of 1520, *Eine kurze Form des Glaubens. Eine kurze Form des Vaterunsers*. WA 7, 204,9-11.

echism ought to be learned and practiced daily, so that one adds experience, just as in study of Scripture: one ought "to read it daily and make it the subject of meditation and conversation. In such reading, conversation and meditation the Holy Spirit is present."[124] This is all the more valid because "God himself is not ashamed to teach it daily, for he knows of nothing better to teach, and he always keeps on teaching this one thing without proposing anything new or different. And all the saints know of nothing better or different to learn."[125] Like study of Scripture, study of the catechism should be both communitarian and personal, that is, both by catechetical preaching or an exercise led by the father of the family and by personal meditation. Luther's catechisms became books of both public worship and private devotion. Their inclusion in *The Book of Concord* in 1580 gave them doctrinal authority at the highest level.

370. The church in her doctrine can only make explicit what Scripture contains. At issue is the church's apostolic character. After Christ, the apostles' and prophets' authority is beyond compare. The successors of the apostles have to follow apostolic authority when they present something as teaching. The church may not issue new articles of faith, but its doctrine may only bring to light the doctrine of Scripture and defend this against errors, in which she can and must say, "This doctrine is not ours, but God's."[126] When Luther sets in opposition God's word and human doctrines, this is not the same as the common distinction made today between divine and human discourse. "We do not censure human doctrine because it comes from human beings, but because it contains lies and blasphemy against Scripture, which itself is written by human beings, but not from themselves, for it is from God."[127] Consequently a council will show that it is gathered in the Holy Spirit and represents the whole church speaking in it, by basing its decisions and utterances on Holy Scripture. A council does not have authority just because according to its own self-understanding it is rightly

---

[124] Preface to the *Large Catechism*, in BC 381.
[125] *Ibid.*, BC 382.
[126] Sermon on Sunday "Judica" (1526). WA 20, 300,18.
[127] *Von Menschenlehre zu meiden und Antwort auf Sprüche* (1522). WA 10/2, 92,4-7.

Church Teaching that Remains in the Truth

gathered in the Holy Spirit. Such authority depends on it working on the basis of the apostles and proceeding not according to its own ideas but according to the analogy of faith.[128]

371. This does not make superfluous the Church Fathers. To be sure they are not an independent source of doctrine which adds to Scripture, which of itself is impossible because of their variety and some internal oppositions between their teachings. But the reformers' appeals to the Fathers served to make clear that they were presenting not new doctrine but teaching that agreed with the Scripture as the Fathers understood and interpreted it. Luther said he was publishing the three ancient creeds, "so that I may again bear witness that I hold to the real Christian Church", in agreement with all of Christendom.[129] Melanchthon, in the *Augsburg Confession* and its *Apology*, refers throughout to Early Church dogma and the Church Fathers.

372. The visitations carried out in Electoral Saxony beginning in 1527 show how highly the reformers valued the transmission of correct doctrine. The *Instructions for the Visitors* set forth important points of doctrine with the practical intention of instructing and examining parish pastors. The office of superintendent was established for oversight over doctrine and life in the communities of a given area and for examining new candidates for pastorates. For the consequences of having capable or incompetent preachers had become clear, whether for good or evil. This led to introducing a regional office of oversight with episcopal tasks, most of all to see to it that the communities of their area remained in the truth.[130]

373. Responsibility for maintaining the church in the truth is not exclusive to superintendents, but also concerns pastors and other members of the community. One can recognize a Christian community by the fact that in it the gospel is preached in its purity and the sacraments are administered in accord with their institution. But this never occurs without bearing fruit, so that such a community is familiar with the

---

[128] Cf. Luther's *Disputation on the Authority of a Council* (1536). WA 39I, 186,18-22.
[129] *The Three Symbols or Creeds of the Christian Faith* (1538). LW 34, 201, from WA 50, 262,8f.
[130] Cf. *Instructions for the Visitors of Parish Pastors in Electoral Saxony* (1528). LW 40, 313f; WA 26, 235,6-39.

voice of its Lord and consequently is able to discern true from false doctrine.[131] This, to be sure, is the case only among Christians well-formed for hearing the truth, who have, through preaching and catechetical instruction, along with personal meditation on Scripture and the catechism, become capable of judging doctrine.

374. The Lutheran confessions, that is, the Augsburg Confession, Luther's Small Catechism, and the other confessions collected in *The Book of Concord*, have taken on particular significance for maintaining Lutheran churches in the truth. Early on, they had a place in local church orders and pastoral office-holders were and still are today bound to them by oath at the time of ordination so that they remain norms of their ministry. The *Book of Concord* declares that Holy Scripture is the sole rule and norm of doctrine, while the three creeds of the Early Church together with the Augsburg Confession and other doctrinal documents of *The Book of Concord* constitute a norm subordinated to that of Scripture. This doctrinal tradition is "well founded in God's word", and with it one can therefore differentiate pure teaching from false doctrine.[132]

375. That the church be maintained in the truth is from beginning to end God's work. "When he deserts us and leaves us to our own resources, our wisdom and knowledge are nothing. Unless he sustains us constantly, the highest learning and even theology are useless."[133] The reformers were certain that the Triune God was laying the foundation and working in the church, and so they were able to give to the human actions of preaching, teaching, meditating, and confessing their proper place with a view to maintaining the church in the truth.

4.4.2 The Ministry of Teaching in Lutheran Churches

376. Lutheran churches have no teaching office in the form of an institution in the church consisting of a particular group of individuals authorized, by belonging to the college of bishops, to issue binding judgments, and in certain circumstances ultimately binding judg-

---

[131] *That a Christian Assembly or Congregation Has the Right and Power to Judge all Teaching and to Call, Appoint, and Dismiss Teachers, Established and Proven by Scripture* (1523). LW 39, 305-314; WA 11, 408-416.

[132] BC 14.

[133] Luther, *Lectures on Galatians* (1535), on Gal 2:13; LW 26, 114; WA 40I, 205,23-25.

ments, concerning the contents of God's revelation or how doctrinal controversies are to be settled. Nonetheless, doctrine does play a major role in Lutheran churches. To be sure, between these churches and even within them, differences exist over the understanding of doctrine and over the importance doctrine has in the church. Similarly differences exist over which normative texts beyond Holy Scripture and which instances should have a role in formulating teaching and just what this role is. But one can still state the following regarding that which one can call the ministry of teaching in Lutheran churches.

377. Holy Scripture is the normative documentation of the apostolic gospel and so it constitutes the norm of all doctrine, both for preaching and the administration of the sacraments, as well as for all activities of the church that could be called "apostolic".

378. The proclamation of the gospel in word and sacrament, taking place in the power of the Holy Spirit, makes present to human beings the gospel and with the gospel Christ himself. In this event the Holy Spirit conveys to men and women the gospel as saving truth for themselves regarding God and humans while the same Spirit awakens in them faith in the gospel of Jesus Christ. Faith and the church are thus grounded in Jesus Christ, while such preaching within worship is the fundamental event of teaching.

379. Because the Holy Spirit opens human hearts to receive the truth of the gospel proclaimed to them, that same Spirit is also the one who maintains them in this truth. But the Holy Spirit makes use of the correct doctrine of the gospel and the rightful administration of the sacraments in leading us to lay hold of the truth of God's word with inner conviction. Thus the Spirit creates and sustains our faith in God. Erroneous doctrine and incorrect administration of the sacraments are obstacles impeding this work of the Spirit. This explains the fierce character of the Reformation-era controversies over correct doctrine and sacramental administration, which remains so to the present day. To be sure, a human teaching is correct only when it takes place within the ambit of the Holy Spirit's work and in trust in the Spirit.

380. Christian teaching is either directly or indirectly interpretation of Holy Scripture, even though Scripture is to this day interpreted by

some differently than by others. This can lead to opposition between teachings and cause an outbreak of controversy. The church has always tried to settle controversies by seeking afresh a consensus over scriptural interpretation and then to formulate this in a binding confession of faith. But this has often led to new controversies, so that lengthy exchanges are often necessary before confessions of faith are widely received. Many Lutheran churches hold as binding doctrine the confessions and confessional documents of the *Book of Concord*, while all the churches of the Lutheran World Federation hold that especially the Augsburg Confession of 1530 and Luther's *Small Catechism* present accurately the word of God.[134]

381. Christian teaching also entails the rejection of doctrines which obscure the gospel or which direct faith to "another gospel" (Gal 1:6-9). However this should be "not with human power but with God's word alone"[135] and without secular penalties for those accused as responsible. For, "by burning heretics . . . we act contrary to the will of the Holy Spirit."[136] Sad to say, during the Reformation era the Lutheran estates did not always observe this basic principle.

382. For Lutherans the doctrine of justification has had from the beginning a special role regarding the whole of Christian teaching, because this doctrine points to the right relation between God who justifies and sinful humans. Justification doctrine makes clear that Christ is the only mediator of salvation and that justification comes to the sinner by grace alone to be accepted by faith alone. Justification doctrine includes the trinitarian and christological confession of the church's faith, directing this toward God's saving encounter with us. God has "given himself to us all wholly and completely, with all that he is and has."[137] God the Father sent Jesus Christ, his Son, into the world, to become salvation for all by his incarnation, life, death, and resurrection. The Holy Spirit makes the person and work of Jesus Christ present to human beings, so that they may attain salvation and the church may come to be and be maintained. The latter

---

[134] *Constitution of the Lutheran World Federation*, Art. II, Doctrinal Basis.

[135] *Augsburg Confession*, Art. XXVIII, 21. BC 95.

[136] Luther, *Explanations of the Ninety-five Theses* (1518). LW 31, 245, translating WA 1, 624,35-625,5.

[137] Luther, *Confession Concerning the Lord's Supper* (1528). LW 37, 366, translating WA 26, 505,38f. What follows is based on LW 37, 366-368, from WA 26, 505,38 – 507,16.

Church Teaching that Remains in the Truth

takes place through the audible and visible word of promise through which the Holy Spirit awakens faith (JDDJ, no. 15). Catholics and Lutherans agree in stating that the doctrine of justification is the "measure and touchstone for the Christian faith. No teaching may contradict this criterion."[138] Justification doctrine "constantly serves to orient all the teaching and practice of our churches to Christ" (JDDJ, no. 18). All churches have to be self-critical by examining whether their teaching, preaching, and whole ecclesial practice agrees with the nature, will, and work of the Triune God, as justification doctrine brings this to expression.

383. Public teaching is the specific task of the ordained ministry. But because this ministerial activity aims to render possible the priesthood of all baptized believers and develop their capacity of judgment, as a consequence ordination cannot be taken as grounding a monopoly regarding Christian insight into the truth. The ministry of teaching is instead cared for through the collaboration of different and diverse personal subjects, in which those who are not ordained have an essential responsibility for teaching. The latter, however, are duty bound, just like the ordained, to give for their doctrinal utterances reasoned arguments derived and worked out from Holy Scripture. In this way the ministry and the community relate to each other in reciprocal responsibility for doctrine.

384. Bishops have the task of public teaching at the supra-local level, where a wider spatial-temporal ministry has been entrusted to them for a special service of the church's unity and teaching. They carry out this ministry both by their own preaching and the positions they take on doctrinal questions, along with their special co-responsibility for correct teaching by pastors. For its remaining in the truth, the church needs this supra-local responsibility for correct teaching (*episcopé*), regarding both the diachronic and synchronic dimensions. Lutheran churches structure this activity in different ways, in most cases by having the bishop or church president exercise this task in collaboration with a synod in which the non-ordained are members. Those responsible for *episcopé* exercise their care for continuity in teaching over time by examining candidates for ordination, by ordination itself, and by visitations.

---

[138] JDDJ, *Annex to the Official Common Statement*, no. 3.

By contacts with those exercising *episcopé* in other churches, they care for unity and catholicity in teaching in their own time. At ordination, pastors pledge themselves to carry out their teaching ministry in agreement with Holy Scripture and with its interpretation in the Reformation-era confessions of faith, for which they can be called to task. If one holding the office of ministry publicly and obstinately goes against Scripture and the Lutheran confessions, he or she may in many Lutheran churches be subject to a doctrinal disciplinary process which can lead after lengthy examination to ascertaining the person's deviance from Scripture and the confessions and because of this even to removal from the ministry and loss of the rights granted along with ordination.

385. Theology has decisive importance for the teaching ministry in its different forms, for it supplies methodical reflection on the God who justifies and sinful human beings, and on all that must be said on this basis about God, human beings, and the world. In theology the word of God and faith are decisively important. Theology reflects the fundamental relation of faith to Holy Scripture by a constantly renewed effort to grasp the meaning of the canonical writings, while it deals with new questions and methods. Theology does this in the context of the binding interpretation of Scripture given in the church's confessions of faith and by its attention to church history, which is as well a history of biblical interpretation. Theology presents doctrinal content in a systematic organization and in relation to questions, insights, and methods of one's own time with its grasp of reason and knowledge. Theology relates its acquired understandings to the fundamental actions of the church in worship, witness, and service, and thus to the pastoral leadership of congregations and the church. Theology, because it is related to its own time and context, is innovative and it contributes essentially to the church being able suitably "to give an account of the hope" that is in her (cf. 1 Pt 3:15). As theology develops new understandings, it gives rise as well to conflicts, but it also provides the place and the means for working through these conflicts.

386. Since Holy Scripture stands in need of interpretation, a mere citing of biblical passages does not suffice to demonstrate that a teaching or practice actually agrees with Scripture. In the face of divergent and mutually contradictory interpretations, the churches have to

Church Teaching that Remains in the Truth

constantly search for a renewed consensus over how to understand Scripture and to relate it to the confessions. Similarly, the confessions, which express the consensus over biblical interpretation attained by previous generations, are themselves in need of interpretation. Here as well the church has to work continually toward agreement. As it moves through history, the church is constantly concerned with handing on the witness of Scripture, with receiving it in new situations, and then again with handing it on further.

387. In all this, a variety of interpretations and explanations have their necessary and legitimate place, corresponding to the differences of time and place, and of subjects and contexts. The ministry of teaching in Lutheran churches has to make such variety possible and encourage it, while at the same time attending carefully and energetically to seeing that amid the variety that which is common and binding is maintained. A variety in which the unity in doctrine is no longer recognizable goes against the unity of the church (cf. Eph 4:3-6). Inversely the attempt to impose uniformity in doctrine to the exclusion of different explanations contradicts the variety of the members of the body of Christ with their different charisms. The teaching ministry has to serve the absolute priority of the word of God over all that takes place in the church. Thus, on the one hand, it has to make sure that the apostolic gospel is heard, believed, understood, and lived out amid the variety of persons and amid the different contexts of church life. On the other hand this ministry has to see to it that the truth of the gospel not be swept away by the undertow of subjectivity in its hearers, readers, and their contexts. This latter requires a clear awareness of the alien character of the word of the cross over against all the assumptions about life and its understanding which humans carry along with themselves. Even believers and church ministers are not exempted from the danger of watering down this alien message by accommodating it to the world. The teaching ministry must be able, by its interpretation of Scripture amid changing contexts, both to distinguish between legitimate variety and necessary agreement, and as well to relate these to each other. To the extent this is realized, teaching gains authority and serves the unity and catholicity of the church.

388. An oversight (*episcopé*) extending beyond single congregations is ecclesially necessary. Lutheran churches institutionalize and prac-

tice this. But the issue arises whether such exercise of oversight should be limited to particular Lutheran churches. For particular Lutheran churches are autonomous churches, with autonomy as well in dealing with doctrinal questions. But there are no convincing theological arguments why this ecclesially necessary oversight should be structured only regionally. Historical facts and factors should not be elevated to the level of theological arguments. The insight given to the Lutheran reformers into the truth of the gospel, expressed for example in Articles I-XXI of the Augsburg Confession, is the confession that unites Lutheran churches. In regard to this, a mutual and shared doctrinal responsibility should be possible and seen as an important task. Since communion between Lutheran churches is made possible by their agreement on the doctrine of the gospel and administration of the sacraments (CA VII), it should also be possible to achieve communion in living out that doctrine, at least by the duty of mutual accountability and regular consultation on doctrinal issues. By extending the exercise of a doctrinal ministry in this way more widely than in a single church, local problems and perspectives would be relativized and correctives from other churches can be seriously considered. The Lutheran World Federation, under mandate of the Lutheran churches, has repeatedly taken on this task in order to bring about a common judgment on doctrinal issues. An example is the decision of the LWF World Assembly in Budapest (1984) to suspend from membership the white churches of southern Africa which had not ended racially-based church divisions and had not unambiguously condemned the apartheid system. Another example is the *Joint Declaration on the Doctrine of Justification* signed in Augsburg in 1999 by representatives of the LWF and of the Roman Catholic Church, which took place after an extensive LWF consultation and a decision-making process in Lutheran churches. Thus the world-wide Lutheran communion does indeed have an instrument for arriving at common doctrinal formulations.

389. From what has been said in nos. 383-385 and 388, above, one sees that Lutheran churches realize the teaching ministry through the collaboration of many different individuals and instances, along with an interplay of many different processes. But for Lutherans

neither this complex collaboration of different instances nor a continuous line of those holding ministerial office can guarantee that the churches preserve the message of salvation it its apostolic identity. It is instead the Holy Spirit, to whom the churches look for their preservation in the truth, and for this they pray. Nonetheless, pastors exercise their teaching ministry in eschatological responsibility for the eternal salvation of those entrusted to them (cf. Acts 20:17-26). In 1528 Luther stated in his "Great Confession": "I desire with this treatise to confess my faith before God and all the world, point by point. I am determined to abide by it until my death and (so help me God!) in this faith to depart from this world and to appear before the judgment seat of our Lord Jesus Christ."[139]

4.5 Catholic Doctrine on the Biblical Canon, Interpretation of Scripture, and the Teaching Office

4.5.1 The Canon of Scripture and its Basis

390. The previous section told of the dispute between Luther and Eck over Second Maccabees and especially concerning the role of the church in establishing the biblical canon (nos. 361-362, above). The widespread Reformation denial of the doctrinal authority of the Old Testament "apocrypha" made it imperative that the Council of Trent should take up this question, and at its Fourth Session, 8 April 1546, the Council formally accepted the "deuterocanonical" books as integral parts of the Old Testament Scripture of the Catholic Church (DS 1502; Tanner, 663-64).

391. The Tridentine decree on the canon did not offer arguments for its decision, but the reasons and the basis of certainty about it can be known from the prior conciliar discussion and from indications in the canon-decree itself (DS 1501-05; Tanner, 663-64). Further insight into the Catholic position on the basis of the canon comes from major theologians and from what Vatican Councils I and II laid down concerning Scripture.

392. The canon came under discussion early at the Council of Trent, after its first action of formally accepting as the "shield of faith"

---
[139] *Confession concerning the Lord's Supper*, LW 37, 360, translating WA 26, 499,6-10.

(Eph 6:16) the Nicene-Constantinoplian Creed, in imitation of previous councils (Tanner, 662). The next step was to identify the sources from which the Council would draw the content of the doctrinal and reform decrees to follow, that is, "what witnesses and supports it will especially use in strengthening its teachings (*dogmata*) and renewing practice (*mores*) in the church" (DS 1505; Tanner, 664). The sources will be the Scriptures and apostolic traditions which communicate the gospel of Christ.

393. On the Old Testament canon, some Tridentine Fathers proposed that the basis had already been given by theologians, such as J. Cochlaeus, J. Eck, A. de Castro, and J. Driedo, who had argued against the reformers that the larger canon had become gradually clear in church tradition under God's enlightenment. One argument for proceeding to a simple declaration of the canon without further deliberation was that previous councils, such as Third Carthage (A.D. 397) and especially Florence (*Decree of Union with the Copts*, 1442, DS 1334-35; Tanner, 572) had treated the matter, with the latter decree confirming a thousand-year tradition of taking the deuterocanonical books as belonging to the Bible. Appeal was also made to the canonical prohibition of taking up again what an earlier council had decided (*Decretum*, Pars II, C. XXIV, Q. 1, c. 2). The Tridentine Canon is thus based on the authority of tradition, both as constant practice has shaped the church's life and as Councils have declared this and thereby made it certain.

394. A further basis for the Tridentine biblical canon appears in the decree itself. The canonical books are the books "as they have, by established custom, been read in the Catholic Church, and as contained in the old Latin Vulgate edition" (DS 1504; Tanner, 664). For the Fathers at Trent, the books contained in the Vulgate made up the Bible by which they in accord with long-standing practice had been schooled in Christian doctrine and spirituality, which they had heard read at Mass, and had recited in the Liturgy of the Hours. Trent called for the text of the Vulgate to be thoroughly revised (DS 1508: Tanner, 665), so that it might better fulfill its role as the official text for public use (DS 1506; Tanner, 664). But, the canonicity of the books offered by the Vulgate could not be

questioned, without implying that the Bible in actual use for centuries had misled the faithful regarding the books conveying God's word.[140]

395. Luther and Eck also clashed over the role of church authority in establishing the canon of Scripture. Today, historians of Catholic doctrine judge that many pre-Tridentine controversialist theologians often practiced an "attack theology" that lacked sensitivity to nuances and to what was valid in their opponents' positions. This is the case in Johann Eck's argument that adherents of the Reformation are caught in a self-contradiction when they cite scriptural authority in arguments against the church's constitution and customary practices, for how do they know that the Scriptures are canonical except from the church?[141]

396. Later, the master controversialist R. Bellarmine was more aware of the complexities of the historical development of the Old Testament canon, with the gradual acceptance of the deuterocanonical books. He also knew of internal criteria by which biblical books show their canonical value. Bellarmine declared that the church did not "make canonical" books which were not so before, but instead declared, in Councils, which books were to be held such, and this not rashly or arbitrarily, for it was based (1) on many testimonies of the Fathers, (2) on similarities recognized between the content of books once held in doubt and the content of other books of undoubted canonicity, and (3) by the discernment of the Christian people, a process to which St. Jerome alluded in reference to the

---

[140] Developments after Vatican II indicate some practical convergence between Protestants and Catholics over the apocrypha or deuterocanonical books. The German Evangelical Lectionary of 1985 contains 24 pericopes from them, while the Lectionary of the Latin Rite of the Catholic Church, in its three year cycle of three readings for Sundays and solemn feast days, includes only a modest selection of 18 passages from them. Among recent inter-confessional translations, the German *Einheitsuebersetzung* (1979) gives the deuterocanonical books according to the Vulgate order, while the *Revised English Bible* (Great Britain, 1989) and the *New Revised Standard Version* (USA 1989) offer these books in a special section between the Prophets and the New Testament, in accord with a practice approved by the Vatican in 1968 and renewed in 1987. But the *New International Version* (1978), widely used by evangelical Protestants, never offers the apocrypha.

[141] *Enchiridion locorum communium* (1525), Loc. I, Response to Objection 3.

way in which the Letter of James gradually came, on its own merits, to be recognized as authoritative.[142]

397. In 1870 Vatican Council I, in its Dogmatic Constitution on the Catholic Faith, *Dei Filius*, made Bellarmine's first point into binding doctrine when it declared that the church does not confer canonical authority, but holds the biblical books "to be sacred and canonical, not because, after having been carefully composed by human industry, they were afterwards approved by her authority", but because "having been written by the inspiration of the Holy Spirit, they have God as their author and have been delivered as such to the Church" (DS 3006; Tanner, 806). The church and its hierarchy are recipients of the inspired and canonical books.

398. What had been implicit at Trent became explicit at Vatican Council II, namely, that knowledge of the biblical canon is a benefit of the tradition which comes from the apostles and is understood progressively in the church. "By means of the same tradition, the full canon of the sacred books is known to the church, and the Holy Scriptures themselves are more thoroughly understood and are constantly made effective" (DV 8.3). The canon is thus a case in which Scripture and tradition go together, for it was in the midst of the ongoing public transmission of the gospel, summarized in the rule of faith and the creeds, along with practices that promote the life of faith, that the canon became fully known.

399. But the same Vatican II document that ascribes to tradition the making known of the canon goes on to urge a many-sided promotion of biblical reading and study in the church, because of the intrinsic efficacy of the Scriptures. "For, since they are inspired by God and committed to writing once and for all time, they present God's own word in an unalterable form, and they make the voice of the Holy Spirit sound again and again in the words of the prophets and apostles. . . . Such is the force and

---

[142] *De Controversiis christianae fidei*, Vol. I (1586), Contr. De Verbo Dei, Lib. I, cap. 10. The third way is "*excommuni sensu et quasi gustu populi Christiani.*" Bellarmine treated the canon in the first of all the controversies because the Scriptures are for the Catholic Church "the Word of God and rule of faith" (cap. 1). He marshals long chains of patristic testimony to show wide recognition of the disputed Old Testament books declared canonical by the Councils (Carthage III, Florence, Trent).

power of the word of God that it is the church's support and strength, imparting robustness to the faith of its daughters and sons and providing food for their souls" (DV 21). Theology and the ministry of the word must take strength and vitality from Scripture (DV 24) and all the faithful are forcefully (*vehementer*) urged to practice prayerful reading of Scripture in which God converses with them (DV 25).

400. Catholic doctrine, thus, does not hold what Reformation theology fears and wants at all costs to avoid, namely, a derivation of scriptural authority as canonical and binding from the authority of the church's hierarchy which makes known the canon.

401. Catholic doctrine furthermore acknowledges what the Reformation stresses, namely, the inherent power of the biblical word to impose itself as a norm and guide, that is, as a "canon" of life before God. This recognition of the inherent quality of Scripture stands, even while Catholic doctrine sees canonicity, that is, public binding authority for doctrine, life, and worship, as coming from Scripture only in intimate connection, first, with the faith-life of believers, who are formed by the expressions of tradition, such as the creeds, and in whom Scripture is recognized as normative and, second, with the ministry of those responsible for articulating, especially in Councils, a clear delineation of the boundaries of the Scriptures which are to shape public teaching, life, and worship in the whole church.

4.5.2 Biblical Interpretation: Trent to Vatican II

402. The previous section set forth the Reformation principles of biblical interpretation (nos. 364-366), especially on Scripture being its own interpreter (nos. 366 and 368). In response, the Council of Trent spoke to the question of Scripture-interpretation as one topic (DS 1507; Tanner, 664) in a longer reform decree which it approved on the same day that it issued the doctrinal decree (DS 1501-05; Tanner, 663-64) on the triad Gospel-Scripture-Traditions and on the biblical canon. The second decree was drafted after the Tridentine Fathers had discussed various abuses in the use of Scripture. First, to bring uniformity to public use of Scripture in the Western church (in Latin texts of the Missal, Liturgy of the Hours, Catechisms, etc.), the decree declared the Vulgate

to be the official Latin version (DS 1506; Tanner, 664).[143] Then Trent issued, in a dense paragraph, norms to correct malpractice in biblical interpretation.

403. On interpretation, two recent precedents had gone before Trent. (1) The Fifth Lateran Council had in 1516 censured preachers who twist the meaning of Scripture by their own rash and idiosyncratic interpretations, e.g., in predicting the day of judgment. Preachers are to preach and explain "the gospel truth and Holy Scripture in accordance with the exposition, interpretation, and commentaries that the church or long use has approved."[144] (2) In France, the Council of Sens, for the region of Paris, had in 1528 taken up issues of early Reformation controversy and first posited the authority and truth of Scripture by citing 2 Pet 2:20-21 and 2 Tim 3:16-17, before going on to decry arbitrary interpretations. Against heretics, who always claim to be interpreting Scripture, one must penetrate to the deeper meaning by following "ecclesiastical interpreters". When conflicts arise over the faith, it is often not enough to amass Scripture texts, but eventually the certain and infallible authority of the church must intervene to settle the dispute. The same church which discerns canonical books from apocryphal ones is able to discern "the catholic meaning from a heretical meaning."[145] The same decree, however, had located the ecclesial authority for settling

---

[143] Trent declared the Vulgate "authentic" for public use in the Western Church of the Roman Rite at a time when new Latin translations were circulating, such as Psalters from the Hebrew by Felice de Prato (1515), Agostino Giustiniani (1516), and in Cardinal Cajetan's Psalms Commentary (1527). Erasmus had published his new Latin version of the New Testament, alongside the Greek text, in 1516. Sante Pagnini, OP, had brought out a Latin Bible in 1528 in which the Old Testament was a new translation from the Hebrew and Isidore Clarius, OSB, published another Hebrew-based Old Testament in a Bible of 1542. A theologian of influence on Trent, J. Dreido of Louvain, had defended the Vulgate in 1535, not as inspired or inerrant, but as a long-used instrument of transmitting the faith. Where it renders the original Hebrew and Greek inadequately, it does not support any heresy nor is it thereby dangerous for public use. The Presidents of the Council of Trent asked the Pope to have the Vulgate revised, so it might be a "pure and genuine" edition, while also calling for preparation of corrected Hebrew and Greek biblical texts. CT, 5, 29 and 1, 37.

[144] Tanner, 636.

[145] Mansi, 52, 1164.

doctrinal questions in Councils, which are guided by the Holy Spirit.[146]

404. Trent's regulatory paragraph combines Fifth Lateran's aim of excluding arbitrary, non-traditional interpretations with the Council of Sens's appeal to the judgment of the church, when Scripture is being interpreted as the source of the faith and Christian practice:

> The council further decrees, in order to control those of unbalanced character, that no one, relying on his personal judgment in matters of faith and customs which are linked to the establishment of Christian doctrine, shall dare to interpret the sacred Scriptures either by twisting its text to his individual meaning in opposition to that which has been and is held by holy mother church, whose function it is to pass judgment concerning the true meaning and interpretation of the sacred Scriptures; or by giving meanings contrary to the unanimous consent of the fathers (DS 1507; Tanner, 664).

Here the Fathers and the church, especially the conciliar tradition, are a negative norm coming from the past, against which the Bible should not be construed. The "judgment of the church" functions in the present, doing what the Council of Sens attributed to councils, namely, assessing and judging what interpreters are putting forth as biblical expressions of the faith and of the right forms of Christian life and worship. Without use of the term, the church's "magisterium" of official teaching is becoming a part of the Catholic doctrinal tradition.

405. In 1870 Vatican Council I renewed Trent's reform decree on biblical interpretation in the Dogmatic Constitution, *Dei Filius* but with a change, because it affirmed that the church's *sensus Scripturae,* a negative norm in Trent, is the true meaning of Scripture (DS 3007; Tanner, 806). But in the wake of Vatican I, the limits of the ecclesial *sensus* became evident as the Magisterium insistently urged Catholics to take up the work of scholarly Scripture study, with the tools of linguistic, historical, and literary expertise. One does not achieve a

---

[146] *Ibid.*, 1163f.

recovery and exposition of the biblical witness to revelation and the life of faith by recourse to what the church, in the teaching of Councils and Popes, holds and teaches, for other interpreters must enter this work.[147]

406. Vatican II declared, as belonging to the apostolic faith, the conviction that Scripture is sacred and canonical, because its authors wrote under the inspiration of the Holy Spirit (DV 11). The Constitution continues by saying that Scripture therefore conveys without error the truth which God, intending to foster our salvation, wanted set down. But the recovery of that truth, by interpretation, is then presented in DV 12 as a many-sided enterprise, involving both (1) a reading based on the application of the scholarly means to recover what the original authors intended to communicate and (2) a reading in faith, attuned to the Holy Spirit, which draws (i) on the whole content and Christ-centered unity of Scripture, (ii) on the church's tradition, in which Scripture has had its ongoing impact; and (iii) on "the analogy of faith," that is, the coherence of the articles of faith in the economy of revelation. Insofar as interpretation is an ecclesial work, (3) it is "ultimately subject to the judgment of the Church", to which God has entrusted the ministry of guarding and interpreting his word. But the Church's judgment, the Council states, develops toward maturity in its teaching activity under the influence of exegetical contributions resulting from the aforementioned scholarly and faith-based readings of the sacred text.

407. Before taking up the question of the magisterium and church doctrine, an interim proposal may be offered on the Lutheran and Catholic views of authentic interpretation of the Bible. First, when Catholic doctrine holds that the "judgment of the church" has a role in authentic interpretation of Scripture, it does not attribute to the church's magisterium a monopoly over interpretation, which adherents of the Reformation rightly fear and reject. Before the

---

[147] The Popes sought to promote Catholic biblical studies in encyclicals of 1893 (Leo XIII, *Providentissmus Deus*), 1920 (Benedict XV, *Spiritus Paraclitus*), and 1943 (Pius XII, *Divino afflante Spiritu*). The Pontifical Biblical Commission, after curtailing scholarly freedom by its anti-modernist guidelines under Pius X (1905-14), became an instance of positive promotion in 1941 (Letter to the Bishops of Italy in defense of philological, historical, and literary analysis of Scripture), 1964 (Instruction on the development of the content of the Gospels), and 1993 (*The Interpretation of the Bible in the Church*).

Reformation, major figures had indicated the ecclesial plurality of interpreters (cf. no. 351, above). When Vatican II speaks of the church having an "ultimate judgment" (DV 12) it clearly eschews a monopolistic claim that the Magisterium is the sole organ of interpretation, which is confirmed both by the century-old official promotion of Catholic biblical studies and the recognition in DV 12 of the role of exegesis in the maturing of magisterial teaching.

408. Because the Scripture comes from God, under the inspiration of the Holy Spirit, no single organ, even an ultimate one, is able to offer an exhaustive interpretation of Scripture's meaning. In fact, the interventions of the teaching office focus primarily, not on biblical texts themselves, but on interpretations of Scripture which are circulating publicly and impinging on the teaching of the doctrinal heritage. The magisterial judgment discerns the value of interpretations, as it assesses them in the framework of the church's ongoing responsibility to carry on public teaching of true doctrine and to promote authentic sacramental worship.

409. Second, one should recall the extensive attention given by Catholics to the doctrine of biblical inspiration, both in authoritative teaching and in theology.[148] This grounds the conviction held in common with the Reformation that the Spirit-inspired biblical text has its own efficacy in conveying revealed truth that forms minds and hearts, as affirmed in 2 Tim 3:17 and stated by Vatican II (DV 21-25; cf. no. 399, above).

410. But Catholics hold that this efficacy has been operative in the church over time, not only in individual believers but as well in the ecclesial tradition, both in high-level doctrinal expressions such as the rule of faith, creeds, and conciliar teaching, and in the principal structures of public worship.[149] The saving truth of Scripture has come to expression in formulations which are both comprehensive of Scripture's witness to God's saving work and at times quite pointed

---

[148] That the Holy Spirit inspired the biblical authors has been declared by Vatican I (DS 3006; Tanner, 806), Leo XIII (DS 3292-93), and Vatican II (DV 11). Between 1870 and 1960, influential theological accounts of inspiration were proposed by J.B. Franzelin, M.-J. Lagrange, A. Bea, K. Rahner, L. Alonso Schoekel, and P. Benoit.

[149] Catholics find central biblical contents conveyed in a vital manner by the yearly cycles of liturgical seasons and feasts, as well as by the binding structure of prayer "to the Father, through Christ, and in the Holy Spirit."

on critical points of dogmatic clarification. Scripture has made itself present *in the tradition,* which is therefore able to play an essential hermeneutical role. Vatican II does not say that the tradition gives rise to new truths beyond Scripture, but that it conveys *certainty* about revelation attested by Scripture.[150] Therefore Catholics are reserved about the statement that "Scripture interprets itself", since it is applied to the formation of a certain faith in God's revelation. But Catholics do not deny the basis of the Reformation's "self-interpreting" Scripture, namely its efficacious power. In Catholic parlance, because of its inspiration Scripture is, in fact, "the highest authority in matters of faith", even when it must be linked, for the reason just stated, with "Sacred Tradition, as indispensable to the interpretation of the Word of God" (Pope John Paul II, *Ut unum sint,* 1995, no. 79).

4.5.3 The Teaching Office in Catholic Doctrine

411. Section 4.4 included an account of the teaching ministries and processes which serve the transmission and communication of doctrine in Lutheran churches (nos. 367, 372-373, and 383-387, above). To carry forward a dialogue in this area, the present section offers fundamental considerations on the church's magisterium as this has developed in the Catholic Church and is understood in Catholic theology.

412. It is only right, first, to register a Catholic appreciation for several Lutheran convictions expressed in section 4.4 of this Part. Catholics agree with Lutherans that correct doctrine is essential in shaping a right relation of faith with God and with his saving work in Christ (cf. no. 367, above). Catholics agree on the importance of a ministry of regional oversight of teaching to care for the unity and catholicity of teaching (nos. 372 and 384, above), even while they see this related to the universal *episcopé* of the Successor of Peter. But along with Lutherans, Catholics also ascribe to the Holy Spirit the effective maintaining of the church in the truth of the gospel and in correct celebration of the sacraments (cf. no. 379, above). Human teachers and office-holders serve this work of the Holy Spirit.

---

[150] After describing the *coordinate* roles of Scripture and Tradition in communicating God's Word, the Council concludes: "Thus it is that the church does not draw its certainty about all revealed truths through Holy Scripture alone" (DV 9).

413. However, beyond these shared convictions, the teaching office of the Catholic Church has taken on a structure and mode of operation notably different from Lutheran teaching ministries, as presented above in Section 4.4.2 (nos. 376-389). As an instance of teaching, the petrine office has exercised a major role, along lines suggested earlier (cf. above, Part 2, no.88). The two Vatican Councils have spoken on magisterial infallibility and the papal office, but also on episcopal collegiality and the *sensus fidelium*. Significant clarifications have been made regarding the different levels of doctrinal binding force of magisterial utterances. In order to advance the Lutheran-Catholic ecumenical exchange, the following paragraphs offer a clarifying sketch of this development.

414. During the nineteenth century, the understanding of the Catholic teaching office (*magisterium*) came to be clearly distinguished and defined in its contemporary meaning as the office of binding teaching exercised by the bishops of the church. Now recognized as distinct from sacramental powers (*potestas ordinis*) and from jurisdiction in church governance (*potestas iudictionis*), the power to teach (*potestas magisterii*) was identified as also essential to the episcopal office in the church. This resulted from a development by which, beginning in the sixteenth century, increased emphasis had fallen on the role of the hierarchy in preserving the truths of faith and as a consequence the church's remaining in the truth became increasingly dependent upon the teaching office of bishops and especially the Pope.

415. Corresponding to this development, emphasis shifted from the indefectibility of the whole church to the infallibility of the teaching office. This resulted, in the centuries after the Council of Trent, from the church finding itself confronted by the modern criticism of revelation and the claim of autonomy of the human subject, which brought to the fore the issue of how to effectively guarantee the objective truth of revelation. An influential current of the nineteenth century Catholic ecclesiology conceived in a juridical manner the infallible authority of the Pope as a type of sovereignty adequate to guarantee the secure preservation of revelation and as supplying the condition making possible a doctrinal judgment of ultimate binding force.

416. Influences from this historical context left their mark on *Pastor aeternus*, the Constitution of Vatican I which defines the authority held by the Pope when he exercises his petrine ministry in essential points of faith and morals by infallibly proclaiming the faith of the church. What Vatican I taught, however, was related to historical factors, since it intended to exclude the Gallican tenet that the certainty of papal *ex cathedra* teachings arises exclusively from the subsequent assent of the church to them. Against this, Vatican I declares that infallible teachings of the Pope are binding "of themselves, and not by the consent of the church" (DS 3074; Tanner, 816), thus ruling out the existence of any instance of decision over the Pope by which his infallible teaching would be subject to a reservation.

417. *Pastor aeternus* teaches that the Pope, when he teaches *ex cathedra* as universal Pastor, is protected from error by the charism of infallibility. This charism is given to him personally, specifically when he exercises his office at its highest level of authority. But while the Fathers of Vatican I were convinced that the Pope would investigate the *sensus ecclesiae* by hearing the testimony of the bishops, they did not make this a formal condition of a doctrinal definition.[151]

418. According to Vatican I, infallible teaching concerns doctrinal matters essential to faith and morals which come from God's revelation. Following Vatican I, a systematic account was worked out concerning the further levels of official church teaching, with their different degrees of binding authority and of force of law.[152] Concerning the interpretation of Scripture, the teaching authority, as indicated above (no. 408) is less concerned with clarifying the exegesis of particular passages than with discerning the coherence of interpretations with the sense of Scripture which the church has received and brought to expression in her creed and articles of faith.

---

[151] The official report on the meaning of *Pastor aeternus*, given by Bp. Vincent Gasser, stresses the essential connection between (1) the agreement of the church in union with the whole teaching office, which is a rule of faith for the Pope, and (2) the action by which the Pope issues an infallible definition of a content of faith. (Mansi, vol. 52, cols. 1213D-1214A, 1216D).

[152] These were set forth recently by the Congregation of the Doctrine of the Faith in its 1990 *Instruction on the Ecclesial Vocation of the Theologian*, nos. 15-17 and 23-24. The document is given in *Origins* 20 (5 July 1990), pp. 118-126.

419. Vatican Council II aimed to broaden the ecclesiological outlook of Vatican I by taking account of the roles in the church of the episcopate and of the whole people of God. Also the Council's return to the original Christian sources produced new orientations, as when the *Constitution on Divine Revelation* declares, "This magisterium is not superior to the Word of God, but is its servant. It teaches only what has been handed on to it. At the divine command and with the help of the Holy Spirit, it listens to this devoutly, guards it with dedication and expounds it faithfully" (DV 10). Vatican II's Dogmatic Constitution on the Church modifies the treatment of the hierarchy and papal infallibility by placing them within the witness given by the whole people of God in its prophetic role.

420. The people as a whole have a faith that does not err, as described in LG 12. The whole body of the faithful, who have received an anointing which comes from the Holy One (cf. 1 Jn 2:20.27), cannot be mistaken in belief. It shows this characteristic through the entire people's supernatural sense of the faith, when "from the bishops to the last of the faithful" (Augustine) it manifests a universal consensus in matters of faith and morals. By this sense of faith, aroused and sustained by the Spirit of truth, the people of God, guided by the sacred magisterium which it faithfully obey, receive not the word of human beings, but truly the word of God (cf. 1 Thess 2:13), "the faith once for all delivered to the saints" (Jude 3). The people unfailingly adhere to this faith, penetrate it more deeply through right judgment, and apply it more fully in daily life.

421. The whole people of God thus become bearers of revelation and subjects who carry ahead tradition. By their *sensus fidei*, stemming from the Holy Spirit's anointing, they cannot err in faith. The text moves beyond a solely passive infallibility in receiving what comes from an active infallibility of the magisterium. The people of God is instead originally addressed by revelation and responds actively by the sense of faith. Led by the magisterium, they accept a specific message of God's word, penetrate it with true discernment, and apply it in life. The *sensus fidei* enables people to recognize revelation and calls forth a relation of connaturality with the truth handed down. In virtue of this vital relationship, the people are able to discern truth and falsehood in questions of faith and

grasp revelation on a deeper level so as to live in correspondence with it.

422. Within the people of God, bishops have a pastoral ministry that includes magisterial teaching. Vatican II restates the doctrine of papal infallibility, but places it within episcopal collegiality (LG 25). The college cannot act without its head, but correspondingly the papal magisterium functions within the communion of the universal episcopal college. All who exercise the magisterium must use the appropriate means to make sure that they teach in accord with revelation: "The Roman Pontiff and the bishops, in virtue of their office and because of the seriousness of the matter, are assiduous in examining revelation by every suitable means and in expressing it properly" (LG 25).

423. *Lumen gentium* repeated Vatican I's statement on the irreformability of papal definitions by their own nature, and not by the consent of the church.[153] But Vatican II also emphasized the *sensus fidelium*, for through the Spirit, "Christ's whole flock is maintained in the unity of the faith and makes progress in it" (LG 25).

424. Thus, while the magisterium is not simply the transmitter of teachings already held by the church, it is also clear that definitions influenced by the charism of the teaching office will find an echo in the faith of the church and call forth assent. If this were not forthcoming, it could well indicate that proper limits were not observed and the necessary conditions had not been fulfilled for a magisterial action to be infallible.

425. The whole body of Christ is anointed by the Holy Spirit, so that a supernatural "sense of faith" gives believers the ability to recognize the word of God in what is taught and to grow in personal understanding of God and his saving work. Thereby, in communion with other instances of witness, the faithful constitute an indispensable means toward maintaining the church in the truth.

---

[153] As stated in the Introduction to this study document, the present Commission has not included in its dialogue an exchange focused on the special teaching ministry of the Bishop of Rome. Other Lutheran-Catholic dialogues have treated this, both in the United States and Germany. Also, papal teaching has not played a major role in our study document, in which at critical points Catholic doctrine has been drawn from the Councils of Trent, Vatican I, and Vatican II.

Church Teaching that Remains in the Truth

426. When one considers the church's teaching office in a broader historical perspective, it becomes clear that magisterial formulations of truths of faith do not in fact communicate the truth in its fullness. They do clarify necessary lines of demarcation which ensure that the church remains faithful to the truth of faith. But the setting of boundaries against theological conceptions incompatible with Catholic doctrine is frequently accompanied by a painful loss that impoverishes the full recognition of the truth of faith. Rejecting an error in a moment of confrontation brings with it the danger of a one-sided fixation on the contrary of what was seen to be erroneous.

427. Also, while magisterial teachings issued as fully obligating represent for Catholics a necessary word of the church in given situations, history shows that they are not the church's last word. Such definitions can settle controversies threatening the identity and integrity of the truth of faith, but beyond this they need to be received by the faith of the church, in order to be recognized in their lasting significance for keeping the church in the truth of the gospel. This reception of magisterial teaching has the support of the same Holy Spirit who maintains the whole church in the truth, and thereby an aspect of truth which was first excluded as contrary to the Catholic faith can subsequently, amid the appropriation of the magisterial teaching, be taken up again in a form reconcilable with the faith of the church.

428. When the teaching authority gives positive expositions of the faith of the church, it intends to show the interconnections of the doctrines of the faith, so as to guide believers toward understand better the entire truth of the gospel. To the extent that such teaching claims to be infallible, its positive content not only serves proclamation in a given moment, but also the future content of the church's faith, which is led by the Holy Spirit to penetrate the truth of faith with a deeper understanding. What is especially emphatic in a given intervention comes in time to find its appropriate location in the hierarchy of truths (UR 11). Presentation by the magisterium of the truth of faith along with clarifications of the binding force of particular contents does not mean that such a presentation prevents the church in the future from finding under the lead of the Holy Spirit new formulations of its faith which correspond better to the challenges of new historical situations. The actual develop-

ment of the Catholic sense of faith shows its ongoing movement through crises and conflicts toward the original fullness of truth concerning God's saving work that the gospel proclaimed once and for all.

4.6 The Church Maintained in the Truth: Conclusions

Introduction

429. This dialogue intends to contribute to bringing about full communion between the Catholic Church and the Lutheran churches of the world. Such communion requires a common profession of the truth given to humankind by God's saving work and word. In moving toward this goal, the differences in faith and doctrine between Lutherans and Catholics must be examined in common, with the aim of discovering convictions held in common and of clarifying whether differing theological explanations are open to reconciliation.

430. This Part has examined how our two traditions understand the means by which the Holy Spirit works in the church to maintain it in the truth of faith and sound doctrine coming from the apostles. It has reported the results of investigations of the New Testament (4.2), of early and medieval expressions and servants of teaching the truth coming from God in Christ (4.3), of Lutheran convictions on the canon, interpretation of Scripture, and the teaching ministry (4.4), and of Catholic doctrine on the canon, biblical interpretation, and the teaching office (4.5).

431. This section now presents the results in two steps. (1) From what has gone before, both in explicit statements and in operative presuppositions, three significant foundational convictions held in common will be named. This is the area of full consensus. (2) Out of what has been discovered in this phase of dialogue, three topics of differentiated consensus will be named, in which the remaining differences have been shown not to be church-dividing. This is the area of reconciled diversity.

4.6.1 Shared Foundational Convictions of Faith

A. *The Gospel of God's Grace in Christ*

432. First, Lutherans and Catholics fully agree that God has issued in human history a message of grace and truth, by word and deed,

which culminated in the saving death and resurrection of Jesus Christ, to which Easter witnesses testify in the power of the Holy Spirit. Jesus Christ is God's definitive and personal word of grace, transcending God's manifestation of himself through Moses and the prophets. As affirmed in the *Joint Declaration on the Doctrine of Justification*, by our common faith in the gospel we hold to the heart of the New Testament witness to God's saving action in Christ, namely that our new life is solely due to the forgiving and renewing mercy that God imparts as a gift and we receive in faith. For we believe that God is with us to deliver us by his free gift from sin and death and to raise us to eternal life (JDDJ 17 and 36).

B. *The Gospel and the Church*

433. Second, Catholics and Lutherans fully agree that God's revelation of himself in Jesus Christ for human salvation continues to be announced in the gospel of Christ that the apostles first preached and taught, as they gathered communities of believers in whose hearts the Holy Spirit inscribed the message of grace and truth. By this gospel, the crucified and risen Lord shows himself to be alive and active to save, as the church continues to proclaim him by word and sacrament. The church of every age stands under the imperative to preserve in continuous succession God's word of saving truth. Made bold by Christ's promise to be with his disciples always, the church carries out his mandate to announce his gospel in every place from generation to generation.

C. *The Gospel, the Canonical Scriptures, and the Church's Teaching and Life*

434. Third, the Scriptures are for Lutherans and Catholics the source, rule, guideline, and criterion of correctness and purity of the church's proclamation, of its elaboration of doctrine, and of its sacramental and pastoral practice. For in the midst of the first communities formed by Christ's apostles, the New Testament books emerged, under the Holy Spirit's inspiration, through the preaching and teaching of the apostolic gospel. These books, together with the sacred books of Israel in the Old Testament, are to make present for all ages the truth of God's word, so as to form faith and guide believers in a life worthy of the gospel of Christ. By the biblical canon, the church does not constitute, but instead recognizes, the inherent au-

thority of the prophetic and apostolic Scriptures. Consequently, the church's preaching and whole life must be nourished and ruled by the Scriptures constantly heard and studied. True interpretation and application of Scripture maintains church teaching in the truth.

4.6.2 Topics of Reconciled Diversity

435. Recalling that, because of the differences of times and places, the one truth of the gospel has to take on a variety of expressions, we turn to show how our different traditions can, on topics of significant differences, mutually recognize in each other the shared truth of the apostolic gospel of Jesus Christ.[154]

A. *The Canon of Scripture and the Church*

436. Lutherans hold that the complex historical process leading to the formation of the canon of Scripture is not to be understood as if the church were conferring on Scripture an authority over faith and life, but instead, that through reading the books and teaching their content, the church was coming to perceive and acknowledge, under the Holy Sprit's guidance, the books' canonical authority, to which the church submitted.

437. Catholics hold, in line with formulations of Vatican Councils I and II, that the books of Holy Scripture are transmitted to the church as inspired, sacred, and canonical (DS 3006; Tanner, 806; DV 11.1). In issuing lists of the canonical books, bishops and church councils were not constituting the books as normative testimonies to God's saving work and word, but were recognizing that they were such in themselves and in their effective contribution to the faith and life of the church. When theological accounts of the canon identify persons in ministries who specified which books were received as canonical, Catholics see in this an indication of those who are responsible for public teaching and the worship of the church, in which the canonical books have primary roles.

438. This conception is compatible with the Lutheran position sketched above, namely, that the core of the canon came to its ecclesial

---

[154] Interim considerations pointing to reconciled diversity were already given above in nos. 400-401, on the biblical canon and the church, and in 407-409, on biblical interpretation in Lutheran and Catholic accounts. Also, no. 412 showed an initial convergence on doctrine and the teaching ministry.

validity because the message of its books validated itself. But certainty about what makes a book canonical does not exclude different conceptions about the outer boundaries of Scripture. The question of the number of canonical books is secondary to the qualitative issue of canonicity, which corresponds to there being among Lutheran churches no magisterial determination of the limits of the canon.

439. Luther's judgment that the Apocrypha are not part of Holy Scripture[155] and the Council of Trent's decision to include them in the canon[156] have led to the traditional Lutheran-Catholic difference over the limits of the canon. Nevertheless Luther also held that the Apocrypha were "useful and valuable for reading"[157] and this led to their being printed, not only in Luther's published Bibles of 1534 and 1545, but as well also in numerous editions of the Bible brought out down to today under Lutheran auspices. Naturally they are given in today's interconfessional editions of the Bible and several readings from the Apocrypha occur in contemporary Lutheran liturgical lectionaries (Cf. no. 394, footnote 133, above).

440. Among Lutherans a new evaluation of the Apocrypha and of their belonging to the canon is presently underway, especially among exegetes. When they face the issue of the unity of Scripture, with an awareness shaped by historical-critical principles, many Scripture scholars are emphasizing three considerations. (1) When the New Testament books were being composed, the canon of the writings that became the "Old Testament" was not yet definitively fixed. (2) The Holy Scripture of earliest Christianity was mainly the Septuagint. (3) If one limits the Old Testament to the Hebrew canon, then a huge gap is left in the tradition-process between the Old and New Testaments, which makes it difficult to grasp the New Testament in its unity with the Old Testament. Thus the question of the unity of Scripture, in the changed context of today, brings with it a change in the controversy over the limits of the canon and reduces its importance.

---

[155] Bible of 1545. WADB 12,3. Cf. the 1534 Bible (WADB 12,2).
[156] DS 1502; Tanner, 663-64.
[157] WADB 12,3 (cf. 12,2).

441. Therefore regarding the biblical canon and the church, Lutherans and Catholics are in such an extensive agreement on the source of the Bible's canonical authority that their remaining differences over the extent of the canon are not of such weight to justify continued ecclesial division. In this area, there is unity in reconciled diversity. However, this fundamental agreement on the canon makes it imperative to clarify the Catholic and Lutheran positions on the role of tradition in biblical interpretation and on the office of teaching in the church.

B. *Scripture and Tradition*

442. Catholics and Lutherans agree, not only that Scripture developed historically from a process of tradition both in Israel and the apostolic church, but as well that Scripture is oriented toward a process of being interpreted in the context of ecclesial tradition.

443. When Catholics affirm that tradition is indispensable in the interpretation of the word of God (*Ut unum sint*, 79; cf. nos. 404-406, above), they are connecting the gospel and Scripture with the Christian faith lived and transmitted in history, where transmission has given rise to valid expressions of that faith. Such expressions are: the rule of faith (nos. 320-322, above); creeds, particularly that of Nicaea-Constantinople (nos. 323-326, above); and conciliar formulations of articles of faith (nos. 337-340, above). These relate to God's saving work as concentrated summaries and clarifications of what is announced in the apostolic gospel and documented in the books of Scripture. Catholics claim that these come from Scripture and, as fundamental expressions of faith and life, they should orient church teaching and biblical interpretation. These expressions of tradition are among the principal means by which, throughout the centuries, the Holy Spirit has maintained the church in the truth of God's saving word and believers have been led to grasp rightly the message of salvation present in Scripture.

444. Catholics have taken hold anew of the patristic and high-medieval conviction that Scripture contains all revealed truth, which leads to a significant distinction. The many "traditions" are the forms of life and practice which apply God's word and are observed out of fidelity to the community of faith. Scripture *is* the inspired word of God, while tradition is the living process which "*transmits* in its

Church Teaching that Remains in the Truth

entirety the Word of God entrusted to the apostles by Christ and the Holy Spirit" (DV 9). This transmission is not the source of new truths by which the content of inspired Scripture would be supplemented, but it does give rise to the elementary expressions mentioned in no. 150, which are not simply "human traditions", for they express and render certain the biblical content of faith.

445. When Lutherans speak of Scripture and tradition, they must first make a conceptual clarification. By "traditions" or, as they often say, "human traditions", the reformers and the confessions often indicate "human ordinances in spiritual or ecclesiastical matters,"[158] which are practices of church life enacted by human beings without grounding in Scripture, but which people should observe because, and insofar as, they promote the good order of the church. A first condition is that people do not observe them believing that they are necessary for salvation or that by their observance one merits salvation. Second, such practices may not go against any commandment of God. If these two conditions are not fulfilled, "human traditions" have to be repudiated. But all enactments "which are not contrary to the Holy Gospel" may be retained.[159]

446. For the reformers the Early Church's creeds are different from the "human traditions" just indicated. They see these as well grounded in Holy Scripture and so having authority as accurate summaries of the gospel and as defenses against errors. The *Augsburg Confession* explicitly holds to these creeds and develops their content in its doctrine of justification. The Confession also adopts the Early Church's condemnation of doctrinal errors. In this way the reformers demonstrate the catholicity of their teaching, to which they add numerous references to the Church Fathers, who are for them witnesses to correct interpretation of Scripture. When Lutherans call these latter expressions of the faith "traditions", they are then seeing Scripture and tradition as belonging to each other. The reformers also gave expression to their faith and understanding of Scripture in confessional documents and the catechism, which have to this day an important role in communicating the apostolic gospel, which Scripture attests in a normative manner. This tradition

---

[158] Luther, *Marburg Articles*, no. 13. LW 38, 88; WA 30III, 168,3f.
[159] *Torgau Articles*. BSLK 107,25.

rightly orients the church in its witness to the gospel and its reading of Scripture, so that the church's teaching prolongs the apostolic witness to the truth of God's revelation.

447. Lutherans further insist that while Scripture and tradition are connected, Scripture should not be absorbed into the tradition-process, but should remain permanently superior as a critical norm, coming from the apostolic origins, which is superior to the traditions of the church. Catholics agree with this, because Scripture is "the highest authority in matters of faith" (*Ut unum sint*, 79) and Scripture continues to direct the church in the "continual reformation" of its life and teaching of which it has need (UR 6).

448. Therefore regarding Scripture and tradition, Lutherans and Catholics are in such an extensive agreement that their different emphases do not of themselves require maintaining the present division of the churches. In this area, there is unity in reconciled diversity.

C. The Teaching Office: Its Necessity and Context in the Church

449. This presentation of Lutheran-Catholic reconciled diversity on the church's teaching office treats the topic at the fundamental level of its necessity and of the context in which it acts. Section 4.5.3 (nos. 411-428, above) related the extensive development of the ecclesial function of the magisterium in the Catholic Church during the centuries of Lutheran-Catholic separation. The historical shifts in Catholic doctrine in this period, along with refinements of recent origin, make the Catholic magisterium considerably different from the functioning of teaching authority in the Lutheran churches with the office of bishops and their synodical forms. Therefore, the present exposition envisages the questions it treats only at a fundamental level, on which nonetheless an ecumenical advance can be proposed.

C.1 The Existence of a Ministry of Public Teaching at the Local and Supra-local Levels

450. Lutheran doctrine locates the ministry of teaching primarily in the local congregation, for which ministers are properly called and ordained to teach publicly and administer the sacraments (*Augsburg Confession*, Art. 14). Linked to sound exegesis and theological reflection, the teaching office is a necessary compo-

nent of church life, by which individuals become responsible in the public life of the church for transmitting the gospel, by which the priesthood of all believers is built up. The Lutheran confessional tradition also holds that a supra-local teaching responsibility is essential in the church, for oversight of discipline and doctrine (*Augsburg Confession*, Art. 28). Such a teaching office brings to expression how every worshipping congregation is linked with other congregations in the church. In current Lutheran church constitutions, the concrete form of this supra-local ministry will differ, but synods which include lay members and represent the whole priestly people are the essential context in which bishops exercise their oversight, so that no single minister has exclusive competence.

451. But in speaking about the teaching ministry in Lutheran churches, one must not focus exclusively on office-holders and institutions, but also take account of the processes of interactions between office-holders, of interventions by Christians practicing the common priesthood of the baptized, and of theologians who contribute the results of their scholarly study and conclusions on doctrinal questions. Lutheran churches earnestly hope that through these processes the Holy Spirit is maintaining them in the truth of the gospel, as they continue to read and listen to Scripture in their own times, while seeking to be faithful to their confessions of faith as they face the challenges of their own day.

452. In Catholic ecclesiology "magisterium" designates the mission of teaching that is proper to the episcopal college, to the Pope as its head, and to individual bishops linked in hierarchical communion with the successor of Peter. It is an essential institutional component of the church for pastoral service, with a proper authority distinct from jurisdiction for governance. But the episcopal teaching office operates within an extensive network of ministers of the word, among whom ordained pastors of parishes have a singular importance in preaching and catechizing. While some ministries of the word, such as that of theologians, are exercised in virtue of intellectual competence, the magisterium functions in virtue of a capacity for discerning the truth of God's word, based on a charism conferred by episcopal ordination.

453. In spite of their different configurations of teaching ministries, Lutherans and Catholics agree that the church must designate members to serve the transmission of the gospel, which is necessary for saving faith. Were a teaching office not present and functioning in specific ways on the levels of both the local congregations and for regions of several or many congregations, the church would be defective.

C.2 The Teaching Office Among Several Instances of Witness to God's Word

454. Lutherans and Catholics agree that those who are responsible for teaching in the church contribute significantly to keeping the church in the truth. Their teaching stands in service to the faith of the whole church. But those who teach function in relation to several instances of witness to the word of God.

455. In Catholic theology, Melchior Cano's influential posthumous work of 1563 presented ten *loci theologici* as domains of knowledge formed by the process of tradition in such a way that each *locus* or area showed forth the truth of revelation. The pastoral magisterium therefore, when it formulates doctrine, even at the highest level, does not act in isolation from Scripture and its interpretation in the *loci*, from the creed and past teaching, from the church's ongoing worship, and from the witness of holy people. The magisterium is in constant interaction with these instances of testimony to God and his revelation. It must, above all, take account of the reality of the inerrant faith of the people as a whole (LG 12; cited in no. 420, above), so that in its service there will be "a unique interplay (*singularis conspiratio*) between bishops and faithful" (DV 10).

456. The Lutheran teaching ministry includes many participating agents and instances, with no one of these able to rightfully claim exclusive competence for itself, as set forth amply in nos. 383-389, above. Responsible persons exercise this ministry in ways that are personal, collegial, and communal, in the midst of the ongoing processes already indicated.

457. Thus Lutherans and Catholics are in fundamental agreement on there being a network of several instances of witness to God's word which constitutes the essential context within which those exercising the teaching office must carry out their responsibilities.

Church Teaching that Remains in the Truth

C.3 The Teaching Office in its Constructive and Critical Functions

458. Lutherans and Catholics agree that the teaching ministry or magisterium serves the faith of the whole church by its public witness to the truth of God's word. It must proclaim the gospel of God's grace, interpret the biblical witness, and further transmit the word of God entrusted to the whole church and expressed in the confessions and articles of faith. The aim is to assist all members of the church toward professing their faith in accord with God's revelation in Christ and in freedom from error. Thus, the teaching office or ministry is a necessary means by which the church is maintained in the truth of the gospel of Christ.

459. Lutherans and Catholics further agree that the teaching ministry must include the authoritative discernment of doctrine offered publicly, leading to judgments that preserve true teaching. Interpretations of the faith contradicting the apostolic gospel must be excluded, in accord with Gal 1:9 (cf. *Apology of the Augsburg Confession*, Art. VII, 48). According to the Augsburg Confession, it pertains to the office of bishop, "to judge doctrine and reject doctrine that is contrary to the gospel" (*Augsburg Confession*, Art. 28, 21). In Lutheran churches today, this task is carried out collegially and in synodical structures.

460. The church's witness to the truth exists in history and thus has aspects of both finality and provisionality. Lutherans and Catholics agree that a particular concern of the teaching ministry is therefore to give public voice in an ongoing manner to the definitive coming of God to humankind in the death and resurrection of Christ, in which believers place their ultimate trust for life and final salvation. But faith is professed and lived out in history, amid cultural changes, which requires an ongoing search for appropriate doctrinal expressions adequate to God's truth in this time before the ultimate eschatological manifestation of Christ as Lord and Savior of all.

Participants
The Lutheran-Roman Catholic Commission on Unity 1995-2006

Roman Catholics

Members

Bishop Dr Walter Kasper, Germany (co-chairperson 1995–2001)
Archbishop Dr Alfons Nossol, Poland
    (member from 1995, co-chairperson 2002-2006)
† Prof. Dr Robert Eno, USA (1995-1996)
Rev. Dr Polykarp Chuma Ibebuike, Nigeria
Prof. Dr Margaret O'Gara, Canada
Prof. Dr Eberhard Schockenhoff, Germany
Bishop Dr Gerhard Schwenzer, Norway
Prof. Dr Lothar Ullrich, Germany (1995-2003)
Prof. Dr Thomas Söding, Germany (2003-2006)

Consultants

Prof. Dr Angelo Maffeis, Italy
Prof. Dr Jared Wicks, S.J., USA (1998-2006)

Staff (Pontifical Council for Promoting Christian Unity)

† Msgr. Dr Heinz-Albert Raem (1995-1996)
Msgr. Dr John Radano (1995-1999)
Rev. Dr Matthias Türk (1999-2005)

Lutherans

Members

Bishop Dr Béla Harmati, Hungary (co-chairperson)
Prof. Dr Kristen Kvam, USA
Bishop Dr Samson Mushemba, Tanzania
Prof. Dr Ricardo Pietrantonio, Argentina
Prof. Dr Turid Karlsen Seim, Norway
Prof. Dr Yoshikazu Tokuzen, Japan
Rev. Dr Pirjo Työrinoja, Finland
Prof. Dr Gunther Wenz, Germany

Consultants

Prof. Dr Theo Dieter, Institute for Ecumenical Research, Strasbourg
Prof. Dr David S. Yaego, U.S.A. (1997-2000)
Prof. Dr Michael Root, U.S.A. (2001-2002)

Staff (The Lutheran World Federation)

Rev. Dr Eugene L. Brand, (co-secretary 1995-1996)
Rev. Sven Oppegaard, (co-secretary 1997-2005)
Mrs. Antonia Bossart, (1995-1999)
Mrs. Sybille Graumann, (2000-2005)

Interpreters

Mrs. Donata Coleman, United Kingdom
Mrs. Ursula Gassmann, Germany

Abbreviations

The following abbreviations give details of works referred to in the present study document.

BC *The Book of Concord, The Confessions of the Evangelical Lutheran Church*, edited by R. Kolb and T. J. Wengert, Fortress Press, Minneapolis, 2000.

BSLK *Die Bekenntnisschriften der evangelisch-lutherischen Kirche.* Vandenhoeck & Ruprecht, Göttingen, 12 ed. 1998.

CT *Concilium Tridentinum. Diariorum, actorum, epistularium, tractatuum Nova Collectio.* Herder, Freiburg/Br., 1901-2001.

DS *Enchiridion symbolorum, definitionum, et declarationum de rebus fidei et morum*, editit Henricus Denzinger et Adolphus Schönmetzer, ed. XXXIII (Herder: Barcinone, Friburgi Brisgoviae, et alibi, 1965). References by paragraph number.

DV *Dei Verbum.* Dogmatic Constitution on Divine Revelation. Second Vatican Council.

JDDJ *Joint Declaration on the Doctrine of Justification* by the Lutheran World Federation and the Roman Catholic Church, Eerdmans, Grand Rapids, USA, 2000.

LG *Lumen gentium.* Dogmatic Constitution on the Church. Second Vatican Council.

LW *Luther's Works.* Published in 55 volumes by Concordia Publishing House and Fortress Press, Philadelphia, USA, 1958-1986.

Mansi *Sacrorum Conciliorum Nova et Amplissima Collectio*, ed. Joannes Dominicus Mansi. Reprint, Akademische Druck- und Verlagsanstalt, Graz, 1960-61.

PO *Presbyterorum Ordinis*, Decree on the Ministry and Life of Priests. Second Vatican Council.

Tanner *Decrees of the Ecumenical Councils*, ed. Norman P. Tanner, 2 vols. (London: Sheed & Ward, and Washington, D.C.: Georgetown University Press, 1990)

UR *Unitatis Redintegratio.* Decree on Ecumenism. Second Vatican Council.

WA "Weimar Ausgabe": *D. Martin Luthers Werke, Kritische Gesamtausgabe*, Hermann Böhlhaus Nachfolger, Weimar, Germany, 1883ff.

www.ingramcontent.com/pod-product-compliance
Lightning Source LLC
Chambersburg PA
CBHW071201070526
44584CB00019B/2871